Rails Recipes

Rails Recipes

Chad Fowler

The Pragmatic Bookshelf
Raleigh, North Carolina   Dallas, Texas

Many of the designations used by manufacturers and sellers to distinguish their products are claimed as trademarks. Where those designations appear in this book, and The Pragmatic Programmers, LLC was aware of a trademark claim, the designations have been printed in initial capital letters or in all capitals. The Pragmatic Starter Kit, The Pragmatic Programmer, Pragmatic Programming, Pragmatic Bookshelf and the linking *g* device are trademarks of The Pragmatic Programmers, LLC.

Every precaution was taken in the preparation of this book. However, the publisher assumes no responsibility for errors or omissions, or for damages that may result from the use of information (including program listings) contained herein.

Our Pragmatic courses, workshops, and other products can help you and your team create better software and have more fun. For more information, as well as the latest Pragmatic titles, please visit us at

http://www.pragmaticprogrammer.com

ISBN 0-9776166-0-6

Printed on acid-free paper with 85% recycled, 30% post-consumer content.

P1.0 printing, June, 2006

Version: 2006-5-15

Contents

Part III—Controller Recipes 133

Part IV—Testing Recipes 171

Part V—Big-Picture Recipes 193

Part VI—Email Recipes   293

Part VII—Appendix   319

A Resources   321

Introduction

What Makes a Good Recipe Book?

If I were to buy a *real* recipe book—you know, a book about cooking food—I wouldn't be looking for a book that tells me how to dice vegetables or how to use a skillet. I can find that kind of information in an overview about cooking.

A recipe book is about how to *make* food you might not be able to easily figure out how to make on your own. It's about skipping the trial and error and jumping straight to a solution that works. Sometimes it's even about making food you never imagined you *could* make.

If you want to learn how to make great Indian food, you buy a recipe book by a great Indian chef and follow his or her directions. You're not just buying any old solution. You're buying a solution you can *trust* to be good. That's why famous chefs sell lots and lots of books. People want to make food that tastes good, and these chefs know how to make (and teach *you* how to make) food that tastes good.

Good recipe books *do* teach you techniques. Sometimes they even teach you about new tools. But they teach these skills within the context and with the end goal of *making something*—not just to teach them.

My goal for *Rails Recipes* is to teach you how to make great stuff with Rails and to do it right on your first try. These recipes and the techniques herein are extractions from my own work and from the "great chefs" of Rails: the Rails core developer team, the leading trainers and authors, and the earliest of early adopters.

I also hope to show you not only *how* to do things but to explain *why* they work the way they do. After reading through the recipes, you should walk away with a new level of Rails understanding to go with a huge list of successfully implemented hot new application features.

Not all of these recipes are long and involved. To spice things up, I've included a number of smaller offerings, which I've called *snacks*. Typically one or two pages long, these snacks will help satisfy those cravings we all get between meals.

Who's It For?

Rails Recipes is for people who understand Rails and now want to see how an experienced Rails developer would attack specific problems. Like with a real recipe book, you should be able to flip through the table of contents, find something you need to *get done*, and get from start to finish in a matter of minutes.

I'm going to assume that you know the basics or that you can find them in a tutorial or an online reference. When you're busy trying to *make* something, you don't have spare time to read through introductory material. So if you're still in the beginning stages of learning Rails, be sure to have a copy of *Agile Web Development with Rails* [TH05] and a bookmark to the Rails API documentation handy.[1]

Rails Version

The examples in this book, except where noted, should work with Rails 1.0 or higher. Several recipes cover new features that were released with Rails 1.1.

Resources

The best place to go for Rails information is the Rails website.[2] From there, you can find the mailing lists, irc channels, and weblogs.

The Pragmatic Programmers have also set up a forum for *Rails Recipes* readers to discuss the recipes, help each other with problems, expand on the solutions, and even write new recipes. While *Rails Recipes* was in beta, the forum served as such a great resource for ideas that more than one reader-posted recipe made it into the book! You can find the forum at http://fora.pragprog.com/rails-recipes.

---

[1] http://api.rubyonrails.org
[2] http://www.rubyonrails.org

The book's errata list is at http://books.pragprog.com/titles/fr_rr/errata. If you submit any problems you find, we'll list them there.

You'll find links to the source code for almost all the book's examples at http://www.pragmaticprogrammer.com/titles/fr_rr/code.html.

If you're reading the PDF version of this book, you can report an error on a page by clicking the "erratum" link at the bottom of the page, and you can get to the source code of an example by clicking the gray lozenge containing the code's file name that appears before the listing.

Acknowledgments

Dave Thomas is a mentor and role model to a constantly growing segment of our industry—particularly within the Ruby world. I can't imagine writing a book for another publisher. Anything else would undoubtedly be a huge step backward. If this book helps you, it's due in no small part to the influence Dave Thomas and Andy Hunt have had on the book and on me.

David Heinemeier Hansson created Rails, which led me and a legion of Rubyists to fulltime work pursuing our passion. David has been a friend and supporter since we met through the Ruby community. His ideas and encouragement made *Rails Recipes* better.

Thanks to Shaun Fanning and Steve Smith for building a great company around a great product and having the guts and vision to start over from scratch in Rails. As a software developer, Naviance is the work environment I've dreamt of, and the depth and complexity of what we do has been a growth catalyst for me as a software developer in general and as a Rails developer in particular.

Mike Clark seemed to pop up on my IM client with an inspiring comment or a killer recipe idea as if he could read my mind and knew when I needed it most.

Sean Mountcastle, Frederick Ros, Bruce Williams, Tim Case, Marcel Molina Jr., Rick Olson, Jamis Buck, Luke Redpath, David Vincelli, Tim Lucas, Shaun Fanning, Tom Moertel, Jeremy Kemper, Scott Barron, David Alan Black, Dave Thomas, and Mike Clark all contributed either full recipes or code and ideas that allowed the recipes to write themselves. This book is a community effort, and I can't thank the contributors enough.

The Rails core team members served as an invaluable sounding board during the development of this book. As I was writing the book, I spent hours talking through ideas and working through problems with the people who created the very features I was writing about. Thanks to Scott Barron, Jamis Buck, Thomas Fuchs, David Heinemeier Hansson, Jeremy Kemper, Michael Koziarski, Tobias Lütke, Marcel Molina Jr., Rick Olson, Nicholas Seckar, Sam Stephenson, and Florian Weber for allowing me to be a (rather loud) fly on the wall and to witness the evolution of this great software as it happened.

Rails Recipes was released as a Beta Book early in its development. We Ruby authors are blessed with what must be the most thoughtful and helpful audience in the industry. *Rails Recipes* was shaped for the better by these early adopters. Thanks for the bug reports, suggestions, and even full recipes.

Most important, thanks to Kelly for tolerating long days of programming Ruby followed by long nights and weekends of writing about it. I couldn't have done this without you.

Chad Fowler
May 2006
chad@chadfowler.com

Tags and Thumb tabs

I've tried to assign tags to each recipe. If you want to find recipes that have something to do with Mail, for example, find the Mail tab at the edge of this page. Then look down the side of the book: you'll find a thumb tab that lines up with the tab on this page for each appropriate recipe.

Ajax

API Tips

Automation

Configuration

Database

Development Process

Extending Rails

HTML

Integration

Rails Internals

Mail

Plugins

Rails 1.1+

Search

Security

Style

Testing

Troubleshooting

XML

Part I

User Interface Recipes

In-Place Form Editing

Your application has one or more pieces of data that are often edited by your users—usually very quickly. You want to give your users an easy way to edit application data *in place* without opening a separate form.

Rails makes in-place editing easy with the script.aculo.us InPlaceEditor control and accompanying helpers. Let's jump right in and give it a try.

First, we'll create a model and controller to demonstrate with. Let's assume we're doing a simple address book application. The following is the Active Record migration we'll use to define the schema:

InPlaceEditing/db/migrate/001_add_contacts_table.rb

```ruby
class AddContactsTable < ActiveRecord::Migration
  def self.up
    create_table :contacts do |t|
      t.column :name, :string
      t.column :email, :string
      t.column :phone, :string
      t.column :address_line1, :string
      t.column :address_line2, :string
      t.column :city, :string
      t.column :state, :string
      t.column :country, :string
      t.column :postal_code, :string
    end
  end

  def self.down
    drop_table :contacts
  end
end
```

Second, we'll use the default generated model for our Contact class. To get things up and running quickly, we can generate the model, controller, and some sample views by just using the Rails scaffolding:

```
chad> ruby script/generate scaffold Contact
      exists  app/controllers/
        :         :        :
      create  app/views/layouts/contacts.rhtml
      create  public/stylesheets/scaffold.css
```

Now we can start script/server, navigate to http://localhost:3000/contacts/, and add a contact or two. Click one of your freshly added contacts' "Show" links. You should see a plain, white page with an undecorated dump of your chosen contact's details. This is the page we're going to add our in-place editing controls to.

The first step in any Ajax enablement is to make sure you've included the necessary JavaScript files in your views. Somewhere in the <head> of your HTML document, you can call the following:

```
<%= javascript_include_tag :defaults %>
```

I usually put that declaration in my application's default layout (in app/views/layouts/application.rhtml) so I don't have to worry about including it (and other application-wide style settings, markup, etc.) in each view I create. If you need Ajax effects in only certain discrete sections of your application, you might choose to localize the inclusion of these JavaScript files. In this case, the scaffolding generator has created the contacts.rhtml layout for us in the directory app/views/layouts. You can include the JavaScript underneath the stylesheet_link_tag() call in this layout.

Open app/views/contacts/show.rhtml in your editor. By default, it should look like this:

InPlaceEditing/app/views/contacts/show.rhtml.default
```
<% for column in Contact.content_columns %>
<p>
  <b><%= column.human_name %>:</b> <%=h @contact.send(column.name) %>
</p>
<% end %>

<%= link_to 'Edit', :action => 'edit', :id => @contact %> |
<%= link_to 'Back', :action => 'list' %>
```

The default show() view loops through the model's columns and displays each one dynamically, with both a label and its value, rendering something like Figure 1.1, on the facing page.

Let's start with this file and add the in-place editing controls to our fields. First we'll remove the "Edit" link, since we're not going to need it anymore. Then we wrap the displayed value with a call to the in-place editor helper. Your show.rhtml should now look like this:

Name: Chad Fowler

Email: chad@chadfowler.com

Phone: 303-555-1212

Address line1: 321 Main St.

Address line2:

City: Gotham

State: CA

Country: USA

Postal code: 12345

Edit | Back

Figure 1.1: BASIC SCAFFOLD VIEW

InPlaceEditing/app/views/contacts/show.rhtml
```
<% for column in Contact.content_columns %>
<p>
  <b><%= column.human_name %>:</b>
  <%= in_place_editor_field :contact, column.name, [], :rows => 1 %>
</p>
<% end %>

<%= link_to 'Back', :action => 'list' %>
```

We're telling the in_place_editor_field() helper that we want it to create an editing control for the instance variable called @contact with the attribute that we're currently on in our loop through the model's column names. To make things a little more concrete, if we weren't in the dynamic land of scaffolding, we would create an edit control for a Contact's name with the following snippet:

```
<%= in_place_editor_field :contact, :name %>
```

Note that the in_place_editor_field() method expects the *name* of the instance variable as its first parameter—not the instance itself (so we use :contact, not @contact).

Refresh the show() page, and you should be able to click one of the contact's values to cause the edit control to automatically open in the current view:

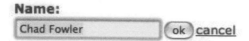

Clicking the ok button now should result in a big, ugly error in a JavaScript alert. That's OK. The in-place edit control has created a form for editing a contact's data, but that form has no corresponding action to submit to. Quickly consulting the application's log file, we see the following line:

```
127.0.0.1 . . . "POST /contacts/set_contact_name/1 HTTP/1.1" 404 581
```

So the application tried to POST to an action called set_contact_name() (notice the naming convention) and received a 404 (not found) response code in return.

Now we could go into our ContactsController and define the method set_contact_name(), but since we're doing something so *conventional*, we can rely on a Rails *convention* to do the work for us! Open the controller app/controllers/contacts_controller.rb, and add the following line right after the beginning of the class definition (line 2 would be a good place):

```
in_place_edit_for :contact, :name
```

Now if you return to your browser, edit the contact's name, and click "ok" again, you'll find that the data is changed, saved, and redisplayed. The call to in_place_edit_for() dynamically defines a set_contact_name() action that will update the contact's name for us. The other attributes on the page still won't work, because we haven't told the controller to generate the necessary actions. We could copy and paste the line we just added, changing the attribute names. But since we want edit controls for all the attributes of our Contact model and the scaffolding has already shown us how to reflect on a model's column names, let's keep it DRY and replace the existing in_place_edit_for() call with the following:

`InPlaceEditing/app/controllers/contacts_controller.rb`

```
Contact.content_columns.each do |column|
  in_place_edit_for :contact, column.name
end
```

Now all the attributes should save properly through their in-place edit controls. Since, as we've seen, in_place_edit_for simply generates appropriately named actions to handle data updates, if we needed to implement special behavior for a given edit, we could define our own custom actions to handle the updates. For example, if we needed special processing for postal code updates, we would define an action called

---

raise() Is Your Friend

If I hadn't just told you how to implement your own custom in-place edit actions, how would you have known what to do?

As we saw in the recipe, we can see what action the Ajax control is attempting to call by looking at our web server log. But since it's making a POST, we can't see the parameters in the log. How do you know what parameters an auto-generated form is expecting without reading through piles of source code?

What I did was to create an action with the name that I saw in the logs that looked like the following:

```
def set_contact_name
  raise params.inspect
end
```

When I submitted the form, I saw the Rails error message with a list of the submitted parameters at the top.

---

set_contact_postal_code(). The in-place edit control form will pass two notable parameters: the contact's id, aptly named id and the new value to use for the update with the parameter key, value.

> The in-place edit control uses Active Record's update_attribute() method to do database updates. This method bypasses Active Record model validations. If you need to perform validations on each update, you'll need to write your own actions for handling the in-place edits.

OK, so these edit fields work. But they're kind of ugly. How would you, for example, make the text field longer? An especially long email address or name would not fit in the default text field size. Many Rails helpers accept additional parameters that will be passed directly to their rendered HTML elements, allowing you to easily control factors such as size.

The InPlaceEditor does things a little differently (and some might say better). It sets a default class name on the generated HTML form, which you can then use as a CSS selector. So to customize the size of the generated text fields, you could use the following CSS:

```
.inplaceeditor-form input[type="text"] {
  width: 260px;
}
```

Of course, since we're using CSS here, we could do anything possible with CSS.

Discussion

You'll notice that our example here assumes that you want to edit all your data with a text box. In fact, it's possible to force the InPlaceEditor to create either a text field or a <*textarea*> field, using the :rows option to the fourth parameter of the in_place_editor_field() method. Any value greater than 1 will tell InPlaceEditor to generate a <*textarea*>.

What if you want to edit with something other than free-form text controls? InPlaceEditor doesn't ship with anything for this by default. See Recipe 2, *Making Your Own JavaScript Helper*, on the next page, to learn how to do it yourself.

Also, you'll quickly notice that if a field doesn't already have a value, the InPlaceEditor will not allow you to click to edit that field. This limitation can be worked around by populating empty fields with default values, such as "Click to edit".

Making Your Own JavaScript Helper

One of the things I love about Rails is that, though I enjoy taking advantage of many of the user interface benefits that JavaScript provides, it saves me from writing JavaScript code that I really don't like to write. Rails is full of magical one-liners that create exciting user interface effects—all without having to touch a line of JavaScript.

Sadly, Rails doesn't solve *every* user interface problem I might ever have. And though its JavaScript helper libraries will continue to grow (either through the core distribution or through user-contributed plugins), no matter how much freely available code is available, if you're doing web applications with rich user interfaces, you're going to eventually encounter something application-specific for which you'll have to write your own JavaScript code.

But most of the time, though not reusable outside your own project or company, these little JavaScript snippets will be reusable for you in your own context.

How can you turn these ugly little inline JavaScript snippets into your own magical one-liners?

This recipe calls for a little bit of JavaScript and a little bit of Ruby. We're going to write a small JavaScript library, and then we're going to wrap it in a Ruby helper that we can then call from our views.

If you've read Recipe 1, *In-Place Form Editing*, on page 3, you know that the built-in InPlaceEditor control supplies a mechanism for generating only text boxes for content editing. To demonstrate how to make a JavaScript helper, we're going to extend the InPlaceEditor, giving it the ability to also generate an HTML <*select*> tag, so clicking an element to edit it could present the user with a list of valid options, as opposed to just a text box into which they can type whatever they like.

We'll assume we're using the same contact management application described in Recipe 1, *In-Place Form Editing*, on page 3. If you haven't already, set the application up, create your migrations, and generate scaffolding for the Contact model. Also, since we're going to be using Ajax, be sure to include the required JavaScript files in your app/views/layouts/contacts.rhtml layout file. We'll start with a simplified view for our show() action. Here's how your app/views/contacts/show.rhtml file should look:

```
MakingYourOwnJavaScriptHelper/app/views/contacts/show.rhtml.first_version
<p>
  <b>Name:</b> <%= in_place_editor_field :contact, :name %> <br />
  <b>Country:</b> <%= in_place_editor_field :contact, :country %>
</p>
<br />

<%= link_to 'Back', :action => 'list' %>
```

This view gives us in-place editing of the name() and country() attributes of any Contact in our database. Clicking the country name will open a text box like the one in the following image:

The call to in_place_editor_field() in the view simply generates the following JavaScript (you can see it yourself by viewing the HTML source of the page in your browser):

```
<b>Country:</b>
<span class="in_place_editor_field" id="contact_country_1_in_place_editor">
    United States of America
</span>
<script type="text/javascript">
    new Ajax.InPlaceEditor('contact_country_1_in_place_editor',
                            '/contacts/set_contact_country/1')
</script>
```

All these magic helpers are really not so magical after all. All they do is generate JavaScript and HTML fragments for us. It's just text generation, but the text happens to be JavaScript.

As you'll remember, our goal is to create our own extension of the InPlaceEditor that will render a <select> tag instead of a text box. Since, as we can see from the HTML source we just looked at, InPlaceEditor generates only a JavaScript call, we're going to have to get into the guts of the InPlaceEditor control to implement this feature.

The InPlaceEditor is defined in the file public/javascripts/controls.js. Browsing its source, we can see that its initializer binds the click event to the function enterEditMode(). We can follow this function's definition through calls to createForm() and then createEditField(). So to summarize (and spare you the details), clicking the text of an in-place edit control calls the createForm() JavaScript function that relies on the createEditField() to set up the actual editable field. The createEditField() function creates either an <input> field of type "text" or a <textarea> and adds it to the form.

This is good news, because createEditField() is a nice, clean entry point for overriding InPlaceEditor's field creation behavior. We have many ways to accomplish this in JavaScript. We won't go into detail on the implementation. The approach we'll use is to take advantage of the Prototype JavaScript library's inheritance mechanism to subclass InPlaceEditor. We'll make our own class called InPlaceSelectEditor, which will simply override InPlaceEditor's createEditField() method.

Let's create our new JavaScript class in the file in_place_select_editor.js in the directory public/javascripts. We can include this file in any page that needs it. Here's what that file should look like:

`MakingYourOwnJavaScriptHelper/public/javascripts/in_place_select_editor.js`

```
Line 1    Ajax.InPlaceSelectEditor = Class.create();
    -     Object.extend(Object.extend(Ajax.InPlaceSelectEditor.prototype,
    -                             Ajax.InPlaceEditor.prototype), {
    -         createEditField: function() {
    5           var text;
    -           if(this.options.loadTextURL) {
    -             text = this.options.loadingText;
    -           } else {
    -             text = this.getText();
    10          }
    -           this.options.textarea = false;
    -           var selectField = document.createElement("select");
    -           selectField.name = "value";
    -           selectField.innerHTML=this.options.selectOptionsHTML ||
    15                      "<option>" + text + "</option>";
    -           $A(selectField.options).each(function(opt, index){
    -             if(text == opt.value) {
```

```
     -                      selectField.selectedIndex = index;
     -                    }
    20                  }
     -                );
     -                selectField.style.backgroundColor = this.options.highlightcolor;
     -                this.editField = selectField;
     -                if(this.options.loadTextURL) {
    25                  this.loadExternalText();
     -                }
     -                this.form.appendChild(this.editField);
     -            }
     -    });
```

Without getting too deep into a discussion of the internals of InPlace-Editor, let's quickly walk through this JavaScript to understand the key points. We start off creating our new InPlaceSelectEditor class, extending InPlaceEditor, and then overriding the createEditField() method. The lines starting at 6 set the text variable to the current value of the field. We then create a new <select> element at line 12 and set its name to "value" on the next line. The generated InPlaceEditor actions on the server will be expecting data with the parameter name "value".

At line 14, we get the value of the selectOptionsHTML parameter, which can be passed into InPlaceSelectEditor's constructor in the third argument (which is a JavaScript Hash). We set the innerHTML of our freshly generated <select> tag to either the options block passed in or a single option containing the current value of the field.[3]

Finally, the loop starting on line 16 goes through each option until it finds the current value of the field and sets that option to be selected. Without this block of code, the select field would unintuitively have a different initial value than the field is actually set to.

Now we have defined our JavaScript, we need to include it in the page via our layout file, app/views/layouts/contact.rhtml. Include it like this:

MakingYourOwnJavaScriptHelper/app/views/layouts/contacts.rhtml

```
<%= javascript_include_tag "in_place_select_editor" %>
```

Now let's make a simple demo view to see this new JavaScript class in action. Create a new view in app/views/contacts/demo.rhtml with the following code:

---

[3]Although this code works as advertised in the Firefox and Safari browsers, Internet Explorer is a bit more finicky when it comes to the use of innerHTML. To make this work with Internet Explorer, you'll need to construct DOM elements programmatically. For the sake of brevity and simplicity, we'll leave that to you as an exercise in JavaScript.

MakingYourOwnJavaScriptHelper/app/views/contacts/demo.rhtml

```
<span class="in_place_editor_field" id="an_element_we_want_to_edit">Some Value</span>
<script type="text/javascript">
  new Ajax.InPlaceSelectEditor(
     'an_element_we_want_to_edit',
     '/an/update/url',
     { selectOptionsHTML: '<option>Blah</option>' +
                          '<option>Some Value</option>' +
                          '<option>Some Other Value</option>'});
</script>
```

Its parameters are the same as those passed to the original InPlaceEditor, except that the third (optional) Hash argument can accept the additional selectOptionsHTML key.

Now we have the JavaScript side working, how can we remove the need for JavaScript programming altogether? It's time to make a helper!

As we saw earlier, the Rails JavaScript helpers essentially just generate text that happens to be JavaScript. What do we need to generate for *this* helper? Basically, we just need to generate the equivalent code that we wrote manually in the previous demo example.

We'll cheat a little by looking at (and copying) the definition of the method in_place_editor_field() from the java_script_macros_helper.rb file in Action Pack. We'll implement our new helpers as a pair of methods, following the pattern of the InPlaceEditor implementation. We'll put them in app/helpers/application_helper.rb to make them available to all our views. We'll call the first method in_place_select_editor_field(). Since we want to be able to pass in an object and a field name, the job of in_place_select_editor_field() is to set up the id and url parameters to pass to the InPlaceSelectEditor JavaScript class, based on the supplied object and field name. Here's the implementation:

MakingYourOwnJavaScriptHelper/app/helpers/application_helper.rb

```
def in_place_select_editor_field(object, method, tag_options = {},
                                 in_place_editor_options = {})
  tag = ::ActionView::Helpers::InstanceTag.new(object, method, self)
  tag_options = { :tag => "span",
                  :id => "#{object}_#{method}_#{tag.object.id}_in_place_editor",
                  :class => "in_place_editor_field"}.merge!(tag_options)
  in_place_editor_options[:url] =
    in_place_editor_options[:url] ||
    url_for({ :action => "set_#{object}_#{method}", :id => tag.object.id })
  tag.to_content_tag(tag_options.delete(:tag), tag_options) +
  in_place_select_editor(tag_options[:id], in_place_editor_options)
end
```

Now as you can see, this method delegates to in_place_select_editor(), whose job is to generate the JavaScript text that will be inserted into the rendered view. Here's what in_place_select_editor() should look like:

```
MakingYourOwnJavaScriptHelper/app/helpers/application_helper.rb
def in_place_select_editor(field_id, options = {})
  function =  "new Ajax.InPlaceSelectEditor("
  function << "'#{field_id}', "
  function << "'#{url_for(options[:url])}'"
  function << (', ' + options_for_javascript(
    {
      'selectOptionsHTML' =>
            %('#{escape_javascript(options[:select_options].gsub(/\n/, ""))}')
    }
    )
  ) if options[:select_options]
  function << ')'
  javascript_tag(function)
end
```

A fortunate side effect of the way the selectOptionsHTML parameter is implemented is that it's easy to use with the Rails form options helpers.

Putting all our work together, here's app/views/contacts/show.rhtml modified to use our new helper. Notice that we are supplying the country list via the built-in Rails country_options_for_select() helper.

```
MakingYourOwnJavaScriptHelper/app/views/contacts/show.rhtml
<p>
  <b>Name:</b>
    <%= in_place_editor_field :contact, :name %> <br />
  <b>Country:</b>
    <%= in_place_select_editor_field(
            :contact,
            :country,
            {},
            :select_options => country_options_for_select) %>
</p>
<br />

<%= link_to 'Back', :action => 'list' %>
```

After clicking the country name, the form now looks like Figure 2.2, on the facing page.

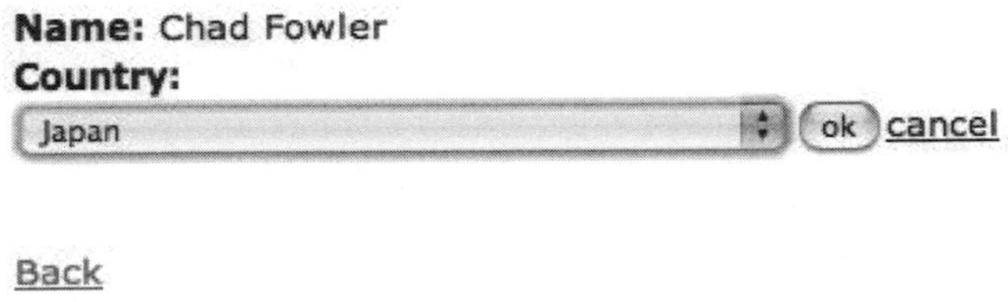

Name: Chad Fowler
Country:

| Japan | ⇕ | (ok) cancel |

Back

Figure 2.2: OUR JAVASCRIPT HELPER IN ACTION

Discussion

Our in_place_select_editor_field( ) and in_place_select_editor( ) helpers contain an ugly amount of duplication. The built-in in_place_editor_field( ) and in_place_editor( ) JavaScript helpers were not made to be extensible. It wouldn't be hard to refactor them to be more pluggable, making our custom helpers smaller and simpler. That would be the *right* thing to do, but it wouldn't serve the purpose of demonstration in a book as well. So here's your homework assignment: refactor the in-place editor helpers to make them extensible, and then plug this helper in. Submit your work.

Showing a Live Preview

Credit

I extracted the technique for this recipe from the Typo weblog engine (see http://typosphere.org/).

Problem

You'd like to give your users the ability to see a live preview of their data *as they are editing it.* You don't want them to have to wait until they submit a form to find out that they've bungled the formatting of, say, a diary entry that's going to be displayed to the world.

Solution

We can easily accomplish a live preview effect using the built-in Rails JavaScript helpers. For this recipe, we'll create a live preview of an extremely simple form for creating a diary entry.

The first step in creating any "Ajaxy" Rails effect is to make sure you're including the right JavaScript libraries. For the live preview effect, we need to include only the Prototype library. I recommend adding it to your application's main layout (in our case, layouts/standard.rhtml) like this:

```
<html>
  <head>
    <%= javascript_include_tag "prototype" %>
  </head>
  <body>
    ...
  </body>
</html>
```

Now that we have the necessary JavaScript libraries loaded, we'll create the model and controller to support our diary entries. We'll call the model class Entry, giving it title and body attributes. If you'd like to follow along without defining the necessary Active Record table, your app/models/entry.rb file should look like this:

```
class Entry
  attr_accessor :title, :body
end
```

The controller will be called DiaryController. We'll create it in the file app/controllers/diary_controller.rb. We'll be radical and name the action for creating a new entry new():

```
def new
  @entry = Entry.new
end
```

Now comes the fun part. This action's view is where the magic happens. Create the file, app/views/diary/new.rhtml, and edit it to look like the following:

```
<%= start_form_tag({:action => "save"},
                    :id => "entry-form")
%>
<%= text_field :entry, :title %><br />
<%= text_area :entry, :body %><br />
<%= submit_tag "Save" %>
<%= end_form_tag %>

<%= observe_form "entry-form",
                 :frequency => 1,
                 :update => "live-preview",
                 :complete => "Element.show('live-preview')",
                 :url => { :action => "preview" } %>

<div id="live-preview" style="display: none; border: 1px solid"></div>
```

What we've created is a standard, vanilla form. We've given the form an id of entry-form so we can reference it from our code. Below the form definition, we have a call to the observe_form() helper. This helper generates the necessary JavaScript to poll each element of a form on the page (referenced by id) looking for a change. It will poll at the interval specified (in seconds) by the :frequency parameter. When it detects a change, it calls the URL specified by the :url parameter, passing the form's values as parameters. Its :update parameter specifies the HTML element (again, by id) to update with the results of the URL call. In this case, the contents of the live preview <div> will be updated with whatever the call to the preview() action ends up rendering.

We have used inline CSS to set the live-preview element to be invisible when the page is initially loaded. Since the user wouldn't have entered any data yet, the live-preview would have nothing to display. The :complete parameter to observe_form() says to execute a snippet of JavaScript after the call to the preview() action completes, which will cause the live-preview element to be displayed.

If only we had a single field element for which we wanted to show a live preview, we could have used the observe_field() helper instead.

The only part left to implement is the preview() action. Here's the code from the controller:

```
def preview
  render :layout => false
end
```

The only job of the action code is to short-circuit the application's usual rendering. Since we're going to be updating the live-preview element of our diary entry creation page with the full results of the preview() action, we don't want it returning a full HTML page. We just want a snippet that will make sense in the larger context of our entry screen.

The preview() action's view, in app/views/diary/preview.rhtml, should look like this:

```
<h2>Diary entry preview</h2>
<h3><%= params[:entry][:title] %></h3>
<%= textilize params[:entry][:body] %>
```

That's all there is to it! This view prints the entry's title as an HTML heading and then generates HTML output via the textilize() method. This method uses the RedCloth library internally to transform simple text markup to HTML.

You can now load the diary entry form and watch your plain text get transformed into HTML before you ever hit the Save button!

Discussion

You can set the :frequency parameter of the methods observe_field() and observe_form() to zero or less, which will cause the field to be observed in real time. Although this might sound like a good way to make your user interface snappier, it will actually drag it down, not to mention add a heavy load to your servers. If you observe changes in real time, *every* change will result in a request to your server, for which you'll have to wait for a result to see the screen update. The changes queue up, and you end up watching the live preview update slowly behind your changes, waiting for it to catch up.

Autocomplete a Text Field

You've seen those nifty "autocomplete" widgets. You know the ones—
you start typing, and the application dynamically starts looking for a
match before you've finished. They're all the rage, and anything less
will make you look oh so 1990s.

For your new killer app, you naturally want to scrve your search in
style.

Solution

As part of the script.aculo.us JavaScript library, Rails ships with a won-
derfully easy-to-use autocompletion widget. With it, you'll be up and
running with a sexily modern search box in fewer than 10 lines of code.

Imagine you have a cookbook application and would like to quickly
search for a recipe by name. We'll assume that we've already created
the necessary database tables and model classes and that the Active
Record migration to create this table looks like the following:

`3_add_recipes.rb`
```
def self.up
  create_table "recipes" do |t|
    t.column "name", :string
    t.column "region", :string
    t.column "instructions", :text
  end
  create_table "ingredients" do |t|
    t.column "recipe_id", :integer
    t.column "name", :string
    t.column "unit", :string
    t.column "quantity", :integer
  end
end
```

Let's create a new controller and view for our search code:

app> `script/generate controller Search`
          :   :   :

We'll create a new view for the search controller—let's call it search.rhtml
for now—from which to perform our fancy autocomplete. As you can
sec, there's not much to it:

`live_search/search.rhtml`

```
<html>
  <head>
    <%= javascript_include_tag :defaults %>
  </head>
  <body>
    <%= text_field_with_auto_complete :recipe, :name %>
  </body>
</html>
```

The first thing you should notice is the line near the top that says javascript_include_tag :defaults. This line is *really* easy to forget and even *harder* to troubleshoot once you've forgotten it. This is the line that includes the JavaScript files that make Rails–Ajax magic. Without this line, depending on your browser, you'll see anything from a cryptic error message to a lifeless HTML form with no explanation for its lack of fanciness. In fact, it can be so annoying that I'll say it again, really loudly: *DON'T FORGET TO INCLUDE THE JAVASCRIPT FILES!*

Now that the magic spells are included, we can invoke them:

```
<%= text_field_with_auto_complete :recipe, :name %>
```

This causes Rails to create a text box for you with all the required JavaScript attached to it. As with most Rails helpers, the method text_field_with_auto_complete() isn't doing anything you couldn't do manually. But, if you've ever had to attach JavaScript events to HTML elements, you know what a blessing these helpers really are.

We've got the client all wired up with JavaScript to observe a text field and make a request back to the server as the user types into the browser. The one final ingredient is to tell the server what to do when it receives these requests. Wiring these client-side requests to a model in your application is trivial. A single line in the SearchController will do the trick:

`live_search/search_controller.rb`

```
class SearchController < ApplicationController
  auto_complete_for :recipe, :name
end
```

This tells Rails to dynamically generate an action method with the name auto_complete_for_recipe_name() that will search for objects matching the entered text and render the results. Those results will fill the inner-HTML of the autocomplete's DHTML *<div>* element in the browser, creating a lovely pop-up effect.

Creating a Drag-and-Drop Sortable List

Credit

Thanks to Bruce Williams for code that inspired this recipe.

Problem

Your application has a model with a list that should be sortable. You want to manage the sort order of the list in the database, and you want to give your users a snazzy, modern, drag-and-drop interface with which to maintain the sort order.

Solution

Let's say we're creating an application for managing grocery lists. With the size of today's American grocery superstore, it's important to devise a shopping strategy before you hit the aisles. Otherwise, you can waste precious hours of your life following unoptimized shopping routes.

The Active Record migration file for our shopping optimization application will look like the following:

DragAndDropSortableList/db/migrate/001_add_person_and_grocery_lists_and_food_items_tables.rb

```
class AddPersonAndGroceryListsAndFoodItemsTables < ActiveRecord::Migration
  def self.up
    create_table :people do |t|
      t.column :name, :string
    end

    create_table :grocery_lists do |t|
      t.column :name, :string
      t.column :person_id, :integer
    end

    create_table :food_items do |t|
      t.column :grocery_list_id, :integer
      t.column :position, :integer
      t.column :name, :string
      t.column :quantity, :integer
    end
  end
```

```
    def self.down
      drop_table :people
      drop_table :grocery_lists
      drop_table :food_items
    end
end
```

As you can see, we have tables to support people, their grocery lists, and the items that go on each list (along with the quantity we need of each item). This is all standard Active Record has_many() fare, except for the position column in the food_items table. This column is special, as we'll see in a moment.

The associated model files are similarly short and sweet. A Person has many GroceryList objects:

DragAndDropSortableList/app/models/person.rb

```
class Person < ActiveRecord::Base
  has_many :grocery_lists
end
```

And each GroceryList has a list of FoodItem objects on it, which will be retrieved by the food_items table's position column:

DragAndDropSortableList/app/models/grocery_list.rb

```
class GroceryList < ActiveRecord::Base
  has_many :food_items, :order => :position
  belongs_to :person
end
```

Finally, we get to the spice. Class FoodItem contains Active Record's acts_as_list() declaration, which allows its containing object (GroceryList) to "automagically" manage its sort order:

DragAndDropSortableList/app/models/food_item.rb

```
class FoodItem < ActiveRecord::Base
  belongs_to :grocery_list
  acts_as_list :scope => :grocery_list
end
```

The :scope parameter tells acts_as_list() that the sort order is relevant within the context of a single grocery_list_id. This is so one grocery list's sort order doesn't affect any other list's order.

The column name position is special to acts_as_list(). By convention, Rails will automatically use this column name to manage sort order when a model is declared acts_as_list(). If we needed to use a nonstandard column name here, we could have passed the :column parameter, but position makes sense for our humble grocery list manager, so we'll leave well enough alone.

After running the migration and creating the model files, let's fire up the Rails console and play with this new structure:

```
chad> ruby script/console
>> kelly = Person.create(:name => "Kelly")
=> #<Person:0x26ec854 ...>>
>> list = kelly.grocery_lists.create(:name => "Dinner for Tibetan New Year Party")
=> #<GroceryList:0x26b9788 ...>>
>> list.food_items.create(:name => "Bag of flour", :quantity => 1)
=> #<FoodItem:0x26a8898 ...>>
>> list.food_items.create(:name => "Pound of Ground Beef", :quantity => 2)
=> #<FoodItem:0x269b60c ...>>
>> list.food_items.create(:name => "Clove of Garlic", :quantity => 5)
=> #<FoodItem:0x26937e0 ...>>
```

So we now have a person named Kelly in our database who seems to be planning a party for the Tibetan New Year celebration. So far, she has three items on her list. She's not done with the list yet, obviously—you can't make momos with just these three ingredients! Let's see what happened to that position column when we created these objects:

```
>> list.food_items.find_by_name("Pound of Ground Beef").position
    => 2
    >> list.food_items.find_by_name("Bag of flour").position
    => 1
```

Cool! Active Record has updated the position column for us! acts_as_list() also sets up a bunch of nice convenience methods for performing tasks such as selecting the next item (in order) in the list or moving an item's position up or down. Let's not get all caught up in the model just now, though. We have enough implemented that we can get to the fun stuff—drag and drop!

As always, if you're going to do fancy Ajax stuff, you need include the necessary JavaScript libraries somewhere in your HTML. I usually create a standard layout and throw the JavaScript in there. Let's create the layout in app/views/layouts/standard.rhtml and then fill it in as follows:

DragAndDropSortableList/app/views/layouts/standard.rhtml

```
<html>
  <head>
      <%= javascript_include_tag :defaults %>
  </head>
  <body>
    <%= yield %>
  </body>
</html>
```

Next, pretending that we already have some kind of interface for creating a list and associating it with a person, let's create the controller and action from whence we'll reorder our list. We'll create a controller in app/views/controllers/grocery_list_controller.rb with an action called show(). The beginning of the controller should look like the following:

`DragAndDropSortableList/app/controllers/grocery_list_controller.rb`

```ruby
class GroceryListController < ApplicationController
  layout "standard"

  def show
    @grocery_list = GroceryList.find(params[:id])
  end
  # ...
```

Note that we've included the standard.rhtml layout, and we've defined a basic action that will simply find a grocery list based on a supplied parameter:

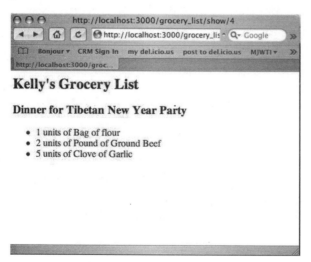

Next we create the associated view in app/views/grocery_list/show.rhtml:

`DragAndDropSortableList/app/views/grocery_list/show.rhtml`

```html
<h2><%= @grocery_list.person.name %>'s Grocery List</h2>
<h3><%= @grocery_list.name %></h3>
<ul id="grocery-list">
  <% @grocery_list.food_items.each do |food_item| %>
  <li id="item_<%= food_item.id %>">
      <%= food_item.quantity %> units of <%= food_item.name %>
  </li>
  <% end %>
</ul>
```

Again, this is nothing too fancy. This is standard Action View read-only material. Do note, though, that we are autogenerating unique element ids for the *<li>* tags. This is necessary when we move on to the sorting code, so don't skip it in this step. We can see what this page looks like by starting our development server and pointing our browser to (assuming the default port) http://localhost:3000/grocery_list/show/*listid*, where *listid* is the id of the GroceryList model object we created in the console.

Now let's make the list sortable. At the end of our show.rhtml, we'll add the following:

`DragAndDropSortableList/app/views/grocery_list/show.rhtml`

```
<%= sortable_element 'grocery-list',
      :url => { :action => "sort", :id => @grocery_list },
      :complete => visual_effect(:highlight, 'grocery-list')
%>
```

This helper generates the JavaScript necessary to turn our unordered list into a dynamic, drag-and-drop sortable form. The first parameter, grocery-list, refers to the ID of the item on the current HTML page that should be transformed into a sortable list. The :url option specifies the elements, such as action and controller, that will make up the URL that will be called when a sorting change is made. We have specified the sort() action of the current controller, appending the current grocery list's ID. Finally, the :complete option sets up a visual effect to take place when the sort() action has finished.

Let's get that sort() action implemented so we can watch this thing in action! In the grocery_list_controller.rb, we'll add a sort() action that looks like this:

`DragAndDropSortableList/app/controllers/grocery_list_controller.rb`

```
def sort
  @grocery_list = GroceryList.find(params[:id])
  @grocery_list.food_items.each do |food_item|
    food_item.position = params['grocery-list'].index(food_item.id.to_s) + 1
    food_item.save
  end
  render :nothing => true
end
```

First we select the grocery list by the supplied ID. Then we iterate through the items on the list and change each item's position to match its index in the grocery-list parameter. The grocery-list parameter is generated automatically by the sortable_element() helper and creates an ordered Array of the list items' IDs. Since our position columns start with 1 and an Array's index starts with 0, we add 1 to the index value before saving the position.

Finally, we explicitly tell Rails that this action should not render anything. Since the visual output of sorting a list is the list itself (which we're already displaying), we let the action complete its work silently. Had we wanted to update the HTML page with the action's results, we could have added the :update option to our sortable_element() call, passing it the ID of the HTML element to populate with our action's results.

If we refresh the grocery list show() page with the sortable_element() addition, we can now drag items up and down the list to change their order both on the page and in the database.

Also See

Chapter 15 of *Agile Web Development with Rails* [TH05] contains a more thorough introduction to acts_as_list().

Update Multiple Elements with One Ajax Request

You've seen how the Ajax form helpers allow you to update a section of the page you're working on with the results of a remote action. For most Ajax actions, you can use the :update parameter to specify an HTML element ID that should be updated with the response of the remote action. This is extremely easy to use and is sufficient in most situations. If you want to add an item to a list, you just update the list's HTML with a rerendered version from the server. If you want to edit a form in place, it's the same thing.

This model starts to break down if you need to update several potentially disconnected elements on the same page with the result of *one* click or action. For example, the mock-up in Figure 6.3, on the next page, shows a fictional shopping cart application. The top of the page displays the number of items in a user's cart, and each product can be added to or removed from the cart without having to refresh the page.

Potential solutions to this problem using the :update parameter are messy and problematic.

Ingredients

• Rails 1.1 or higher

Solution

Rails 1.1 introduces a new type of template called Remote JavaScript, or RJS. Just as with Builder templates and their .rxml extension, templates with a file name extension of .rjs are automatically handled as RJS templates.

RJS provides simple, succinct Ruby methods that generate verbose JavaScript code for you. You call methods such as

```
page.hide 'element-id'
```

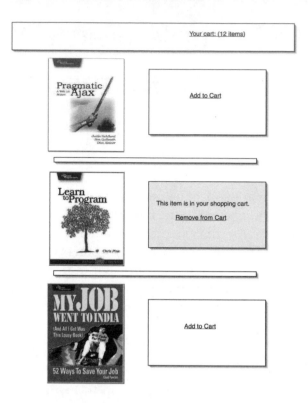

Figure 6.3: MOCK-UP OF SHOPPING CART

and RJS generates the JavaScript to set the display of the named element to none and then streams that JavaScript to the browser. The content is returned to the browser with a Content-type of text/javascript. The Prototype JavaScript library that ships with Rails recognizes this Content-type and calls JavaScript's eval() with the returned content.

Let's cook up a quick example to see this in action. Assuming we already have an application generated, we'll generate a new controller to play with:

```
chad> ruby script/generate controller AjaxFun
    exists  app/controllers/
      :         :
```

Next we'll make a simple index.rhtml view for this controller, which will serve as our Ajax playground. The index.rhtml should look like the following, keeping in mind that the HTML element ID names are important:

`UpdateMultiplePageElementsWithAjax/app/views/ajax_fun/index.rhtml`

```
<html>
  <head>
    <%= javascript_include_tag :defaults %>
  </head>
  <body>
    <h2 id="header">Ajax Fun</h2>
    <div>
      This page was initially loaded at <%= Time.now %>
    </div>
    <div>
      This page was updated at <span id="time_updated"><%= Time.now %></span>
    </div>
    <ul id="the_list">
      <li>Initially, the first item</li>
      <li>Another item</li>
      <li id="item_to_remove">This one will be removed.</li>
    </ul>
    <div id="initially_hidden" style="display: none;">
      This text starts out hidden.
    </div>
    <%= link_to_remote "Ajax Magic", :url => {:action => "change"} %><br/>
  </body>
</html>
```

We've taken the time to label the elements that we want to be dynamically updated with HTML ID attributes. The remote link at the bottom of the page will fire an XMLHttpRequest to the controller's change() method. That's where we'll have our fun. Notice there's no :update parameter given to link_to_remote(). Let's look first at the controller:

`UpdateMultiplePageElementsWithAjax/app/controllers/ajax_fun_controller.rb`

```
class AjaxFunController < ApplicationController
  def change
    @rails_version = Rails::VERSION::STRING
  end
end
```

We simply set an instance variable called @rails_version that we'll use in our view. The real work happens in the view for this action, change.rjs:

`UpdateMultiplePageElementsWithAjax/app/views/ajax_fun/change.rjs`

```
Line 1    page.replace_html 'time_updated', Time.now.to_s
     -    page.visual_effect :shake, 'time_updated'

     -    page.insert_html :top, 'the_list', '<li>King of the Hill</li>'
     5    page.visual_effect :highlight, 'the_list'

     -    page.show 'initially_hidden'
```

```
  -    page.delay(3) do
 10      page.alert @rails_version
  -    end
  -
  -    page.remove 'item_to_remove'
```

You'll notice that RJS implicitly supplies an object called page that provides all the JavaScript generation methods. Line 1 replaces the HTML for the time-updated span tag with the current time. The following line alerts the user with a not-so-subtle shake, indicating that the time was updated.

Line 4 inserts a new list item into the page's unordered list element, followed by an instance of the 37signals-coined *Yellow Fade Technique*. Note that insert_html() and replace_html() can each accept either a String as we've supplied here or the same parameters that render() accepts. So you could, for example, insert the result of rendering a partial view template into the page.

On line 7, we cause the page's hidden element to appear. The opposite of this is the hide() method, not to be confused with remove(), which we use on line 13 to actually *delete* an element from the HTML page.

Finally, on line 9, we use the rather unusual delay() method to cause a JavaScript alert to pop up three seconds after the page has loaded. The delay() method generates a JavaScript timeout function, which will execute any JavaScript generated inside its supplied block.

Notice that the alert() method uses the instance variable, @rails_version, that we set in the controller. Instance variables and helper methods are available in an RJS template, just like in any other view.

As we said earlier, the RJS template generates JavaScript and passes it back to the browser for evaluation. For this particular RJS template, the generated JavaScript would look something like the following:

```
Element.update("time-updated", "Sat Jan 28 15:40:45 MST 2006");
new Effect.Shake('time-updated',{});
new Insertion.Top("the-list", "<li>King of the Hill</li>");
new Effect.Highlight('the-list',{});
Element.show("initially-hidden");
setTimeout(function() {
alert("0.14.3");
}, 3000);
["item-to-remove"].each(Element.remove);
```

And there it is. Easy as pie. With RJS, Ajax is no longer an ordeal.

Discussion

The Content-type of an RJS template *must* be set to text/javascript. The RJS handler does this for you, but if you have any code in your application that explicitly sets the Content-type, you may find that your RJS templates aren't doing *anything*. If your RJS templates don't seem to be doing anything at all, make sure your application doesn't have an after filter that's setting the Content-type.

Another issue you need to be aware of when you're dealing with RJS templates is that since RJS templates generate JavaScript to be evaluated by the browser, errors can be a little harder to detect. For example, if you were to create a syntax error in your controller or view, Rails would return its usual HTML-formatted stack trace. The problem with this is that it's fired in the background, and since there's no JavaScript to evaluate, *nothing* will end up happening in the browser. So if you find yourself staring at your browser's lifeless face as you wait infinitely for an RJS-powered Ajax action to complete, you might want to check the log to find out whether the request ended in an error.

Lightning-Fast JavaScript Autocompletion

When your users have to perform a function over and over again, you want it to be as fast as it possibly can be. Google understood this when it designed the email address autocompletion feature of Gmail. You start typing, and there's no lag. The addresses pop up almost as fast as you can type.

How does Google do it so fast? How does Google do it without beating its servers to death? Google prefetches the addresses and autocompletes them from an in-browser cache.

First we need to serve up something that the browser can download *once* and that an autocompleter can access. How about a JavaScript Array? The JavaScript source files we usually include at the top of our HTML files, such as prototype.js, controls.js, and effects.js, are static text files that get directly served to the browser. But there's no reason we can't serve up a *dynamically* generated JavaScript file too.

Say we were trying to do an autocompleted search field for all the authors who write for a publisher. We might have, say, a BookController with the following action:

`LightningFastJavaScriptAutoCompletes/app/controllers/book_controller.rb`

```ruby
def authors_for_lookup
  @authors = Author.find(:all)
  @headers['content-type'] = 'text/javascript'
end
```

We selected all of the authors and then, most important, set the content-type to text/javascript. Some browsers don't care, but some do. We might as well do it right. Also note that if you are using layouts, you'll need to call the following at the end of the action to make sure the JavaScript doesn't get mixed with your application's HTML layout:

```ruby
render :layout => false
```

Now let's look at the corresponding view:

LightningFastJavaScriptAutoCompletes/app/views/book/authors_for_lookup.rhtml

```
var authors = new Array(<%= @authors.size %>);

<% @authors.each_with_index do |author, index| %>
  authors[<%= index %>] = "<%= author.name %>";
<% end %>
```

You see, even though we tend to put HTML in our ERb templates, ERb really doesn't care *what* we're dynamically generating as long as it's text and it doesn't contain syntactically incorrect ERb code. So in this template, we're generating a little JavaScript snippet that takes our Ruby Array and turns it into the source code for a JavaScript one.

Now that we're able to serve it up, we can include it in our templates just like any other JavaScript file. Here's the top of a template from which we'll use this file. Note that we also include the default Rails JavaScript files, since we're going to need them for our dynamic auto-complete.

LightningFastJavaScriptAutoCompletes/app/views/book/search_page.rhtml

```
<head>
  <%= javascript_include_tag :defaults %>
  <script src="/book/authors_for_lookup" type="text/javascript"></script>
```

We inserted a <*script*> tag. In it we put relative path to our JavaScript action. It's as easy as pie. Now we have access to the authors variable from our dynamically generated script. We can do as many Ajax requests as we want on this page, and we won't have to reload this Array again. The browser already has it.

Now that the authors variable is accessible to our browser, we can put it to use. Rails ships with an easy-to-use autocompletion library, complete with Ruby helper methods and a rich JavaScript library to back it up. The Ruby helper methods assume that we want to perform our autocompletion against the results of a remote request back to the server. However, the JavaScript library that supports this functionality also has a "local" mode.

The JavaScript class we need to use is called Autocompleter.Local[4]. Its constructor accepts three mandatory arguments: the id of the text element to attach itself to, the id of a <*div*> element to update with the

---

[4]http://wiki.script.aculo.us/scriptaculous/show/Autocompleter.Local has the official documentation.

autocompletion results, and a JavaScript Array of character strings to use as the data source for the control (this is our authors variable).

An example invocation of the local autocompleter might look like this:

```
<%= javascript_tag("new Autocompleter.Local('author_lookup',
                                  'author_lookup_auto_complete',
                                  authors);") %>
```

The first two arguments to the Autocompleter.Local constructor imply the existence of two HTML elements that we haven't yet created. The first is the text field into which our users will type their searches. The second is a (initially empty) <div> to fill with the autocompletion results. We can define those like this:

```
<input type="text" id="author_lookup" name="author_lookup" />
<div class="auto_complete" id="author_lookup_auto_complete"></div>
```

Notice the class attribute we applied to the empty <div>. To give our autocompletion results a look that our users are familiar with, we'll need to style the <div> ourselves. The Rails autocompletion helpers give us the necessary styling by default, but since we're creating our own JavaScript autocompleter, we can't use the helpers.

Not wanting to re-invent the wheel (which is a euphemism for "I suck at CSS"), I temporarily added the built-in autocompletion helper to my template, viewed it in my browser, and snagged the generated <style> tag to add to the template here. To save you that work, here it is:

LightningFastJavaScriptAutoCompletes/app/views/book/search_page.rhtml

```
<style>
  div.auto_complete {
    width: 350px;
    background: #fff;
  }
  div.auto_complete ul {
    border:1px solid #888;
    margin:0;
    padding:0;
    width:100%;
    list-style-type:none;
  }
  div.auto_complete ul li {
    margin:0;
    padding:3px;
  }
  div.auto_complete ul li.selected {
    background-color: #ffb;
  }
```

```
div.auto_complete ul strong.highlight {
  color: #800;
  margin:0;
  padding:0;
}
</style>
```

Just add that anywhere in your page's <head> tag, and your autocompleters should behave as you expect them to behave.

Putting it all together, here's the entire page with the form, JavaScript, and necessary CSS:

LightningFastJavaScriptAutoCompletes/app/views/book/search_page.rhtml

```
<html>
  <head>
    <%= javascript_include_tag :defaults %>
    <script src="/book/authors_for_lookup" type="text/javascript"></script>
    <style>
      div.auto_complete {
        width: 350px;
        background: #fff;
      }
      div.auto_complete ul {
        border:1px solid #888;
        margin:0;
        padding:0;
        width:100%;
        list-style-type:none;
      }
      div.auto_complete ul li {
        margin:0;
        padding:3px;
      }
      div.auto_complete ul li.selected {
        background-color: #ffb;
      }
      div.auto_complete ul strong.highlight {
        color: #800;
        margin:0;
        padding:0;
      }
    </style>
  </head>
  <body>
    <label for="author_lookup">Author Search</label>
    <input type="text" id="author_lookup" name="author_lookup" />
    <div class="auto_complete" id="author_lookup_auto_complete">
    </div>
    <%= javascript_tag("new Autocompleter.Local('author_lookup',
                                     'author_lookup_auto_complete',
```

```
                authors,
                {fullSearch: true,
                   frequency: 0,
                   minChars: 1
                }
                );") %>
  </body>
</html>
```

I wanted the autocompleter to be really responsive, so I added a fourth argument to the Autocompleter.Local initializer. The fourth argument is a Hash of options, similar to the convention followed by many of the Rails helper methods. I wanted to be able to match a first name or a last name, so I set fullSearch to true. To minimize the delay in a result coming up, I set the polling frequency to 0 (which makes it event-based rather than time-based) and minChars to 1. This means as soon as our users start typing, they'll start seeing matching results. Very snappy!

Viewing this action against the Pragmatic Bookshelf authors list gives us a really fast and responsive autocompleter that looks like this:

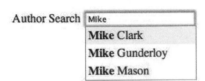

Cheap & Easy Theme Support

Thanks to David Alan Black for the idea for this recipe.

It's possible to spend a lot of time adding theme support to your application. If an application requires different layouts for different themes, this level of effort might be worthwhile.

More often than not, though, you can get by with a lightweight, entirely CSS-driven approach to themes.

Simply add a String field called style to your application's User (or equivalent) model, and you can implement theme support in a matter of minutes with an application layout like the following:

CheapAndEasyThemeSupport/app/views/layouts/application.rhtml

```
<html>
  <head>
   <%= stylesheet_link_tag(session[:user].style || "default") %>
  </head>
  <body>
    <div id='main'>
      <div id='header'>
        <h1>Welcome, <%= session[:user].name %>!</h1>
      </div>
      <div id='content'>
        <%= yield %>
      </div>
    </div>
  </body>
</html>
```

Any user who doesn't have a configured style attribute will get the default CSS style sheet (literally called default.css). All it takes to alter a user's visual experience is the following:

```
chad> ruby script/console
>> User.find_by_name("Chad").update_attribute(:style, "hideous")
=> true
```

The next time poor Chad reloads the page, he'll be confronted with the usual page, styled using public/stylesheets/hideous.css.

Trim Static Pages with Ajax

With the heavy emphasis on Ajax being used to drive ultradynamic Web *applications*, you might overlook one of its simpler benefits. If you have a page with both summary and detail data for a set of items (for example, a product catalog), you might want to enable users to view an overview of each item in a list and then click for details without having to refresh the page. You could just, for example, assign an empty *<div>* to each product to store its detail information and then show that *<div>* when the user clicks the "detail" link.

You could just embed all of this detail in every listing, but the resulting HTML pages could get really big and lead to long download times and browser instability. So, grabbing the detail from a remote location makes a lot of sense.

Remote links can even be made to static HTML pages. Take the following view snippet as an example:

`StaticAjax/app/views/products/index.rhtml`

```
<ul>
  <li>
    <div id="product-1" class="product-overview">
        <span class="title">Learn to Program (Chris Pine)
            <%= link_to_remote "detail",
                    :update => 'product-1-detail',
                    :method => 'get',
                    :url => '/catalog/details/1.html'  %>
        </span>
    </div>
    <div id='product-1-detail'></div>
  </li>
</ul>
```

When a user clicks the "detail" link, an Ajax request will be made that will simply retrieve the file, 1.html, from the web server and replace the product-1-detail HTML *<div>* with its contents.

Notice that we've instructed Rails to make an HTTP GET request to the server. It defaults to a POST for remote links, which is not appropriate for getting static files.

Smart Pluralization

An annoying little problem that we all have to deal with sometimes in application development occurs when you need to conditionally use the plural or singular version of a word depending on how many items were returned from a database. How many messages does a user have in his or her inbox? How many failed transactions does a financial operations team need to resolve?

Rails comes with a wonderful tool called the Inflector, which is the thing that (among doing other tasks) figures out what a table name should be called based on the name of its associated model. This logic involves a great deal of smarts, and it has thankfully been exposed for use anywhere in a Rails application. In fact, a handy wrapper method in Action View was made to handle the most common pluralization need as described previously. Here's how you use it:

`SmartPluralizationOfWords/app/views/recipes/index.rhtml`

```
Hi <%= @user.name %>.
You have <%= pluralize @recipes.size, "unread recipe" %> in your inbox.
```

What if your application isn't in English or you want to support the (horrible) geek-culture tendency to refer to server boxes as *boxen*? Casting aside good taste, you can do that by customizing the Inflector's pluralization rules. Just add something like the following to your config/environment.rb:

`SmartPluralizationOfWords/config/environment.rb`

```
Inflector.inflections do |inflect|
  inflect.plural /(ox)$/i, '\1en'
  inflect.singular /(ox)en/i, '\1'
end
```

Now, the plural form of *box* is *boxen* and vice versa.

You can also use the Inflector's uncountable() method to signify words that have no plural and the irregular() method to configure words whose pluralization rules don't follow a pattern:

```
inflect.uncountable "fish", "information", "money"
inflect.irregular "person", "people"
```

Debugging Ajax

All of this fancy Ajax stuff is cool. But because Ajax is something that has recently taken hold, the methods of developing software with these techniques are still maturing. This immaturity shows most strongly when trouble strikes.

A bad Ajax request can leave you staring at a lifeless screen for precious minutes and hours of your life while you try to figure out why a list isn't updating or an effect isn't being applied.

Here are three simple tips you can use to make Ajax debugging easier.

First, if you're running Rails 1.1 and using RJS templates, you can add the following line to your config/environments/development.rb:

```
config.action_view.debug_rjs = true
```

For applications *generated* with Rails 1.1 or higher, this is the default behavior, as configured in config/environments/development.rb. If you *really* need to, you can turn on debugging for your production environment in the corresponding file, but it's best not to do that unless it's absolutely necessary.

This will result in some helpful JavaScript alerts when there is an RJS-driven JavaScript exception. Don't be alarmed if you add this line and no alerts pop up when there is an exception raised in the RJS template itself. These alerts show up only when there is a JavaScript exception, for example when referencing a nonexistent element by ID.

Second, you can register your own Ajax responder to update the page with every Ajax request. Rick Olson suggests something like this:

```
DebuggingAjax/app/views/ajax/index.rhtml
```
```
<% if ActionView::Base.debug_rjs %>
 <script type="text/javascript">
   Ajax.Responders.register({
     onComplete: function(request, transport) {
       new Insertion.Bottom('debug',
         '<div style="border: 1px solid">' +
           transport.responseText.escapeHTML() +
         '</div>')
     }
   });
 </script>
<% end %>
```

Now in your template, simply add an empty *<div>* with id="debug", and if you have configured your application to be in RJS debug mode, every Ajax request will result in a line being appended to this *<div>*. Seeing the raw contents of every request can be an incredible time saver.

Finally, if you're using Firefox, you shouldn't be without Joe Hewitt's FireBug.[5] FireBug lets you log JavaScript errors, inspect the elements of a page, and inspect XMLHttpRequest output (similar to our *<debug>* trick).

---

[5]Available from http://www.joehewitt.com/software/firebug/

Creating a Custom Form Builder

Credit

Thanks to Mike Clark and Bruce Williams for the ideas they contributed to this recipe.

Problem

You have your own style of form that your application needs to use constantly. You want to create a helper that can be used to create customized form types.

Ingredients

- Rails 1.1 or higher

Solution

Through the new form_for() family of helpers, Rails 1.1 introduces the notion of a form builder. A vanilla Rails 1.1 form might look like this:

```
<% form_for :contact do |f| %>
  <%= f.text_field :name %>
  <%= f.text_field :email %>
  <%= f.text_field :phone %>
<% end %>
```

This generates a form for the variable contact. The syntax is much nicer, but this generates the same tired old HTML form we've seen since Rails introduced start_form_tag() in its initial release. It gets more exciting when you take advantage of form_for()'s :builder option. The builder is the object that is yielded to form_for()'s block. Because you call the helpers on that object, it's the builder that actually generates the HTML for the form and its tags.

What if we wanted to always generate a tabular form, with each field getting its own table row (<tr>) containing columns for a field label and the field itself? The form_for() call would look something like this:

```erb
<% form_for :contact, :builder => TabularFormBuilder do |f| %>
  <%= f.text_field :name %>
  <%= f.text_field :email %>
  <%= f.text_field :phone %>
<% end %>
```

Then we would define the TabularFormBuilder in a helper. I've put this one in application_helper.rb, because I want it to be available to all my views. Here's its definition:

CustomFormBuilder/app/helpers/application_helper.rb

```ruby
class TabularFormBuilder < ActionView::Helpers::FormBuilder
  (field_helpers - %w(check_box radio_button hidden_field)).each do |selector|
    src = <<-END_SRC
      def #{selector}(field, options = {})
        @template.content_tag("tr",
          @template.content_tag("td", field.to_s.humanize + ":") +
            @template.content_tag("td", super))
      end
    END_SRC
    class_eval src, __FILE__, __LINE__
  end
end
```

If you haven't done a lot of metaprogramming in Ruby, this class might be a little jarring at first. It's OK to take this on faith to some extent, so don't let it bog you down. You can use this as a template for creating your own builders. Just know that what we're doing is looping through all the helpers defined on FormBuilder and overriding them with our own autogenerated method definitions. If you turn your head to the side and squint at this code, you can see that, in the loop, it defines a method with the same name as each helper (such as text_field() and text_area()) that sets up a table row, a table column with a label in it, and an empty table column into which the output of the original helper from FormBuilder is placed.

Our new form_for() now generates the following (some newlines were added to make this listing fit the width of the page):

```html
<form action="/contacts/new" method="post">
  <tr>
    <td>Name:</td>
    <td>
      <input id="contact_name" name="contact[name]" size="30" type="text" />
    </td>
  </tr>
  <tr>
    <td>Email:</td>
    <td>
```

```
      <input id="contact_email" name="contact[email]" size="30" type="text" />
    </td>
  </tr>
  <tr>
    <td>Phone:</td>
    <td>
      <input id="contact_phone" name="contact[phone]" size="30" type="text" />
    </td>
  </tr>
</form>
```

Now we're getting somewhere! The only problem is that our form_for() is generating table rows but no enclosing table. We could, of course, simply insert <*table*> tags wherever we use this builder, but that would lead to a lot of ugly duplication. Instead, let's create our own wrapper for form_for(), which will not only take care of inserting the <*table*> tags but will also save us from having to enter the builder option every time we create a form. We'll put this method definition in application_helper.rb:

CustomFormBuilder/app/helpers/application_helper.rb

```
def tabular_form_for(name, object = nil, options = nil, &proc)
    concat("<table>", proc.binding)
    form_for(name,
             object,
             (options||{}).merge(:builder => TabularFormBuilder),
             &proc)
    concat("</table>", proc.binding)
end
```

This method is simple. It wraps the same old standard call to form_for() with concat() calls, which concatenate the opening and closing <*table*> tags to the output.

Our view code would now create the form like this:

CustomFormBuilder/app/views/contacts/new.rhtml

```
<html>
<head>
    <%= stylesheet_link_tag "application" %>
</head>
<body>
<% tabular_form_for :contact do |f| %>
  <%= f.text_field :name %>
  <%= f.text_field :email %>
  <%= f.text_field :phone %>
<% end %>
</body>
</html>
```

Now that you have that working, you can't help but ask yourself what *other* elements you constantly find yourself putting into forms. How about alternate the color of each row in a form? Here's a form builder that does that:

CustomFormBuilder/app/helpers/application_helper.rb

```ruby
class TabularAlternatingColorFormBuilder < ActionView::Helpers::FormBuilder
  (field_helpers - %w(check_box radio_button hidden_field)).each do |selector|
    src = <<-END_SRC
      def #{selector}(field, options = {})
        @template.content_tag("tr",
          @template.content_tag("td", field.to_s.humanize + ":") +
          @template.content_tag("td", super),
            :class => (@alt = (@alt ? false : true)) ? "alt-row" : ""  )
      end
    END_SRC
    class_eval src, __FILE__, __LINE__
  end
end

def tabular_form_with_alternating_colors_for(name,
                                              object = nil,
                                              options = nil,
                                              &proc)
  concat("<table>", proc.binding)
  form_for(name,
           object,
           (options||{}).merge(:builder => TabularAlternatingColorFormBuilder),
           &proc)
  concat("</table>", proc.binding)
end
```

This builder uses the instance variable @alt to toggle the CSS class name with each table row. Adding a CSS snippet like the following to your application's style sheet will give you a nice, readable alternating table row effect:

```css
.alt-row {
  background: #fab444;
}
```

Make Pretty Graphs

You want to dynamically generate attractive graphs of data in your application.

- ImageMagick. Get it from http://www.imagemagick.org.

- Ruby's ImageMagick binding, RMagick. Installable via gem install rmagick. ImageMagick and RMagick can be a bit difficult to set up (sometimes). Have a look at the RMagick installation FAQ at http://rmagick.rubyforge.org/install-faq.html before you try to install them. You'll be glad you did.

- Geoffrey Grosenbach's beautiful Gruff graphing library, installable via gem install gruff.

In this recipe, we'll see how to use Gruff to make pretty graphs and how to include them in our application's views. Let's get right down to business.

We'll put all our graph logic together in a controller called GraphController. Although it's not necessary to put graphing logic in a separate controller, we'll do so in this case so that we can keep all our Gruff-related code together. Generate the controller now.

Gruff supports several different types of graphs: line, bar, area, pie, and stacked bar graphs. We'll start with a simple pie chart. Normally you would graph data that you calculated based on model objects or some other statistic relevant to your domain.[6] To keep this example simple and relevant to *all* Rails programmers, we'll use our application's statistics as the data model for our graphs.

Let's add the following stats() action to our new GraphController:

---

[6]See Recipe 27, *Perform Calculations on Your Model Data*, on page 123 for further information.

MakePrettyGraphs/app/controllers/graph_controller.rb

```
require 'gruff'

  STATS_DIRECTORIES = [
    %w(Helpers              app/helpers),
    %w(Controllers          app/controllers),
    %w(APIs                 app/apis),
    %w(Components           components),
    %w(Functional\ tests    test/functional),
    %w(Models               app/models),
    %w(Unit\ tests          test/unit),
    %w(Libraries            lib/),
    %w(Integration\ tests test/integration)
  ].collect { |name, dir|
      [ name, "#{RAILS_ROOT}/#{dir}" ]
    }.select { |name, dir|
      File.directory?(dir)
    }
  def stats
    code_stats = CodeStatistics.new(*STATS_DIRECTORIES)
    statistics = code_stats.instance_variable_get(:@statistics)
    g = Gruff::Pie.new(500)
    g.font = "/Library/Fonts/Arial"
    g.title = "Code Stats"
    g.theme_37signals
    g.legend_font_size = 10
    0xFDD84E.step(0xFF0000, 1500) do |num|
      g.colors << "#%x"  % num
    end
    statistics.each do |key, values|
      g.data(key, [values["codelines"]])
    end
    send_data(g.to_blob,
                :disposition => 'inline',
                :type => 'image/png',
                :filename => "code_stats.png")
  end
#END
end
```

Running this action results in a beautiful graph that looks like Figure 13.4, on the next page.

Let's walk through the code. First we require the gruff library and then set up the STATS_DIRECTORIES constant. I ripped this out of the stats() Rake task that ships with Rails. Its function is simply to supply a list of directories for the CodeStatistics class to process.

Then, moving into the stats() action, the first two lines set up our model data that will be fed to the graphing engine. We have to play an ugly

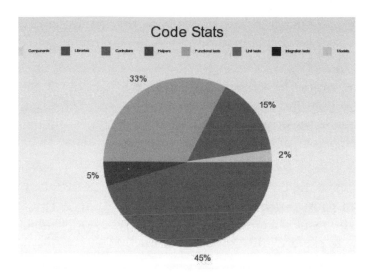

Figure 13.4: GRUFF PRODUCED A PIE CHART

trick to get access to the raw statistics data, since there is no accessor for it. That's why we're using instance_variable_get() here. In your own applications, this part would be replaced with a call to select your application-specific models.

We spend the next several lines setting up the graph. The number 500, which we pass into the constructor, indicates the width of the image. We set the font and the title and then select (optionally) from one of Gruff's included themes. The other theme choices are theme_keynote, theme_rails_keynote, and theme_odeo. Next, since our legend contains some pretty long words, we set the font size of the legend. To finish up the graph configuration, we loop through a series of hexadecimal values to set a range of graph colors. With a small data set, this isn't necessary because the default themes have enough colors to accommodate every row of data.

Our last bit of graph work is to actually populate the graph with data. We loop through our code statistics Hash and add one row of data to the graph for each entry in the Hash. The second parameter of the graph's data() method is an Array of actual values. In this case, we're tracking only one value for each row, but we still need to pass an Array, so we pass a single-value Array containing the number of lines of code for this directory.

Finally, to avoid having to write a file to the file system, we use the Rails built-in send_data() method to stream the raw image data to the browser.

What if we wanted to convert this graph to a bar chart? Simple! Just change the line that reads Gruff::Pie to read Gruff::Bar. That's it! The same is true of the other Gruff-included graph types, though there are some, such as Line and Area, that wouldn't make sense to use with our two-dimensional data set.

Once you have the basics down (and ImageMagick installed properly!), Gruff is an easy-to-use, consistent graphing library. The interface is basically the same throughout the various types of graphs, making it really easy to explore and experiment with.

Part II

Database Recipes

Rails without a Database

"Opinionated software" as it is, Rails assumes you want to develop with a database. This is *usually* the case, which is the reason the assumption. But what if you're developing an application with a file-based back end? Or perhaps you're simply front-ending an external service-based API. Rails is a little less friendly to you in this case—particularly when testing your application.

By default, Rails assumes that you want to connect to and initialize a database whenever you run your tests. This means that if you don't have a database, testing is difficult to do. Of course, you could just create a database for nothing, but that would mean you'd have extra infrastructure to support for no reason. A little hacking on a generated Rails application will get it into testable shape without a database.

To keep things simple and repeatable, we'll start with a fresh application. You'll be able to easily apply what we do here to your own application. Let's generate an application now. You can call it whatever you like. Mine is named DatabaselessApplication.

Next we'll create a simple class in lib for which to write some tests. Let's be really simple and create a class called Adder that adds numbers together:

`DatabaselessApplication/lib/adder.rb`

```ruby
class Adder
  def initialize(first, second)
    @first = first
    @second = second
  end

  def sum
    @first + @second
  end
end
```

Now we'll create a simple test case for it in test/unit/adder_test.rb:

```
DatabaselessApplication/test/unit/adder_test.rb
```

```ruby
require File.join(File.dirname(__FILE__), "..", "test_helper")
require 'adder'
class AdderTest < Test::Unit::TestCase
  def test_simple_addition
    assert_equal(4, Adder.new(3,1).sum)
  end
end
```

Let's try to run the test:

```
chad> rake test_units
    (in /Users/chad/src/FR_RR/Book/code/DatabaselessApplication)
rake aborted!
#42000Unknown database 'databaselessapplication_development'
```

It seems that the Rails test_units() Rake task does some database initialization. In fact, rake -P confirms this:[7]

```
chad> rake -P |tail
    prepare_test_database
rake stats
rake test_functional
    prepare_test_database
rake test_plugins
    environment
rake test_units
    prepare_test_database
rake unfreeze_rails
rake update_javascripts
```

Sure enough, test_units() depends on the prepare_test_database() task. What if we tried to run the tests directly, not using our Rake task?

```
chad> ruby test/unit/adder_test.rb
Loaded suite test/unit/adder_test
Started
EE
Finished in 0.052262 seconds.

  1) Error:
test_simple_addition(AdderTest):
Mysql::Error: #42000Unknown database 'databaselessapplication_test'
(abbreviated)
```

---

[7]Note that a significant upgrade of Rake was released during the development of this book. Rake now supports the ability to place tasks in a namespace. You may find that the task names displayed here are syntactically different. For example, the prepare_test_database task has been renamed to db:test:prepare.

Some digging shows that somewhere in the chain of having required test_helper.rb, we inherited the database-centric setup() and teardown() methods. We could just use require "test/unit" manually right here in the test, but then we'd have to replicate this in every test we create. We would also find that this wouldn't initialize the Rails environment as necessary. So instead, we'll modify test_helper.rb itself.

Specifically, test_helper.rb's inclusion of test_help.rb is the source of the problem. So instead of the require() call to test_help.rb, we'll just cherry-pick what we want from it. And since we're removing the fixture-related definitions, we'll remove all of the generated fixture-related code as well. Here's our new test_helper.rb:

DatabaselessApplication/test/test_helper.rb

```
ENV["RAILS_ENV"] = "test"
require File.expand_path(File.dirname(__FILE__) + "/../config/environment")
require 'application'
require 'test/unit'
require 'action_controller/test_process'
require 'action_web_service/test_invoke'
require 'breakpoint'
```

If you don't plan to use ActionWebService, it's safe to remove the line that requires action_web_service/test_invoke.

Running our test as we did before now passes!

```
chad> ruby test/unit/adder_test.rb
Loaded suite test/unit/adder_test
Started
.
Finished in 0.002703 seconds.

1 tests, 1 assertions, 0 failures, 0 errors
```

Now that we have a unit test working, let's try a functional test. We'll first need to generate a controller (and the related tests):

```
chad> ruby script/generate controller MyController
      exists  app/controllers/
      exists  app/helpers/
      create  app/views/my_controller
      create  test/functional/
      create  app/controllers/my_controller_controller.rb
      create  test/functional/my_controller_controller_test.rb
      create  app/helpers/my_controller_helper.rb
```

Let's just try to run this test as is. Maybe it'll work:

```
chad> ruby test/functional/my_controller_controller_test.rb
Loaded suite test/functional/my_controller_controller_test
Started
.
Finished in 0.002624 seconds.

1 tests, 1 assertions, 0 failures, 0 errors
```

Well, that was easy, wasn't it? All that's left is to get these tests working with Rake. Having to manually invoke our test files one at a time is a real step backward from the default Rails way of testing. The Rails built-in testing tasks work really well, so we'd rather not lose any functionality as we implement our own tasks. We also don't want to have to copy and paste their code into our own Rake tasks. If we did that, we wouldn't receive the benefits of bug fixes and upgrades to the built-in tasks. If only the built-in tasks didn't have that prepare_test_database() prerequisite!

Fortunately, with the way Rails loads user-defined Rake tasks, we aren't limited to simply defining our own *new* tasks. We can also use drop-in Rakefiles to modify the behavior of the built-in Rake tasks before they are executed. The three tasks we're specifically interested in are test_units(), test_functional(), and recent() (a really handy task that runs only those tests that have recently changed). If we create the following file in lib/tasks/clear_database_prerequisites.rake, it will do the trick for us:

DatabaselessApplication/lib/tasks/clear_database_prerequisites.rake

```
[:test_units, :test_functional, :recent].each do |name|
  Rake::Task[name].prerequisites.clear
end
```

Rake 0.7.0 introduced a slight incompatibility in its API. If you're using a Rake version *prior to* 0.7.0, you'll need this instead:

DatabaselessApplication/lib/tasks/clear_database_prerequisites.rake

```
[:test_units, :test_functional, :recent].each do |name|
  Rake::Task.lookup(name).prerequisites.clear
end
```

This single line looks up each Task using Rake's API and clears the Task's dependencies. With this file installed, we can now successfully run any of the three built-in testing tasks without a database!

Discussion

Though it's not necessary to get our application running without a database, we can save memory and improve performance by controlling which Rails frameworks get loaded when our applications initialize. In a freshly generated Rails 1.0 application, the file config/environment.rb contains a section that looks like the following:

```
# Skip frameworks you're not going to use
# config.frameworks -= [ :action_web_service, :action_mailer ]
```

If we uncomment this line, we can specify any of the frameworks that we *do not* plan on using. For this recipe, it would make sense to add :active_record to this list.

Connecting to Multiple Databases

Credit

Thanks to Dave Thomas for the real-world problem and the inspiration for this solution.

Problem

The simple default Rails convention of connecting to *one* database per application is suitable *most* of the time. That's why it was made so easy to do. The task you most often want to do should be easy. The problem, though, is that sometimes it's so easy that you don't know how it works. Rails is full of magic, and database connectivity is a particularly magical area of the framework.

By default, on initialization a Rails application discovers which environment it's running under (development, test, or production) and finds a database configuration in config/database.yml that is named for the current environment. Here's a simple sample:

```
ConnectingToMultipleDatabases/config/typical-database.yml
```

```
development:
  adapter: mysql
  database: ConnectingToMultipleDatabases_development
  username: root
  password:
  socket: /tmp/mysql.sock

test:
  adapter: mysql
  database: ConnectingToMultipleDatabases_test
  username: root
  password:
  socket: /tmp/mysql.sock

production:
  adapter: mysql
  database: ConnectingToMultipleDatabases_production
  username: root
  password:
  socket: /tmp/mysql.sock
```

If you've done *any* database work with Rails, you've already seen (and probably configured) a file that looks like this. The naming conventions make it quite obvious what goes where, so you may find yourself blindly editing this file and achieving the desired effect.

But what if you need to step outside the norm and connect to multiple databases? What if, for example, you need to connect to a commercial application's tables to integrate your nifty new Web 2.0–compliant application with a legacy tool that your company has relied on for years? How do you configure and create those connections?

Solution

To understand how to connect to multiple databases from your Rails application, the best place to start is to understand how the *default* connections are made. How does an application go from a YAML configuration file to a database connection? How does an Active Record model know which database to use?

When a Rails application boots, it loads its config/environment.rb file. This file invokes the Rails Initializer. The Initializer has the big job of making sure all the components of Rails are properly set up and glued together. One of its jobs is to initialize database connections.

With the default Rails configuration, the Initializer then calls the method ActiveRecord::Base.establish_connection(). If you call this method with no arguments, it will check the value of the RAILS_ENV constant and will look that value up in the loaded config/database.yml. The default value for RAILS_ENV is development. So, by default, if you start a Rails application, it will look up the database configuration section named development in its config/database.yml file and set up a connection to that database.

Note that an actual connection has not yet been *established*. Active Record doesn't actually make the connection until it needs it, which happens on the first reference to the class's connection() method. So if you're following along and watching open database connections, don't be surprised if you don't see an actual connection made immediately after your application boots.

Having set up a connection to a database solves only part of the puzzle. That connection still has to be referenced by the model classes that need it. Things get interesting here. When the default connections are made by the Initializer, they are made directly from the ActiveRecord::Base class, which is the superclass of all Active Record models. Because the call to establish_connection() was made on ActiveRecord::Base, the connection is associated with the ActiveRecord::Base class and is made available to all of its child classes (your application-specific) models.

So, in the default case, all your models get access to this default connection. But, ActiveRecord::Base. If you make a connection from one of your model classes (by calling establish_connection()), that connection will be available from that class and any of its children but *not* from its superclasses, including ActiveRecord::Base.

The behavior of a model when asked for its connection is to start with the exact class the request is made from and work its way up the inheritance hierarchy until it finds a connection. This is a key point in working with multiple databases.

Now that we know how Active Record connections work, let's put our knowledge into action. We'll contrive a couple of example databases with which to demonstrate. The following is our config/database.yml file. We have two databases. One is labeled as development and will be our default database. The other is called products, simulating the hypothetical scenario of having an existing, external product database for a new application.

ConnectingToMultipleDatabases/config/database.yml

```
development:
  adapter: mysql
  database: myrailsdatabase_development
  username: root
  password:
  socket: /tmp/mysql.sock

products:
  adapter: mysql
  database: products
  username: root
  password:
  socket: /tmp/mysql.sock
```

We'll also create some tables in these databases so we can hook them up to Active Record models. For our default Rails database, we'll create a migration defining tables for users and shopping carts.

```
ConnectingToMultipleDatabases/db/migrate/001_add_tables_for_users_and_carts.rb
class AddTablesForUsersAndCarts < ActiveRecord::Migration
  def self.up
    create_table :users do |t|
      t.column :name, :string
      t.column :email, :string
    end
    create_table :carts do |t|
      t.column :user_id, :integer
    end
    create_table :carts_products, :id => false do |t|
      t.column :cart_id, :integer
      t.column :product_id, :integer
    end
  end

  def self.down
    drop_table :users
    drop_table :carts
    drop_table :carts_products
  end
end
```

In a typical scenario like this, the second database would be one that already exists and that you wouldn't want to (or be able to) control via Active Record migrations. As a result, Active Record's migrations feature wasn't designed to manage multiple databases. That's OK. If you have that level of control over your databases, you're better off putting them all together anyway. For this example, we'll assume that the products database already has a table called products, with a varchar field for the product name and a float for the price. For those following along, the following simple DDL can be used to create this table on a MySQL database:

```
ConnectingToMultipleDatabases/db/products.sql
DROP TABLE IF EXISTS 'products';
CREATE TABLE 'products' (
  'id' int(11) NOT NULL auto_increment,
  'name' varchar(255) default NULL,
  'price' float default NULL,
  PRIMARY KEY ('id')
) ENGINE=InnoDB DEFAULT CHARSET=latin1;
```

Now that we have our databases set up, we'll generate models for User, Cart, and Product. The User model can have an associated Cart, which can have multiple Products in it. The User class is standard Active Record fare:

ConnectingToMultipleDatabases/app/models/user.rb

```
class User < ActiveRecord::Base
  has_one :cart
end
```

Things start to get a little tricky with the Cart class. It associates with User in the usual way. We'd like to use has_and_belongs_to_many() to link to :products but we can't, because our products table is not in the same database. The has_and_belongs_to_many() method will result in a table join, which we can't do across database connections. Here's the Cart without any association with the Product class:

ConnectingToMultipleDatabases/app/models/cart.rb

```
class Cart < ActiveRecord::Base
end
```

Before we deal with hooking Carts to Products, let's look at our Product model:

ConnectingToMultipleDatabases/app/models/product.rb

```
class Product < ActiveRecord::Base
  establish_connection :products
end
```

As we learned earlier, by Active Record establishes connections in a hierarchical fashion. When attempting to make a database connection, Active Record models looks for the connection associated with either themselves or the nearest superclass. So in the case of the Product class, we've set the connection directly in that class, meaning that when we do database operations with the Product model, they will use the connection to our configured products database.

If we were to load the Rails console now, we could see that we are indeed connecting to different databases depending on the model we're referencing:

```
chad> ruby script/console
    >> Cart.connection.instance_eval {@config[:database]}
    => "myrailsdatabase_development"
    >> Product.connection.instance_eval {@config[:database]}
    => "products"
```

Great! Now if we were to call, say, Product.find(), we would be performing our select against the products database. So how do we associate a Cart with Products? We have many different ways to go about doing this, but I tend to favor the laziest solution.

To make the connection, we'll create a mapping table in our application's default database (the same one the cart table exists in):

ConnectingToMultipleDatabases/db/migrate/002_add_product_reference_table.rb

```ruby
class AddProductReferenceTable < ActiveRecord::Migration
  def self.up
    create_table :product_references do |t|
      t.column :product_id, :integer
    end
  end

  def self.down
    drop_table :product_references
  end
end
```

This table's sole purpose is to provide a local reference to a product. The product's id will be stored in the product reference's product_id field. We then create a model for this new table:

ConnectingToMultipleDatabases/app/models/product_reference.rb

```ruby
class ProductReference < ActiveRecord::Base
  belongs_to :product
  has_and_belongs_to_many :carts,
                          :join_table => "carts_products",
                          :foreign_key => "product_id"
  def name
    product.name
  end
  def price
    product.price
  end
end
```

We've created the has_and_belongs_to_many() relationship between our new ProductReference class and the Cart class, and we've associated each ProductReference with a Product. Since our Product class is simple, we have also manually delegated calls to name() and price() to the Product, so for read-only purposes, the product *reference* is functionally equivalent to a Product.

All that's left is to associate the Cart with its products:

ConnectingToMultipleDatabases/app/models/cart.rb

```ruby
class Cart < ActiveRecord::Base
  has_and_belongs_to_many :products,
                          :class_name => "ProductReference",
                          :join_table => "carts_products",
                          :association_foreign_key => "product_id"
end
```

We can now say things such as User.find(1).cart.products.first.name and get the desired data. This solution would, of course, require the necessary rows to be created in the product_references table to match any products we have in the alternate database. This could be done either in batch or automatically at runtime.

Now what if you would like to connect to multiple tables in the same external database? Based on what we've done so far, You'd think you could add calls to establish_connection() in the matching models for each of the new tables. But, what you might not expect is that this will result in a separate connection for every model that references your external database. Given a few tables and a production deployment that load balances across several Rails processes, this can add up pretty quickly.

Thinking back to what we learned about how database connections are selected based on class hierarchy, the solution to this problem is to define a parent class for all the tables that are housed on the same server and then inherit from that parent class for those external models. For example, if we wanted to reference a table called tax_conversions on the products database, we could create a model called External as follows:[8]

ConnectingToMultipleDatabases/app/models/external.rb

```
class External < ActiveRecord::Base
  self.abstract_class = true
  establish_connection :products
end
```

Then, our Product and TaxConversion models could inherit from it like so:

ConnectingToMultipleDatabases/app/models/product.rb

```
class Product < External
end
```

ConnectingToMultipleDatabases/app/models/tax_conversion.rb

```
class TaxConversion < External
end
```

---

[8]At the time of this writing, the Oracle connection adapters don't seem to be very well behaved when calling establish_connection(). The code as presented here may cause a new connection to be opened with every subclass of External. To work around this limitation, you can wrap the call to establish_connection() with a conditional that checks the connected?() property for the model to determine whether a connection is already open.

Note that we've moved the establish_connection( ) call from Product to External. All subclasses of External will use the same connection. We also set abstract_class to true to tell Active Record that the External class does not have an underlying database table.

You won't be able to instantiate an External, of course, since there is no matching database table. If there *is* a table in your external database called externals, choose a different name for your class to be on the safe side.

Discussion

Though it's possible to configure multiple database connections, it's preferable to do things the Rails Way. If you can, try to eventually migrate all of your data to the same place. And, given the choice, for new tables, always house them in the same database. There's no sense in making things harder than they have to be.

If you *have* to continue to use an external database, you might consider migrating your data via a batch process. Though batch processes offer their own set of management challenges, if your external data is updated infrequently, batch data migration can make your Rails code cleaner *and* dramatically improve database performance. Data housed in the same database can often be retrieved via single SQL queries, whereas externally housed data will always require a separate query for retrieval.

Integrating with Legacy Databases

Credit

Thanks to reader Frederick Ros for ideas he contributed to this recipe.

Problem

You need to connect to a database that doesn't follow the Rails conventions. You may have an old legacy system you're replacing piece by piece. Or perhaps you need to integrate with an external, non-Rails application that follows its own naming conventions.

One of the Rails mantras is "convention over configuration." It's a great idea. But the problem with conventions is there can be more than one. In this recipe, you'll learn how to not only buck the Rails conventions but also how to snap your model onto *another* convention using the Wordpress[9] database schema.

Solution

Let's start by looking at the definition of one of Wordpress's more representative tables. Here's the Wordpress comments table:

```
CREATE TABLE 'wp_comments' (
  'comment_id' bigint(20) unsigned NOT NULL auto_increment,
  'comment_post_id' int(11) NOT NULL default '0',
  'comment_author' tinytext NOT NULL,
  'comment_author_email' varchar(100) NOT NULL default '',
  'comment_author_url' varchar(200) NOT NULL default '',
  'comment_author_IP' varchar(100) NOT NULL default '',
  'comment_date' datetime NOT NULL default '0000-00-00 00:00:00',
  'comment_date_gmt' datetime NOT NULL default '0000-00-00 00:00:00',
  'comment_content' text NOT NULL,
  'comment_karma' int(11) NOT NULL default '0',
  'comment_approved' enum('0','1','spam') NOT NULL default '1',
  'comment_agent' varchar(255) NOT NULL default '',
  'comment_type' varchar(20) NOT NULL default '',
```

---

[9]Wordpress is a popular, open source weblog engine written in PHP and available from http://www.wordpress.org.

```
'comment_parent' int(11) NOT NULL default '0',
'user_id' int(11) NOT NULL default '0',
PRIMARY KEY ('comment_id'),
KEY 'comment_approved' ('comment_approved'),
KEY 'comment_post_id' ('comment_post_id')
)
```

The first step in hooking Active Record into this table is to generate a model for it. By Rails conventions, the model name for this table would have to be WpComment. That's ugly, so we'll generate a model called Comment and deal with the incompatibility.

Active Record has a configuration option to set the table name prefix for models. We can simply call ActiveRecord::Base.table_name_prefix=() to set it. Since we want that setting to affect our entire application, we'll put it at the bottom of config/environment.rb:

LegacyDatabases/config/environment.rb

```
ActiveRecord::Base.table_name_prefix = "wp_"
```

There is also a _suffix form of this attribute for setting the suffix of table names.

At this point, we can start the console and query the wp_comments table with our model. Note that if the table names were really unusual, you could always call set_table_name() in your model's definition, passing in the name of the table.

```
>> spam = Comment.find(:all).last
=> #<Comment:0x2524830 @attributes={"comment_date_gmt"=>"2006-01-20 18:50:05",
"comment_approved"=>"0", "comment_parent"=>"0", "comment_content"=>
"<a href=\"http://some-poker-spam.blogeasy.com\" ...
                   "comment_author"=>"texas holdem",
..."comment_id"=>"340"}>
>> spam.destroy
ActiveRecord::StatementInvalid: Mysql::Error:
                   Unknown column 'id' in 'where clause':
DELETE FROM wp_comments
          WHERE id = NULL
```

Oops. No id field.

```
>> Comment.column_names.grep(/id/i)
=> ["comment_id", "comment_post_id", "user_id"]
```

The key is called comment_id. Scanning the other Wordpress tables, it looks like this is a standard convention used throughout (most of) the product. Fortunately, it's also used widely enough throughout the industry that Rails provides an easy way to accommodate it. Adding the following to the end of config/environment.rb will cause Active Record to work correctly with this convention:

`LegacyDatabases/config/environment.rb`

```
ActiveRecord::Base.primary_key_prefix_type = :table_name_with_underscore
```

If we were working with a schema that used a convention such as commentid, we could have set this parameter to :table_name.

Now we can find and destroy records by their primary keys:

```
<![[CDATA
>> Comment.find(441)
=> #<Comment:0x221a504 @attributes={"comment_date_gmt"=>"2006-02-08 13:24:35",
..."comment_id"=>"441"}>
>> Comment.destroy(441)
=> #<Comment:0x2218010 @attributes={"comment_date_gmt"=>"2006-02-08 13:24:35",
..."comment_id"=>"441"}>
]]>
```

Now what if the table had been called wp_comment and all the other tables used singular forms of the name as well? Simply add the following to config/environment.rb, and you'll be in business:

```
ActiveRecord::Base.pluralize_table_names = false
```

Finally, if your schema were to use an arbitrary (but repeatable) primary key field name throughout, such as identifier, much in the same way Rails uses id, you could set the primary key name using the following:

```
ActiveRecord::Base.set_primary_key = "identifier"
```

Discussion

Though Rails allows some configuration to adapt to schemas outside of its usual convention, the path of least resistance (and greatest joy!) with Rails is to stick to its conventions when you can. Use these tips if you have a legacy database to which you must adapt. But if you're creating a new application or migrating an old one, do yourself a favor and just stick to the defaults. You'll save a lot of time and have a lot more fun.

DRY Up Your Database Configuration

Problem

DRY. It's Pragmatic Programmer–speak for "Don't Repeat Yourself."[10] Duplication is a waste of your time and a source of bugs and rework.

As programmers, we spend a lot of time learning how to design systems that eliminate code duplication. How do you apply this same rule when you're dealing with a configuration file, such as the Rails database.yml? Many applications will share host or login information across multiple databases. How do you remove this duplication?

Solution

The database.yml file is so small and simple (by default) that it's easy to forget that it is written in a pretty robust markup language: YAML. YAML has a little-used feature called *merge keys*. A merge key allows you to literally *merge* one Hash into another.

Guess what the database.yml configuration entries are. That's right: they're hashes. This means you can use YAML merge keys to convert a duplication-ridden file like this one:

`DRYUpYourDatabaseConfig/config/database.yml.yuck`

```
development:
  adapter: mysql
  database: DRYUpYourDatabaseConfig_development
  username: root
  password:
  socket: /tmp/mysql.sock

test:
  adapter: mysql
  database: DRYUpYourDatabaseConfig_test
  username: root
  password:
  socket: /tmp/mysql.sock
```

---

[10]*The Pragmatic Programmer* [HT00]

```
production:
  adapter: mysql
  database: DRYUpYourDatabaseConfig_production
  username: root
  password:
  socket: /tmp/mysql.sock
```

into something DRY and respectable like this:

DRYUpYourDatabaseConfig/config/database.yml

```
defaults: &defaults
  adapter: mysql
  username: root
  password: secret
  socket: /tmp/mysql.sock

development:
  database: DRYUpYourDatabaseConfig_development
  <<: *defaults

test:
  database: DRYUpYourDatabaseConfig_test
  <<: *defaults

production:
  database: DRYUpYourDatabaseConfig_production
  <<: *defaults
```

They're functionally equivalent, but the second one is much less likely to cause an embarrassing head-smacking moment down the road.

Discussion

We didn't go into detail about how merge keys work. YAML is a rich language with many features you might want to take advantage of in your database configuration or your fixtures. Make an afternoon project out of reading through the YAML specification, which is freely available at http://yaml.org/spec/.

Self-referential Many-to-Many Relationships

Credit

Thanks to Luke Redpath for the ideas that led to this recipe.

Problem

You have a model that needs a many-to-many relationship with itself. For example, you might want to keep track of a bunch of people and who their friends are. In Active Record–speak, a Person has and belongs to many friends, who are also people. But how do you represent a has_and_belongs_to_many relationship when both ends of the relationship are of the same class?

Solution

Let's start by setting up a simple data model representing people and their friends. To keep things simple, we'll give people the bare minimum of information in our system. The following is the Active Record migration to create our data model:

```ruby
class AddPeopleAndTheirFriendsRelationship < ActiveRecord::Migration
  def self.up
    create_table :people do |t|
      t.column "name", :string
    end

    create_table :friends_people, :id => false do |t|
      t.column "person_id", :integer
      t.column "friend_id", :integer
    end
  end

  def self.down
    drop_table :people
    drop_table :friends_people
  end
end
```

We now have a table structure that is capable of storing a dead-simple Person and a link between people and friends. This looks like a typical has_and_belongs_to_many relationship, given the existence of both a Person model *and* a Friend model. Since we want to have Person objects on both ends of the relationship, we'll have to get more explicit than usual as we specify the has_and_belongs_to_many relationship. The following is the Person code.

```
class Person < ActiveRecord::Base
  has_and_belongs_to_many :friends,
    :class_name => "Person",
    :join_table => "friends_people",
    :association_foreign_key => "friend_id",
    :foreign_key => "person_id"
end
```

This declaration creates an attribute on Person called friends. Since we're bucking the usual Rails naming conventions, we have to specify the class name of the model that we are relating to—in this case, the class Person. We have to specify :join_table, because the default naming convention for a table relating people and people would be people_people. We then set :association_foreign_key, which will store the IDs for our people's friends and :foreign_key, which will hold the ID of the person who has the friends.

Loading the console, we can see that this works as expected:

```
chad> ruby script/console
Loading development environment.
>> person1 = Person.create(:name => "Chad")
=> #<Person:0x233db98 @errors=#<ActiveRecord::Errors:0x2312ee8 @errors={},
   @base=#<Person:0x233db98 ...>>, @attributes={"name"=>"Chad", "id"=>7},
   @new_record_before_save=false, @new_record=false>
>> person2 = Person.create(:name => "Erik")
=> #<Person:0x230e0f0 @errors=#<ActiveRecord::Errors:0x230d5ec @errors={},
   @base=#<Person:0x230e0f0 ...>>, @attributes={"name"=>"Erik", "id"=>8},
   @new_record_before_save=false, @new_record=false>
>> person1.friends << person2
=> [#<Person:0x230e0f0 @errors=#<ActiveRecord::Errors:0x230d5ec @errors={},
   @base=#<Person:0x230e0f0 ...>>, @attributes={"name"=>"Erik", "id"=>8},
   @new_record_before_save=false, @new_record=false>]
```

Great! But now that I think of it, as an idealist, I like to think that if I count someone as being my friend, they reciprocate the feeling....

```
>> person2.friends
=> []
```

That makes me sad, though I'm convinced that the problem is not of human nature but just a limitation of Active Record's naming conventions. Because we need one key for the possessor and another key for the possessed party of a has_and_belongs_to_many relationship, there's no way for the relationship to be fully reciprocal on naming convention alone. Thankfully, as of Rails 0.13.1, Active Record gives us the ability to make the world a friendlier place by introducing association callbacks.

A quick change to our Person model gives us the following:

```
class Person < ActiveRecord::Base
  has_and_belongs_to_many :friends,
    :class_name => "Person",
    :join_table => "friends_people",
    :association_foreign_key => "friend_id",
    :foreign_key => "person_id",
    :after_add => :be_friendly_to_friend,
    :after_remove => :no_more_mr_nice_guy

  def be_friendly_to_friend(friend)
    friend.friends << self unless friend.friends.include?(self)
  end

  def no_more_mr_nice_guy(friend)
    friend.friends.delete(self) rescue nil
  end
end
```

You'll notice two new lines at the end of our has_and_belongs_to_many declaration. The :after_add option expects either a Proc or the symbol for a method to call, either of which will be executed after an object is added to this association. Not surprisingly, the :after_remove option takes a similar set of arguments, but to be called when an object is removed from the association. So, now when we call the following code:

```
person.friends << another_person
```

Person's be_friendly_to_friend() method will be called, with another_person passed in as a argument. Our code will now encourage—OK, *force*—another_person to accept person as his friend.

Tagging Your Content

Problem

By now, it's a fairly safe bet that you (and many of the users of your software) have heard of this thing called *social networking*. It was recently all the rage. Cutting edge. A delight to use and a differentiator for applications that used it.

Now, though, it's *expected* that web applications will employ some kind of social networking effect where relevant. If you're looking for books, you expect the online bookstore to leverage the shopping behavior of the masses to help you find books you might like. Or music. Or whatever you might be trying to do or explore. And, though it's possible to hire computer scientists to develop algorithms for predicting what each user is going to be looking for, it's a lot cheaper and easier to let your users do the work.

So after the dust has settled, the heart of what's left in the "social" applications arena is *tagging*. You put simple, textual, nonhierarchical identifiers on items in an application, and the cumulative effect of all the application's users doing this creates a self-organizing system. It's an idea made popular by sites like del.icio.us and Flickr that has now taken over the Web. If you're lucky, tags on your site will help users find new favorite things they didn't even know they liked.

So, how do we do this in Rails?

Ingredients

- David Heinemeier Hansson's acts_as_taggable plugin, installable from the root of your Rails application with the following:

```
chad> ruby script/plugin install acts_as_taggable
+ ./acts_as_taggable/init.rb
+ ./acts_as_taggable/lib/README
+ ./acts_as_taggable/lib/acts_as_taggable.rb
+ ./acts_as_taggable/lib/tag.rb
+ ./acts_as_taggable/lib/tagging.rb
+ ./acts_as_taggable/test/acts_as_taggable_test.rb
```

- Rails 1.1 or higher. acts_as_taggable() relies on polymorphic associations, a feature added after Rails 1.0 (see Recipe 23, *Polymorphic Associations—has_many :whatevers*, on page 109).

Solution

Assuming you have already installed the acts_as_taggable plugin, the first step in adding tagging to your application is to set up the database to hold the tags and their associations with your models. The migration for the database should look something like the following:

`Tagging/db/migrate/001_add_database_structure_for_tagging.rb`

```
class AddDatabaseStructureForTagging < ActiveRecord::Migration
  def self.up
    create_table :taggings do |t|
      t.column :taggable_id, :integer
      t.column :tag_id, :integer
      t.column :taggable_type, :string
    end
    create_table :tags do |t|
      t.column :name, :string
    end
  end

  def self.down
    drop_table :taggings
    drop_table :tags
  end
end
```

So now we have the ability to tag something. We just need something to tag! Let's make a simple model to tag. In your own application, of course, you'd already have models to tag. But for the sake of demonstration, let's create a simple model for tracking contacts in an address book application. As always, we'll use an Active Record migration:

`Tagging/db/migrate/002_add_contacts_table.rb`

```
class AddContactsTable < ActiveRecord::Migration
  def self.up
    create_table :contacts do |t|
      t.column :name, :string
      t.column :address_line1, :string
      t.column :address_line2, :string
      t.column :city, :string
      t.column :state, :string
      t.column :postal_code, :string
    end
  end
```

```
    def self.down
      drop_table :contacts
    end
end
```

Next we'll generate the model and make it taggable. We don't need to create models for the actual Tag objects, because they're included in the acts_as_taggable plugin.

Tagging/app/models/contact.rb

```
class Contact < ActiveRecord::Base
  acts_as_taggable
end
```

Believe it or not, we now have taggable contacts. Let's look in the console:

```
chad> ruby script/console
Loading development environment.
>> c = Contact.create(:name => "Josef K", :address_line1 => "123 Main St.",
    :address_line2 => "Apt. 2", :city => "Vienna",
    :state => "Colorado", :postal_code => "54321")
=> #<Contact:0x267a8f8 @new_record=false, @base=#<Contact:0x267a8f8 ...>>
>> c.tag_with("friends colorado existentialists")
=> ["friends", "colorado", "existentialists"]
```

Here we created an instance of Contact and used the tag_with() method to tag it with a space-delimited list of tags. The acts_as_taggable plugin automatically parses the list and either creates new Tag instances or associates existing ones. The associated tags are then available via the tags() method on the model:

```
>> c.tags
    => [#<Tag:0x264f450 @attributes={"name"=>"friends", "id"=>"1"}>,
        #<Tag:0x264f414 @attributes={"name"=>"colorado", "id"=>"2"}>,
        #<Tag:0x264f3d8 @attributes={"name"=>"existentialists", "id"=>"3"}>]
```

Now if we were to create a new contact and tag it with an already existing tag, we'll see that the existing instance of the tag in the database is reused and associated with the model:

```
>> c2 = Contact.create(:name => "John Barth", :address_line1 => "432 South End Rd.",
    :city => "Gotham", :state => "North Carolina", :postal_code => "12345")
=> #<Contact:0x26463c8 @new_record=false, @base=#<Contact:0x26463c8 ...>>
>> c2.tag_with("friends carolina pragmatists")
=> ["friends", "carolina", "pragmatists"]
>> c2.tags
=> [#<Tag:0x2605bc0 @attributes={"name"=>"friends", "id"=>"1"}>,
    #<Tag:0x2605b84 @attributes={"name"=>"carolina","id"=>"4"}>,
    #<Tag:0x2605b48 @attributes={"name"=>"pragmatists", "id"=>"5"}>]
```

OK. Our models are ready to be tagged! Let's get our heads out of the console and put the tags to use on a real web application. Most tag-enabled applications will want to do three tasks: assign tags to an item, view an item's tags, and search for items by tag. We'll start with the easiest part: viewing an item's tags.

The first thing we need is the ability to actually view an item, so we'll whip up a simple action for that. The following is the beginning of our ContactsController class:

Tagging/app/controllers/contacts_controller.rb

```ruby
class ContactsController < ApplicationController
  def list
    @contacts = Contact.find(:all)
  end
```

This is a typical list action. We'll get a little fancier with the view and throw in some user-friendly Ajax effects. After all, these days tagging without Ajax is like wearing a mink coat with an old, worn-out pair of tennis shoes. Our contacts/list.rhtml is a simple wrapper for a partial template that contains the real display logic for our contacts:

Tagging/app/views/contacts/list.rhtml

```html
<ul id="contacts-list">
  <% if @contacts.blank? %>
    <li class="no-contacts">No contacts to display</li>
  <% else %>
  <%= render :partial => "detail", :collection => @contacts %>
  <% end %>
</ul>
```

We use a partial template because it separates the code into smaller more manageable chunks and and also because we're going to use the same partial view as the rendered response of our Ajax requests. The template contacts/_detail.rhtml consists of two parts: the contact display and a form for editing a contact's tags. To support subsequent Ajax requests, the display part is separated into another partial template, contacts/_content.rhtml:

Tagging/app/views/contacts/_content.rhtml

```erb
<div class="name"><%= contact.name %>
  <%=
    if contact.tags.blank?
      ""
    else
      "(" + contact.tags.collect{|tag| tag.name}.join(", ") + ")"
    end
```

```
        %>
        <%= link_to_function("Edit Tags", "Element.toggle($('#{form_id}'))") %>
      </div>
      <div class="address">
        <%= contact.address_line1 %><br/>
        <%= contact.address_line2 %><br/>
        <%= contact.city %>, <%= contact.state %>  <%= contact.postal_code %>
      </div>
    </div>
```

This is mostly typical display code. We display a contact's tags, if any, in parentheses next to the contact's name. Here's what it looks like in the browser:

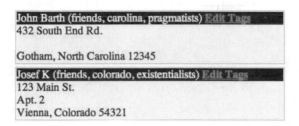

Each contact gets its own separate form for editing the contact's tags. This form starts out hidden and is displayed via the Element.toggle()() JavaScript call when a user clicks the "Edit Tags" link. Completing the contact display implementation, here's the full contacts/_detail.rhtml code that creates the form for editing a contact's tags and references the display partial:

> Don't forget to include the necessary JavaScript files for the Ajax effects to work. Somewhere in the *<head>* section of your view, you'll need this:
>
> `<%= javascript_include_tag :defaults %>`

Tagging/app/views/contacts/_detail.rhtml

```
<li class="contact-item">
<% form_id = "tag-form-for-#{detail.id}" %>
<%= form_remote_tag :url => {:action => "tag", :id => detail},
                    :complete => "Element.toggle($('#{form_id}'))",
                    :success => visual_effect(:shake, "contact-#{detail.id}"),
                    :update => "contact-#{detail.id}",
                    :html => {:id => form_id, :style => "display:none"} %>

  <%= text_field_tag "tag_list",
                     detail.tags.collect{|t| t.name}.join(" "),
                     :size => 40 %>

  <%= hidden_field_tag "form_id", form_id %>
  <%= submit_tag "save" %>
```

```
<%= end_form_tag %>
<div id="contact-<%=detail.id%>" class="contact-details">
<%= render :partial => "content",
          :locals => {:contact => detail, :form_id => form_id} %>
</div>
</li>
```

We first generate an HTML ID for the form, which we use to toggle the form's display on and off. Then, since we want tag updates to be as painlessly easy as possible, we create the form via form_remote_tag(). When a user submits the form, it will make an asynchronous HTTP request in the background to the tag action of our ContactsController. On successful completion of that request, the tag form will be toggled closed, the contact display will be updated, and we'll give the contact's display a little shake to let the user know something happened.

All that's left to actually make tagging happen is to implement the tag action. We already learned how to do this in our script/console session earlier, so the implementation is easy:

Tagging/app/controllers/contacts_controller.rb

```
def tag
  contact = Contact.find(params[:id])
  contact.tag_with(params[:tag_list])
  contact.save
  render :partial => "content",
         :locals => {:contact => contact, :form_id => params[:form_id]}
end
```

Now that we can display and edit a contact's tags, all we lack is the ability to search for a contact by tag. Since we already created the list() action, it makes sense to modify it for our needs instead of creating yet another action that displays a list. Here's the revised version of our action:

Tagging/app/controllers/contacts_controller.rb

```
def list
  @contacts = if tag_name = params[:id]
    Tag.find_by_name(tag_name).tagged
  else
    Contact.find(:all)
  end
end
```

This code reads a tag name supplied in the URI and finds items tagged with that name. So, for example, you could call the application with the URI /contacts/list/colorado to list only those contacts tagged with colorado. If no tag is supplied on the URI, it returns a list of *all* the contacts in the database as before.

A nice feature of the acts_as_taggable() library is that you can use it to tag more than one model type. For example, let's say our little contact database were to blossom into a full-blown personal information manager and we added the ability to create both notes and calendar appointments. Naturally, it would make sense to tag these features along with our contacts.

Because acts_as_taggable() uses Active Record's new polymorphic associations feature, we can tag any model we'd like. All we need to do is declare each model as acts_as_taggable(), and the plugin takes care of the rest for us.

Discussion

In our schema, we haven't yet added any database indexes. For a large application, it would make sense to create indexes on various fields in the supplied tables, including but not limited to the name column of the tags table.

Versioning Your Models

Problem

Your application contains user-editable data. Sometimes users make mistakes as they edit the data, and they'd like an "Undo" feature like they're used to in their spreadsheets and word processors. Sometimes you'd just like to be able to compare two versions of a piece of data to see what has changed. In some cases you might even have a *legal* requirement to keep track of your data and its changes through time.

Ingredients

• Rick Olson's acts_as_versioned plugin. Install with the following:

```
script/plugin discover
script/plugin install acts_as_versioned
```

Solution

The acts_as_versioned plugin allows you to easily cause a model to save each version of its data in a special table, complete with a version identifier that can be used to list, retrieve, or roll back to previous arbitrary versions of that data.

For demonstration, we'll work on the model for a simple, collaborative book-writing tool. In this application, each Book is divided into Chapters, for which version history is stored. If one of the authors of a book comes along and wipes out an important plot twist, our users will be able to easily roll back to the previous version as well as to see a history of the chapter's development.

We'll start by defining the model for our version-controlled Chapter objects. Notice that we're doing the model first. You'll see why this is important as we start defining the database tables to support the model.

```
chad> ruby script/generate model Chapter
      exists  app/models/
      exists  test/unit/
      exists  test/fixtures/
      create  app/models/chapter.rb
      create  test/unit/chapter_test.rb
      create  test/fixtures/chapters.yml
```

Now we'll edit chapter.rb to declare that our Chapter model should be version controlled. Because we already installed the acts_as_versioned plugin, this is a simple one-liner.

```
class Chapter < ActiveRecord::Base
  acts_as_versioned
end
```

That single call to acts_as_versioned() is, in the background, defining a bunch of filters that will stand between our code and the actual saving of our Chapter objects. Now that we have defined Chapter to be versioned, the acts_as_versioned plugin takes care of everything else.

With our model defined, we'll create the migration that will define the tables to support a versioned Chapter model. (If you're using Rails 1.1 or higher, the migration will have been created automatically when you created the Chapter model, and will be called 001_add_chapter.rb.)

```
chad> ruby script/generate migration add_chapter_and_version_tables
    create  db/migrate
    create  db/migrate/001_add_chapter_and_version_tables.rb
```

The migration should look like the following:

```
class AddChapterAndVersionTables < ActiveRecord::Migration
  def self.up
    create_table :chapters do |t|
      t.column "title", :string
      t.column "body", :text
      t.column "version", :integer
    end
    Chapter.create_versioned_table
  end

  def self.down
    drop_table :chapters
    Chapter.drop_versioned_table
  end
end
```

Notice the call to Chapter.create_versioned_table() and its inverse, Chapter.drop_versioned_table(). These special methods were added to our model dynamically by the acts_as_versioned plugin. They define what is essentially a copy of the table for a given model. If we hadn't created our model class first, we wouldn't have been able to use these methods in our migration file. Run rake migrate now to add these tables.

Now that we have a versioned model and a database schema to support it, let's load up script/console and see what this thing can do.

```
chad> ruby script/console
>> chapter = Chapter.create(:title => "Ligeti's Legacy", :body =>
   "Ligeti turned in time to see a look of terror sweep over his wife's face..")
=> #<Chapter:0x232ad68 @attributes={ "body"=>
   "Ligeti turned in time to see a look of terror sweep over his wife's face..",
   "title"=>"Ligeti's Legacy", "id"=>1, "version"=>1},
   @changed_attributes=[], @new_record_before_save=false,
 @new_record=false, =#<Chapter:0x232ad68 ...>, @errors={}>>
>> chapter.version
=> 1
>> chapter.title = "Ligeti's Legacy of Lunacy"
=> "Ligeti's Legacy of Lunacy"
>> chapter.version
=> 1
>> chapter.save
=> true
>> chapter.version
=> 2
>> chapter.body << "Ligeti didn't know what to think."
=> "Ligeti turned in time to see a look of terror sweep over
    his wife's face..Ligeti didn't know what to think."
>> chapter.save
=> true
>> chapter.version
=> 3
```

We created a Chapter instance, and it was automatically assigned a version of 1. Note that when we changed the title of the chapter, the version didn't get updated until we saved the object. Now we have a Chapter instance with three versions. What can we do with them?

```
>> chapter.versions.size
=> 3
>> chapter.version
=> 3
>> chapter.find_version(1).title
=> "Ligeti's Legacy"
>> chapter.revert_to(2)
=> true
>> chapter.body
=> "Ligeti turned in time to see a look of terror sweep over his wife's face.."
>> chapter.versions.size
=> 3
>> chapter.title = "Another version's title"
=> "Another version's title"
>> chapter.save
=> true
>> chapter.version
=> 4
```

We can access data from previous versions and even revert the object to a previous version. However, as we can see by the ending version number from this session, reverting an object is itself a change that acts_as_versioned tracks. To revert without saving a revision, we can use the *bang* version of revert_to(). We'll start a fresh Chapter object to demonstrate:

```
>> chapter = Chapter.create(:title => "The Next Day",
 :body => "Liget woke up with a throbbing headache...")
=> #<Chapter:0x231e4b4 @attributes={"title"=>"The Next Day",
    "body"=>"Liget woke up with a throbbing headache...",
   "id"=>1, "version"=>1}, @changed_attributes=[],
   @base=#<Chapter:0x231e4b4 ...>, @errors={}>>
>> chapter.title = "different title"
=> "different title"
>> chapter.save
=> true
>> chapter.title = "different title again"
=> "different title again"
>> chapter.save
=> true
>> chapter.versions.size
=> 3
>> chapter.version
=> 3
>> chapter.revert_to!(1)
=> true
>> chapter.version
=> 1
>> chapter.title
=> "The Next Day"
>> chapter.versions.size
=> 3
```

So we see that calling Chapter's revert_to!() method brings the version and accompanying database back to the state of the referenced version number without saving a new revision in the process. This is more akin to a typical "Undo" scenario. You'll also see that, though we've reverted to version 1, versions 2 and 3 are still intact:

```
>> chapter.versions.size
=> 3
>> chapter.title = "What will my version be?"
=> "What will my version be?"
>> chapter.save
=> true
>> chapter.version
=> 4
>> chapter.versions(true).size
=> 4
```

Under the covers, acts_as_versioned is managing your model's versions through the additional table it set up when you ran your migration. This is done, not surprisingly, using an Active Record model. The model for your version tables is constructed in memory at runtime. You can access it via the method versioned_class(), which acts_as_versioned adds to your model's class. With this class, you can do all the usual stuff you'd expect to be able to do with an Active Record model. So, for example, if you wanted to look at all the versions of every instance of Chapter, you would do something like this:

```
>> Chapter.versioned_class.find(:all).collect do |version|
     [version.chapter_id, version.title]
   end
=> [[1, "Ligeti's Legacy"], [1, "Ligeti's Legacy of Lunacy"],
    [1, "Ligeti's Legacy of Lunacy"], [1, "Another version's title"],
    [2, "What will my version be?"]]
```

Converting to Migration-Based Schemas

Credit

Thanks to Rails core developer Jamis Buck (http://jamis.jamisbuck.org), whose original weblog post on this topic got *me* converted to migrations.

Problem

Active Record migrations are a wonderful, database-independent way to evolve a database schema as your application's code evolves. And as a Ruby programmer, the ability to define schemas in a language that I have some chance of remembering is a welcome relief from the inevitable Google searches and head scratching every time I have to go back to SQL DDL.

Unfortunately, many of our Rails applications either were started before the migration functionality was added to Rails or were started before we had the time to learn how migrations work. So now it feels like a catch-22. You want to use migrations, but you can't because you're not already using migrations! How do you go from a traditional, SQL-managed schema to an Active Record migrations-managed schema?

Solution

To see a real conversion to migrations in action, let's start with a small set of example tables. The following is the DDL for three simple tables, backing an online cooking recipe database. We'll assume that these tables already exist in our database and that they have data in them.

`ConvertExistingAppToMigrations/db/initial_schema.sql`

```sql
CREATE TABLE 'ingredients' (
  'id' int(11) NOT NULL auto_increment,
  'recipe_id' int(11) default NULL,
  'name' varchar(255) default NULL,
  'quantity' int(11) default NULL,
  'unit_of_measurement' varchar(255) default NULL,
  PRIMARY KEY ('id')
);
```

```
CREATE TABLE `ratings` (
  `id` int(11) NOT NULL auto_increment,
  `recipe_id` int(11) default NULL,
  `user_id` int(11) default NULL,
  `rating` int(11) default NULL,
  PRIMARY KEY  (`id`)
);

CREATE TABLE `recipes` (
  `id` int(11) NOT NULL auto_increment,
  `name` varchar(255) default NULL,
  `spice_level` int(11) default NULL,
  `region` varchar(255) default NULL,
  `instructions` text,
  PRIMARY KEY  (`id`)
);
```

The challenge is to move from this SQL-driven approach of maintaining the schema to using Active Record migrations without losing any data.

Active Record migrations are managed using a domain-specific language called ActiveRecord::Schema. ActiveRecord::Schema defines a pure-Ruby, database-independent representation of a database schema. Of Rails 1.0, Rails ships with a class called ActiveRecord::SchemaDumper whose job is to inspect your databases and print their schema definitions in ActiveRecord::Schema format.

After requireing active_record/schema_dumper (it's not loaded by Rails by default), a call to ActiveRecord::SchemaDumper.dump() will result in your default database's schema being dumped to your console. To see it in action, do the following. (We've split the command across two lines to make it fit.)

```
chad> ruby script/runner 'require "active_record/schema_dumper";
                  ActiveRecord::SchemaDumper.dump'
```

But the Rails developers have made it even easier than this. Using the supplied Rake task, db:schema:dump,[11] you can dump your schema into the file db/schema.rb at any time. Let's do that with our existing schema:

```
chad> rake db:schema:dump
(in /Users/chad/src/FR_RR/Book/code/ConvertExistingAppToMigrations)
```

Now we have our existing schema converted to an ActiveRecord::Schema format in db/schema.rb. Here's what it looks like:

---

[11] Or db:schema:dump if you're using Rails 1.0

ConvertExistingAppToMigrations/db/schema.rb

```
Line 1    # This file is autogenerated. Instead of editing this file, please use the
    -     # migrations feature of ActiveRecord to incrementally modify your database, and
    -     # then regenerate this schema definition.
    -
    5     ActiveRecord::Schema.define(:version => 1) do
    -
    -       create_table "ingredients", :force => true do |t|
    -         t.column "recipe_id", :integer
    -         t.column "name", :string
   10         t.column "quantity", :integer
    -         t.column "unit_of_measurement", :string
    -       end
    -
    -       create_table "ratings", :force => true do |t|
   15         t.column "recipe_id", :integer
    -         t.column "user_id", :integer
    -         t.column "rating", :integer
    -       end
    -
   20       create_table "recipes", :force => true do |t|
    -         t.column "name", :string
    -         t.column "spice_level", :integer
    -         t.column "region", :string
    -         t.column "instructions", :text
   25       end
          end
```

That was nice and simple. And, because this format is the same format that migrations use, the create_table() code in this file will be the very code that makes up our first migration! Let's create that migration now:

```
chad> ruby script/generate migration InitialSchema
exists  db/migrate
create  db/migrate/001_initial_schema.rb
```

Now we can take the code from db/schema.rb and paste it into our freshly generated migration file, db/migration/001_initial_schema.rb. Here is what the migration file should look like (note: don't jump the gun— read ahead before you run this migration, or you might lose data!):

ConvertExistingAppToMigrations/db/migrate/001_initial_schema.rb

```
class InitialSchema < ActiveRecord::Migration
  def self.up
    create_table "ingredients" do |t|
      t.column "recipe_id", :integer
      t.column "name", :string
      t.column "quantity", :integer
      t.column "unit_of_measurement", :string
    end
```

```ruby
    create_table "ratings" do |t|
      t.column "recipe_id", :integer
      t.column "user_id", :integer
      t.column "rating", :integer
    end

    create_table "recipes" do |t|
      t.column "name", :string
      t.column "spice_level", :integer
      t.column "region", :string
      t.column "instructions", :text
    end
  end

  def self.down
    drop_table :ingredients
    drop_table :ratings
    drop_table :recipes
  end
end
```

Notice that we also added drop_table() calls to the migration's self.down() definition, which tell Active Record to remove those tables if we ever downgrade beyond this version (though that's unlikely to happen given that this is the initial version of the schema). If you do this, remember to drop the tables in such a way that you don't break any foreign key constraints.

At this point, our *application* has been converted to use migrations. On a fresh database, we can run rake migrate to install our schema. We can also start generating subsequent migrations and evolve our database. But we still have a problem. Our migration isn't *quite* ready yet. In its present form, this migration will wipe out our existing data:

```
chad> ruby script/runner 'puts Recipe.count'
253
chad> rake migrate
chad> ruby script/runner 'puts Recipe.count'
0
```

Oops! You may have noticed that in our migration, the create_table() calls are passed the :force parameter with a value of true. This parameter causes Active Record to first *drop* the table if it already exists and then re-create it. And with the initial table goes all of its rows.

Remove the :force parameter from your migration before you try to run it. It won't get us all the way there, but we should get rid of it to avoid losing any data. Here's what happens when we try to run the migration now:

```
chad> rake migrate
(in /Users/chad/src/FR_RR/Book/code/ConvertExistingAppToMigrations)
rake aborted!
Mysql::Error: #42S01Table 'ingredients' already exists:
CREATE TABLE ingredients ('id' int(11) DEFAULT NULL auto_increment PRIMARY KEY,
'recipe_id' int(11), 'name' varchar(255), 'quantity' int(11),
'unit_of_measurement' varchar(255)) ENGINE=InnoDB
```

It can't create the tables, because they already exist. At this point, we have two choices.

The first choice is the brute-force solution. We could dump our existing data as fixtures (see Recipe 42, *Extracting Test Fixtures from Live Data*, on page 179 to learn now). This would allow us to drop and re-create our entire database, starting over using migrations from the beginning. After re-creating the database, we would run rake migrate and then rake load_fixtures to restore the data. Our application would then be ready for any future migrations without any hassle.

The alternative is probably both easier and safer. Active Record was trying to re-create tables that already exist because its method of determining which version of the schema it's on wasn't available. Active Record uses a special table called schema_info to keep track of the database's current schema version. This table contains a single row with a single column called version. You probably noticed when you generated the migration file that its file name started with the number 001. It's this number, prepended to every migration's file name, that Active Record uses to determine which files are newer than the last run of rake migrate and therefore in need of processing.

So our file, labeled as version 1 of the schema, was newer than the version number 0 that Active Record assigned for this first run. (If you check your database, you'll see that it did in fact create the schema_info table and set the version to 0 during your failed run.)

The alternative way to make things work, therefore, is to set the schema version before the migration runs. Here's a command that will do just that (again, split onto two lines for formatting reasons):

```
chad> ruby script/runner 'ActiveRecord::Base.connection.execute(
        "UPDATE schema_info SET version = 1")'
```

Sure enough, after setting the schema version to 1, a call to rake migrate works as advertised. Congratulations! You are now one step closer to

Rails Nirvana. Be careful, though. Migrations will spoil you. Once you've used them, you'll never want to go back.

> **Also See**
>
> For more information about using migrations, see the Rails API documentation.[12]

---

[12]http://api.rubyonrails.org/classes/ActiveRecord/Migration.html

Many-to-Many Relationships with Extra Data

Credit

Thanks to Marcel Molina Jr. for the example idea for this recipe.

Problem

Usually, a relationship between two models is just a relationship. For example, a person has and belongs to many pets, and you can leave it at that. This kind of relationship is straightforward. The association between the two models is all there is to track.

But sometimes the relationship has its own data. For example, a magazine has (and belongs to) many readers by way of their subscriptions. Subscriptions are interesting entities in their own right that a magazine-related application would probably want to track.

How can you achieve a many-to-many relationship while enabling the *relationship* to have attributes of its own?

Ingredients

- Rails 1.1 or higher.

Solution

We're taught that when we have a many-to-many relationship to model in a Rails application, we should use the has_and_belongs_to_many() (habtm) macro with its associated join table. But habtm is best suited to relationships that have no attributes of their own. It is *possible* to add attributes to the join table in a has_and_belongs_to_many() setup, but it has proven unwieldy in many cases and is on the list of features to be deprecated in a future release of Rails.

Rails 1.1 introduces a new idea called *join models*. Don't panic: this isn't a whole new type of model you have to learn. You'll still be using and extending ActiveRecord::Base. In fact, join models are more of a technique or design pattern than they are a technology. The idea with join models is that if your many-to-many relationship needs to have some richness in the association, instead of putting a simple, dumb join table in the middle of the relationship, you can put a full table with an associated Active Record model.

Let's look at an example. We'll model a magazine and its readership. Magazines (they hope) have many readers, and readers can potentially have many magazines. So a typical way to model that in Rails would be to use habtm. Here's a sample schema to implement this:

`ManyToManyWithAttributesOnTheRelationship/db/migrate/001_add_tables_for_typical_habtm.rb`

```
def self.up
  create_table :magazines do |t|
    t.column :title, :string
  end
  create_table :readers do |t|
    t.column :name, :string
  end
  create_table :magazines_readers, :id => false do |t|
    t.column :magazine_id, :integer
    t.column :reader_id, :integer
  end
```

You would then say that the Magazine model has_and_belongs_to_many :readers, and vice versa.

Now imagine you needed to track not only current readers but everyone who has ever been a regular reader of your magazine. The natural way to do this would be to think in terms of subscriptions. People who have subscriptions are the readers of your magazine. Subscriptions have their own attributes, such as the length of the subscription and the date it was last renewed.

It is possible with Rails to add these attributes to a habtm relationship and to store them in the join table (magazines_readers in this case) along with the foreign keys for the associated Magazine and Reader entities.

But, what this technique does in effect is relegate a *real*, concrete, first-class concept in our domain to what amounts to an afterthought. We'd be taking what should be its own class and making it hang together as a set of attributes hanging from an association. It feels like an afterthought because it is.

This is where join models come in. Using a join model, we can maintain the convenient, directly accessible association between magazines and readers while representing the relationship itself as a first-class object: a Subscription in this case.

Let's put together a new version of our schema, but this time supporting Subscription as a join model. Assuming we already have a migration that set up the previous version, here's the new migration:

```
ManyToManyWithAttributesOnTheRelationship/db/migrate/002_create_join_model_readership_schema.rb
def self.up
  drop_table :magazines_readers
  create_table :subscriptions do |t|
    t.column :reader_id, :integer
    t.column :magazine_id, :integer
    t.column :last_renewal_on, :date
    t.column :length_in_issues, :integer
  end
end
```

Our new schema uses the existing magazines and readers tables but replaces the magazines_readers join table with a new table called subscriptions. Now we'll also need to generate a Subscription model and modify all three models to set up their associations. Here are all three models:

```
ManyToManyWithAttributesOnTheRelationship/app/models/subscription.rb
class Subscription < ActiveRecord::Base
  belongs_to :reader
  belongs_to :magazine
end
```

```
ManyToManyWithAttributesOnTheRelationship/app/models/reader.rb
class Reader < ActiveRecord::Base
  has_many :subscriptions
  has_many :magazines, :through => :subscriptions
end
```

```
ManyToManyWithAttributesOnTheRelationship/app/models/magazine.rb
class Magazine < ActiveRecord::Base
  has_many :subscriptions
  has_many :readers, :through => :subscriptions
end
```

Subscription has a many-to-one relationship with both Magazine and Reader, making the *implicit* relationship between Magazine and Reader a many-to-many relationship. Although this was indeed possible with Rails 1.0, a bit of magic is happening in both the Magazine and Reader classes.

We can now specify that a Magazine object has_many() readers, *through* their associated subscriptions. This is both a conceptual association and a technical one. Let's load the console to see how it works:

```
chad> ruby script/console
>> magazine = Magazine.create(:title => "Ruby Illustrated")
=> #<Magazine:0x26a3708 @errors=#<ActiveRecord::Errors:0x26a227c @errors={},
...@attributes={"title"=>"Ruby Illustrated", "id"=>1}>
>> reader = Reader.create(:name => "Anthony Braxton")
=> #<Reader:0x26993c0 @errors=#<ActiveRecord::Errors:0x2697b74 @errors={},
...@attributes={"name"=>"Anthony Braxton", "id"=>1}>
>> subscription = Subscription.create(:last_renewal_on => Date.today,
    :length_in_issues => 6)
=> #<Subscription:0x26da3d4 @errors=#<ActiveRecord::Errors:0x26b6204
    ... "length_in_issues"=>6, "reader_id"=>nil, "magazine_id"=>nil}>
>> magazine.subscriptions << subscription
=> [#<Subscription:0x26da3d4 @errors=#<ActiveRecord::Errors:0x26b6204
...}>]
>> reader.subscriptions << subscription
=> [#<Subscription:0x26da3d4 @errors=#<ActiveRecord::Errors:0x26b6204
... "reader_id"=>1, "magazine_id"=>1}>]
>> subscription.save
=> true
```

This doesn't contain anything new yet. But, now that we have this association set up, look what we can do:

```
>> magazine.readers
=> [#<Reader:0x267cc20 @attributes={"name"=>"Anthony Braxton", "id"=>"1"}>]
>> reader.magazines
=> [#<Magazine:0x267aed4 @attributes={"title"=>"Ruby Illustrated", "id"=>"1"}>]
```

Though we never explicitly associated the reader to the magazine, the association is implicit through the :through parameter to the has_many() declarations.

Behind the scenes, Active Record is generating an SQL select that joins the tables for us. For example, calling reader.magazines generates the following:

```
SELECT magazines.*
  FROM subscriptions, magazines
 WHERE (magazines.id = subscriptions.magazine_id AND
        subscriptions.reader_id = 1)
```

With a join model relationship, you still have access to all the same has_many options you would normally use.[13] For example, if we wanted an easy accessor for all of a magazine's semiannual subscribers, we could add the following to the Magazine model:

---

[13]One exception to this is the :class_name option. When creating a join model, you should instead use :source, which should be set to the name of the association to use, instead of the class name.

ManyToManyWithAttributesOnTheRelationship/app/models/magazine.rb

```
class Magazine < ActiveRecord::Base
  has_many :subscriptions
  has_many :readers, :through => :subscriptions
  has_many :semiannual_subscribers,
           :through => :subscriptions,
           :source => :reader,
           :conditions => ['length_in_issues = 6']
end
```

We could now access a magazine's semiannual subscribers as follows:

```
chad> ruby script/console
>> Magazine.find(1).semiannual_subscribers
=> [#<Reader:0x26ba05c @attributes={"name"=>"Anthony Braxton", "id"=>"1"}>]
```

Polymorphic Associations—has_many :whatevers

Active Record's has_many() and belongs_to() associations work really well when the two sides of the relationship have fixed classes. An Author can have many Books. A Library can have Books.

But sometimes you may want to use one table and model to represent something that can be associated with many types of entities. For example, how do you model an Address that can belong to both people *and* companies? It's clear that both a person and a company can have one or more addresses associated with them. But a has_many() relationship relies on a foreign key, which should uniquely identify the owner of the relationship. If you mix multiple owning tables, you can't rely on the foreign key to be unique across the multiple tables. For instance, there may be a person with id number 42 *and* a company with id number 42.

• Rails 1.1 or higher.

Rails 1.1 introduced *polymorphic associations*. Although its name is daunting, it's actually nothing to fear. Polymorphic associations allow you to associate one type of object with objects of *many* types. So, for example, with polymorphic associations an Address can belong to a Person or a Company or to any other model that wants to declare and use the association.

Let's work through a basic example. We'll create a simple set of models to represent people, companies, and their associated addresses. We'll start with an Active Record migration that looks like the following:

```
PolymorphicAssociations/db/migrate/001_add_people_company_and_address_tables.rb

class AddPeopleCompanyAndAddressTables < ActiveRecord::Migration
  def self.up
    create_table :people do |t|
      t.column :name, :string
    end
    create_table :companies do |t|
      t.column :name, :string
    end
    create_table :addresses do |t|
      t.column :street_address1, :string
      t.column :street_address2, :string
      t.column :city, :string
      t.column :state, :string
      t.column :country, :string
      t.column :postal_code, :string
      t.column :addressable_id, :integer
      t.column :addressable_type, :string
    end
  end

  def self.down
    drop_table :people
    drop_table :companies
    drop_table :addresses
  end
end
```

You'll immediately notice something unusual about the addresses table. First, the name of the foreign key is neither people_id nor company_id, which is a departure from the usual Active Record convention. It's called addressable_id instead. Also, we've added a column called address-able_type. You'll see in a moment how we're going to use these columns. You get extra credit if you can guess before reading on!

Now that we have a database schema to work with, let's create models using the generator. We'll generate models for Person, Company, and Address. We'll then add has_many() declarations to the Person and Company models, resulting in the following:

```
PolymorphicAssociations/app/models/person.rb

class Person < ActiveRecord::Base
  has_many :addresses, :as => :addressable
end
```

```
PolymorphicAssociations/app/models/company.rb

class Company < ActiveRecord::Base
  has_many :addresses, :as => :addressable
end
```

As you can see, the has_many() calls in the two models are identical. And now we start to get some insight into the addressable columns in the addresses table. The :as option, part of the new polymorphic associations implementation, tells Active Record that the current model's role in this association is that of an "addressable," as opposed to, say, a "person" or a "company." This is where the term *polymorphic* comes in. Though these models exist as representations of people and companies, in the context of their association with an Address they effectively assume the *form* of an "addressable" thing.

Next we'll modify the generated Address model to say that it belongs_to() addressable things:

PolymorphicAssociations/app/models/address.rb

```
class Address < ActiveRecord::Base
  belongs_to :addressable, :polymorphic => true
end
```

If we had omitted the :polymorphic option to belongs_to(), Active Record would have assumed that Addresses belonged to objects of class Addressable and would have managed the foreign keys and lookups in the usual way. However, since we've included the :polymorphic option in our belongs_to() declaration, Active Record knows to perform lookups based on both the foreign key *and* the type. The same is true of the has_many() lookups and their corresponding :as options.

The best way to understand what's going on here is to see it in action. Let's load the Rails console and give our new models a spin:

```
chad> ruby script/console
Loading development environment.
>> person = Person.create(:name => "Egon")
=> #<Person:0x22c2434 @new_record_before_save=true,
      @errors=#<ActiveRecord::Errors:0x2293a94 @errors={},
      @base=#<Person:0x22c2434 ...>>, @new_record=false,
      @attributes={"name"=>"Egon", "id"=>1}>
>> address = Address.create(:street_address1 => "Wiedner Hauptstrasse 27-29",
      :city => "Vienna", :country => "Austria", :postal_code => "091997")
=> #<Address:0x2289864 @errors=#<ActiveRecord::Errors:0x2285160 @errors={},
      @base=#<Address:0x2289864 ...>>,
      @new_record=false, @attributes={"city"=>"Vienna", "postal_code"=>"091997",
      "addressable_type"=>nil, "country"=>"Austria", "id"=>1,
      "addressable_id"=>nil,
      "street_address1"=>"Wiedner Hauptstrasse 27-29",
      "street_address2"=>nil, "state"=>nil}>
>> address.addressable = person
=> #<Person:0x22c2434 @new_record_before_save=true,
      @errors=#<ActiveRecord::Errors:0x2293a94
```

```
        @errors={}, @base=#<Person:0x22c2434 ...>>, @new_record=false,
        @attributes={"name"=>"Egon", "id"=>1}>
>> address.addressable_id
=> 1
>> address.addressable_type
=> "Person"
```

Aha! Associating a Person with an Address populates both the address-able_id field *and* the addressable_type field. Naturally, associating a Company with an Address will have a similar effect:

```
>> company = Company.create(:name => "TCB, Inc.")
=> #<Company:0x2262df4 @new_record_before_save=true,
     @errors=#<ActiveRecord::Errors:0x2260194 @errors={},
     @base=#<Company:0x2262df4 ...>>, @new_record=false,
     @attributes={"name"=>"TCB, Inc.", "id"=>1}>
>> address = Address.create(:street_address1 => "123 Main",
     :city => "Memphis", :country => "US", :postal_code => "38104")
=> #<Address:0x2256dc4 @errors=#<ActiveRecord::Errors:0x2255bb8
     @errors={}, @base=#<Address:0x2256dc4 ...>>,
     @new_record=false, @attributes={"city"=>"Memphis",
     "postal_code"=>"38104", "addressable_type"=>nil,
     "country"=>"US",  "id"=>3, "addressable_id"=>nil,
     "street_address1"=>"123 Main",
     "street_address2"=>nil, "state"=>nil}>
>> address.addressable = company
=> #<Company:0x2262df4 @new_record_before_save=true,
     @errors=#<ActiveRecord::Errors:0x2260194 @errors={},
     @base=#<Company:0x2262df4 ...>>, @new_record=false,
      @attributes={"name"=>"TCB, Inc.", "id"=>1}>
>> address.addressable_id
=> 1
>> address.addressable_type
=> "Company"
```

Notice that in both examples, the addressable_id values have been set to 1. If the relationship wasn't declared to be polymorphic, a call to Company.find(1).addresses would result in the same (incorrect) list that Person.find(1).addresses would return, because Active Record would have no way of distinguishing between *person* number 1 and *company* number 1.

Instead, a call to Company.find(1).addresses will execute the following SQL:

```
SELECT *
  FROM addresses
 WHERE (addresses.addressable_id = 1 AND
        addresses.addressable_type = 'Company')
```

You could achieve a similar effect by hand with Rails 1.0. To do so, you would have to manually manage the addressable_type field in the addresses table. When you saved a new association, you would need to set the addressable_type field, and as you declared any associations, you would need to set the :conditions option to include a query for the right addressable_type. For example, the has_many() declaration in the Person model would need to look like the following:

```
has_many :addresses,
         :foreign_key => "addressable_id",
         :conditions => ['addressable_type = ?', 'Person']
```

Add Behavior to Active Record Associations

When you access a has_many or has_and_belongs_to_many association on an Active Record model object, it returns an array-like object that provides access to the individual objects that are associated with the object you started with. Most of the time, the stock array-like functionality of these associations is good enough to accomplish what you need to do.

Sometimes, though, you might want to add behavior to the association. Adding behavior to associations can make your code more expressive and easier to understand. But, since these associations are generated by Rails, how do you extend them? There isn't an easily accessible class or object to add the behavior to. So how do you do it?

Before we get started, let's create a simple model with which to demonstrate. For this example, we'll create models to represent students and their grades in school. The following is the Active Record migration to implement the schema:

AddingBehaviorToActiveRecordAssociations/db/migrate/001_add_students_tables.rb

```ruby
class AddStudentsTables < ActiveRecord::Migration
  def self.up
    create_table :students do |t|
      t.column :name, :string
      t.column :graduating_year, :integer
    end
    create_table :grades do |t|
      t.column :student_id, :integer
      t.column :score, :integer # 4-point scale
      t.column :class, :string
    end
  end

  def self.down
    drop_table :students
    drop_table :grades
  end
end
```

We'll next create simple Active Record models for these tables. We'll declare the Student class has_many() Grades. Here are the models:

```
AddingBehaviorToActiveRecordAssociations/app/models/student.rb

class Student < ActiveRecord::Base
  has_many :grades
end
```

```
AddingBehaviorToActiveRecordAssociations/app/models/grade.rb

class Grade < ActiveRecord::Base
end
```

Now that we have a working model, let's create some objects:

```
chad> ruby script/console
>> me = Student.create(:name => "Chad", :graduating_year => 2006)
=> #<Student:0x26d18d8 @new_record=false, @attributes={"name"=>"Chad",
"id"=>1, "graduating_year"=>2006}>
>> me.grades.create(:score => 1, :class => "Algebra")
=> #<Grade:0x269cb10 @new_record=false, @errors={}>, @attributes={"score"=>1,
"class"=>"Algebra", "student_id"=>1, "id"=>1}>
```

(I was never very good at math—a 1 is a failing grade.)

If you're paying close attention, you'll notice that this has already gotten interesting. Where does this create() method come from? I don't recall seeing create() defined for the Array class. Maybe these associations don't return arrays after all. Let's find out:

```
>> me.grades.class
=> Array
>> Array.instance_methods.grep /create/
=> []
```

Just *what* is going on here? The association claims to return an Array, but where's the create() method coming from?

Ruby is a very dynamic language. When I encounter something magical like this, I find myself mentally working through all the possible ways it could be implemented and then ruling them out. In this case, I might start by assuming that the association is indeed an instance of Array with one or more singleton methods added.

But, looking at the Rails source code for verification, it turns out I'd be wrong. What's really going on is that the call to grades() returns an instance of ActiveRecord::Associations::AssociationProxy. This sits between your model's client code and the actual objects the model is associated with. It masquerades as an object of the class you expect (Array in this example) and delegates calls to the appropriate application-specific model objects.

So, where does create() come from? It is defined on the association itself, and it delegates to the Grade class to create grades.

Understanding that an association call really returns a proxy, it's easy to see how you could add behaviors to the association. You would just need to add the behavior to the proxy. Since each access to an association can create a new instance of AssociationProxy, we can't just get the association via a call to grades() and add our behaviors to it. Active Record controls the creation and return of these objects, so we'll need to ask Active Record to extend the proxy object for us.

Fortunately, Active Record gives us *two* ways to accomplish this. First, we could define additional methods in a module and then extend the association proxy with that module. We might, for example, create a module for doing custom queries on grades, including the ability to select below-average grades. Such a module might look like the following:

AddingBehaviorToActiveRecordAssociations/lib/grade_finder.rb

```
module GradeFinder
  def below_average
    find(:all, :conditions => ['score < ?', 2])
  end
end
```

This is a simple extension that adds a below_average() method to the grades() association, which will find all grades lower than a C (represented as a 2 on the 4-point scale). We could then include that module in our model with the following code:

AddingBehaviorToActiveRecordAssociations/app/models/student.rb

```
require "grade_finder"
class Student < ActiveRecord::Base
  has_many :grades, :extend => GradeFinder
end
```

The new method is now accessible on the association as follows:

```
chad> ruby script/console
>> Student.find(1).grades.below_average
=> [#<Grade:0x26aecc0 @attributes={"score"=>"1", "class"=>"Algebra",
"student_id"=>"1", "id"=>"1"}>]
```

Alternatively, we could have defined this method directly by passing a block to the declaration of the has_many() association:

AddingBehaviorToActiveRecordAssociations/app/models/student.rb

```ruby
class Student < ActiveRecord::Base
  has_many :grades do
    def below_average
      find(:all, :conditions => ['score < ?', 2])
    end
    def foo
      raise self.inspect
    end
  end
end
```

These association proxies have access to all the same methods that would normally be defined on the associations, such as find(), count(), and create().

Discussion

An interesting point to notice is that inside the scope of one of these extended methods, the special variable self refers to the Array of associated Active Record objects. This means you can index into the array and perform any other operations on self that you could perform on an array.

Dynamically Configure Your Database

The Rails database configuration file, config/database.yml is a YAML file. But before it is fed to the YAML parser, it is preprocessed using ERb. This means you can embed Ruby code in the file just like you do with your view templates, giving you the full power of the language.

I work with a team of three developers. We all use Macintoshes at work, so our configurations are usually the same. But sometimes we each find ourselves developing in a Linux environment, and our configurations vary. This can get annoying, because our database.yml files all need to point to different MySQL socket files. If one of us makes a local change and accidentally checks it in, the next person who updates is confronted with an error message.

So now we use ERb in our database.yml file to look for the MySQL socket file in all the places our various computers may store it and then select the right one:

DynamicDatabaseConfiguration/config/database.yml

```
development:
  adapter: mysql
  database: DynamicDatabaseConfiguration_development
  username: root
  password:
  socket: <%=  ["/tmp/mysqld.sock",
                "/tmp/mysql.sock",
               "/var/run/mysqld/mysqld.sock",
               "/var/lib/mysql/mysql.sock"].detect{|socket|
                 File.exist?(socket)
               } %>
```

This is just one example of the ways you can use ERb to add smarts to your database.yml. Keep your mind open, and you're likely to find other ways to save time and avoid frustration with dynamic database configuration.

Use Active Record Outside of Rails

The Rails environment is really well configured. It's so well configured that we rarely (if ever) have to concern ourselves with the process of initializing the Rails subframeworks.

In fact, you might not even realize it's *possible* to use, for example, Active Record outside of the context of a Rails application. It's not only possible, but it's really easy.

Here's a script that uses Active Record to connect to a database and search for pending orders. It then shells out to an external program that sends those orders to a legacy mainframe system for fulfillment.

```
UseActiveRecordOutsideOfRails/process_orders_nightly.rb
require 'active_record'
ActiveRecord::Base.establish_connection(
  :adapter  => "mysql",
  :host     => "localhost",
  :username => "nightlybatch",
  :password => "secret",
  :database => "web_orders"
)

class Order < ActiveRecord::Base
end
ActiveRecord::Base.logger = Logger.new(STDOUT)

Order.find(:all).each do |o|
  puts "Processing order number #{o.id}"
  `./sendorder -c #{o.customer_id} \
    -p #{o.product_id} \
    -q #{o.quantity}`
end
```

If you work in an environment that has any non-Rails applications, this kind of lightweight script can really come in handy. You don't need to create an entire Rails application or to incur the start-up overhead of the full Rails environment for something this simple.

Perform Calculations on Your Model Data

Credit

Thanks to Rails core team member Rick Olson for his help on this recipe and for writing the Active Record calculations code.

Problem

You want to perform numeric calculations on the data in your database. You don't want to have to drop to SQL, but your data sets are too big to select all the data and perform the calculations in Ruby.

Ingredients

• Rails 1.1 or higher.

Solution

The ActiveRecord::Calculations module, introduced in Rails 1.1, is just what you need. It wraps the SQL necessary to perform in-database applications while also providing a friendly interface that will be comfortably familiar to everyone who already uses Active Record.

ActiveRecord::Calculations provides model-level methods for querying the count, sum, average, maximum, and minimum values of data in a model. For example, if you wanted to find out the number of people older than 21 in your system, you could do this:

```
>> Person.count("age > 21")
=> 23
```

Under the covers, Active Record generates something like this:

```
SELECT count(*) AS count_all FROM people WHERE (age > 21)
```

To find the average, minimum, and maximum ages of all the people in your system you could do this:

```
>> Person.average(:age)
=> 26.1765
>> Person.minimum(:age)
=> 1
```

```
>> Person.maximum(:age)
=> 42
```

Because ActiveRecord::Calculations uses much of the same code that find() uses, its interface is similar. For example, you can pass in the :conditions option just like you would with find(). The following code averages the ages of everyone whose name contains the letter *T*:

```
>> Person.average(:age, :conditions => ["name like ?", '%T%'])
=> 20.6
```

You can also group your calculations by an attribute of the model. For example, to sum the number of donations to a charity for each day in a pledge drive, you could do this:

```
>> Donation.sum(:amount, :group => :created_at)
=> [[Sun Mar 26 18:48:43 MST 2006, 3053], [Mon Mar 27 18:48:43 MST 2006,
   1597], [Tue Mar 28 18:48:43 MST 2006, 3809], ....etc.
```

You can also use SQL functions in the :group parameter. To perform the same operation but group by year, you could do this:

```
>> Donation.sum(:amount, :group => 'YEAR(created_at)')
=> [[2005, 450243], [2006, 23503]]
```

> If you need your code to be database-agnostic, beware of using SQL in the :group. Not all databases support the same functions.

You can group by associations, too. If you had a weblog with a rating system and wanted to get the average rating for each post in the system, you could do this:

```
>> Rating.average(:value,
                  :group => :post).collect{|post, rating| [post.title, rating]}
=> [["Increase your life time earnings chadfowler", 3.6667],
   ["All m3mory enhancers on one portal!", 0.6667],
   ["300 free welcome bonus!", 4.0], ["A Free ...etc.
```

Grouping on associations yields an OrderedHash whose key is the full, instantiated associated object. So if you wanted to get the average of a specific post, given the full list, you could do this:

```
>>  Rating.average(:value, :group => :post)[Post.find(2)]
=> 0.6667
```

Finally, if you wanted to perform calculations within a certain scope, they work the same as the rest of Active Record. For example, to average the rating of posts by a specific person, you could do this:

```
>> Person.find_by_name("Adam").ratings.average(:value)
=> 2.0
```

DRY Up Active Record Code with Scoping

You often need to limit most or all of your application's queries based on some kind of key. Maybe you have a bunch of users who share documents with each other within the context of a single account. Or you want to let a user work with to-do lists but you don't want to show them any lists that they didn't create.

You could sprinkle :conditions throughout your find() calls and always throw a parameter into your create() calls. That would create a lot of duplication and make your code more brittle (not to mention ugly).

Active Record gives you a few tools for DRYing up your code in a situation like this. A good one to start with is with_scope(). Here's an example. Say you're creating a user administration page that account owners can use to manage users within their companies. You want to allow them to see or create users only within their context.

```
User.with_scope(
  :find => {:conditions => ["account_id = ?", current_account()]},
  :create => {:account_id => current_account()}) do
    @users = User.find(:all)
    @new_user = User.create(:name => "Jerry")
end
```

with_scope() sets the scope of database operations within its block. If current_account() returns the account number of the currently logged in user, any calls involving Users inside this block are automatically scoped for you. Wrap actions in a before_filter() method and you end up with not only a cleaner code base but much less of a chance of *forgetting* to scope your database queries (which would result in users seeing other users outside their accounts—not good!).

Another trick you can use to scope things properly is to find() objects through associations. For example, if you want to select only the users in a certain account, instead of doing this:

```
User.find(:all, :conditions => ['account_id = ? AND name = ?',
                                 current_account, "Chad"])
```

you can do this:

```
@account.users.find(:all, :conditions => ['name = ?', "Chad"])
```

Make Dumb Data Smart with composed_of()

Sometimes, though it makes sense to store simple data in flattened structures in your database tables, you want a rich, object-oriented representation of the data in your Ruby code. How do you construct intelligent, structured objects from flat data?

For a long time, Active Record has shipped with a powerful but poorly understood macro called composed_of(). The basic syntax of the macro looks like this:

```
class SomeModel < ActiveRecord::Base
  composed_of :some_attribute,
              :class_name -> 'SomeSpecialClass',
              :mapping => [%w(model_attr_name special_class_attr)]
end
```

The problem here is that it reads like: "SomeModel is composed of some attribute." That doesn't quite capture the meaning of composed_of(). How it should really read is as follows: "Add some attribute, composed of SomeSpecialClass, and map SomeModel's model_attr_name field to special_class_attr."

Imagine we're managing student records for a school. We want to use each student's course history to determine whether they meet the academic requirements to participate in various school-sponsored extracurricular activities. For example, we might say that a student has to have completed Algebra II with a grade of B or better to be part of the math club.

For each record of a student having completed a course, we store the letter grade that student received for the course. Letter grades can be A through F and be modified with a plus or minus sign such as B+. We store the letter grade as a string in the database.

This is a perfect place to use a composed_of() mapping. Our internal field is "dumb": it's just a string with no grade-specific behavior. But we need to ensure that A- is higher than F without case sensitivity.

Here's what the relevant code from our CourseRecord class would look like:

MakeDumbDataSmart/app/models/course_record.rb

```ruby
class CourseRecord < ActiveRecord::Base
  composed_of :grade,
              :class_name => 'Grade',
              :mapping => [%w(letter_grade letter_grade)]
end
```

The CourseRecord model has a table attribute called letter_grade that will be mapped to an identically named field in the class, Grade, which will be accessible via CourseRecord's grade() attribute. The class name Grade is determined by the same conventions used to translate model and controller class names to their associated source files.[14] The composed_of() macro assumes that it can instantiate the composing class, passing each of the mapped values into its constructor. So, we'll make sure our Grade class accepts a single argument. Here's the class now:

MakeDumbDataSmart/app/models/grade.rb

```ruby
class Grade
  include Comparable
  attr_accessor :letter_grade
  SORT_ORDER = ["f", "d", "c", "b", "a"].inject({}) {|h, letter|
    h.update "#{letter}-" => h.size
    h.update letter => h.size
    h.update "#{letter}+" => h.size
  }
  def initialize(letter_grade)
    @letter_grade = letter_grade
  end
  def <=>(other)
    SORT_ORDER[letter_grade.downcase] <=> SORT_ORDER[other.letter_grade.downcase]
  end
end
```

We've defined the <=> method and included the Comparable module, which is all any Ruby class needs to do to implement comparison functionality. The <=> method returns one of 1, 0, or -1 depending on whether the receiving object is semantically greater than, equal to, or

---

[14]You can override the naming convention by passing the :class_name option to the composed_of() method.

less than the supplied argument. The SORT_ORDER hash defines how letter grades should be sorted, including the pluses and minuses.

Let's take a look at how this works in the console:

```
chad> ruby script/console
>> grade = CourseRecord.find(:first).grade
=> #<Grade:0x2241618 @letter_grade="a">
>> grade > Grade.new("a-")
=> true
>> grade > Grade.new("a+")
=> false
```

The value objects that we create in a composed_of() scenario should be treated as immutable. You can modify these objects in place all you want, but the values will never get saved:

```
>> course = CourseRecord.find(:first)
=> #<CourseRecord:0x2237514 @attributes={"student_id"=>..."letter_grade"=>"a"...>
>> course.grade
=> #<Grade:0x22364c0 @letter_grade="a">
>> course.grade.letter_grade = "f"
=> "f"
>> course.save
=> true
>> course = CourseRecord.find(:first)
=> #<CourseRecord:0x222e900 @attributes={"student_id"=>..."letter_grade"=>"a"...>
```

To actually modify the value stored in the database, you have to create a new Grade object and assign it to the CourseRecord class:

```
>> course.grade = Grade.new("f")
=> #<Grade:0x222c54c @letter_grade="f">
>> course.save
=> true
>> course = CourseRecord.find(:first)
=> #<CourseRecord:0x2226d90 @attributes={"student_id"=>"..."letter_grade"=>"f",...>
```

Discussion

You can also use the composed_of() macro to make a flat structure look normalized. If for some reason you needed to store structured data, such as an address, in the same table with the entity that data belongs to, you could map multiple fields into a single object. For example:

```
class Person < ActiveRecord::Base
  composed_of :address, :mapping => [ %w(address_street street),
                                      %w(address_city city),
                                      %w(address_state state),
                                      %w(address_country country) ]

end
```

This would map the fields address_street, address_city, address_state, and address_country of the people table to the Address class, allowing you to work with addresses as first-class objects, even though they're stored as flat attributes in the database.

Safely Use Models in Migrations

Thanks to Tim Lucas for inspiring and supplying code for this recipe.

Active Record migrations are wonderful things in that they support constant evolution of your database schema. Where it used to be painful to rename, add, or drop columns, migrations makes it easy.

But with this flexibility comes the increasing probability that we'll want to not only add, drop, and rename tables and columns but we'll want and need to do the same with our models as well. This can lead to problems. Since you sometimes need to manipulate data during a migration, it's tempting to use your Active Record models in the migrations themselves. After all, Active Record is usually quite a bit easier and less wordy to use than raw SQL.

But what if you rename your models? Early migrations will cease to work, since your file system (and even your source control tool) doesn't have a built-in versioning system that would be compatible with migrations. Your earlier migrations would be relying on models that were either deleted or removed.

The solution? Define your models (even if they already exist in the usual place) *in the migration itself*. For example:

```ruby
class AddPositionToProducts < ActiveRecord::Migration
  class Product < ActiveRecord::Base; end
  class SoftwareProduct < Product; end
  class CourseProduct < Product; end
  def self.up
    add_column :products, :position, :integer
    Product.reset_column_information

    # Set default list orders
    SoftwareProduct.find(:all).each_with_index {|p, i| p.position = i; p.save!) }
    CourseProduct.find(:all).each_with_index {|p, i| p.position = i; p.save! }
  end
  def self.down
    remove_column :products, :position
  end
end
```

Regardless of what models exist on your file system, this migration will *always* work. Take notice that the models are defined *inside* the migration class. This is important, because they are separated by namespace, just in case you need to use different versions of the model classes in other migrations. For example, the Product class is really AddPositionToProducts::Product. This guarantees that the model will be unique among your migrations.

Part III

Controller Recipes

Authenticating Your Users

Credit

Thanks to reader Tom Moertel for his suggestions and for the salt-related code in this recipe.

Problem

You're developing an application that has a separate piece of functionality supporting administrative features. Perhaps it's an online trivia game that has an interface for adding questions and their answers. Naturally, you don't want all the players to have access to the answers, so you'd like to protect the administrative interface with a username and password.

Solution

Although several authentication libraries are available as plugins and generators, simple authentication is so easy to do with Rails, that it is often not worth the extra baggage of depending on a third-party add-on to handle authentication. A quick mixture of a new user model and an Action Controller before_filter can have you up and running with login-protected actions in a matter of minutes.

For the sake of simplicity, it's best to put all the sensitive functionality in a separate controller. For our example, let's assume we have a controller named AdminController for which we would like to shield all actions behind a username and password.

The first step is to create a model to hold our authentication information. We'll do this by generating an Active Record migration to create a simple table. From the root directory of our application, we use the generate script to create the migration skeleton. (If you're using Rails 1.1 or higher, the migration will have been created automatically when you created the User model and will be called 001_add_user.rb.)

```
chad> ruby script/generate migration add_user_table
```

We then fill out the migration to look like this:

```
Authentication/db/migrate/001_add_user_table.rb
```

```ruby
class AddUserTable < ActiveRecord::Migration
  def self.up
    create_table :users do |t|
      t.column "username", :string
      t.column "password_salt", :string
      t.column "password_hash", :string
    end
  end

  def self.down
    drop_table :users
  end
end
```

The schema is simple. Users have a username, a hashed password, and a salt, which, as you'll see shortly, we'll use to generate the hashed password. We'll then use the migration to generate the database table with the following:

chad> **rake migrate**

Next, we'll need an Active Record model to support our new table. We can generate that as well:[15]

chad> **ruby script/generate model User**

Next we'll add some authentication-specific code to the User model. Here's the user.rb file:

```
Authentication/app/models/user.rb
```

```ruby
require 'digest/sha2'
class User < ActiveRecord::Base
  def password=(pass)
    salt = [Array.new(6){rand(256).chr}.join].pack("m").chomp
    self.password_salt, self.password_hash =
      salt, Digest::SHA256.hexdigest(pass + salt)
  end
end
```

Since we don't want to store plain-text passwords in the database, we use Ruby's SHA2 library to create a hash of the plain-text password for storage. We're not actually storing the password. We're storing only a string that can be reproducibly generated *given* the plain-text pass-

---

[15]Note that in Rails 1.1 or higher, the generation of a model automatically results in the generation of a migration for that model's matching table. If you are running Rails 1.1 or higher, you'll need to append --skip-migration to any model-generation commands in this recipe or simply use the migrations created with the model.

word. We're also adding a string (the *salt*) to the prehashed password to make it extra-difficult for malicious users to guess passwords by brute force. We store the salt and the hashed password in the database. When we want to authenticate a user, we look them up by username and then hash the salt and the supplied password to see whether they match the stored hash.

Now that we have a data model to support our User objects, we need to create a user. This is a simple model, so we could easily create a user administration form (probably also under our new AdminController) or even use simple scaffolding. But for now, we'll just create one using the Rails console:

```
chad> ruby script/console
Loading development environment.
>> chad = User.create(:username => "chad")
=> #<User:0x2416350 @errors=#<ActiveRecord::Errors:0x241598c...@new_record=false>
>> chad.password = "secret"
=> "secret"
>> chad.password_hash
=> "fa56838174d3aef09623ea003cb5ee468aa1b0aa68a403bd975be84dd999e76c"
>> chad.password_salt
=> "luBKiKLa"
>> chad.save
=> true
```

Now that we have a User with which to sign in, we can modify our AdminController to require authentication before executing any actions. We can do this using the before_filter macro included with Action Controller. At the top of the AdminController's class definition, let's add the following:

Authentication/app/controllers/admin_controller.rb

```
before_filter :check_authentication

def check_authentication
  unless session[:user]
    session[:intended_action] = action_name
    session[:intended_controller] = controller_name
    redirect_to :action => "signin"
  end
end
```

This tells Rails to always execute the method check_authentication() before executing any actions in this controller. This method checks for a user id in the session object. If the user does not exist (which means the user hasn't yet authenticated), the application redirects to the signin action, which will collect the user's username and password. As you'll soon see, saving session[:intended_action] and session[:intended_controller] will allow us to keep track of what the user was trying to do before authenticating, so we can place them gently back on their intended paths after checking their credentials. This is especially important to support bookmarks.

With the code in its current state, we have a problem. The method check_authentication() will redirect us to the signin action, which will again fire the controller's before_filter, bringing us full circle. To avoid an infinite loop, we'll need to modify the call to before_filter to exclude the sign-in–related action from the authentication check:

```
before_filter :check_authentication, :except => [:signin]
```

Now we can always access the signin action.

The signin action will handle both the display of the sign-in form and the actual authentication process that this form posts to. Here's the HTML form, app/views/admin/signin.rhtml, for collecting the user's credentials:

```
<html>
  <head>
    <title>Signin for Admin Access</title>
  </head>
  <body>
    <%= start_form_tag :action => "signin" %>
      <label for="username">Username:</label>
      <%= text_field_tag "username" %><br />
      <label for="password">Password:</label>
      <%= password_field_tag "password" %><br />
      <%= submit_tag "Sign in" %>
    <%= end_form_tag %>
  </body>
</html>
```

The user then submits their username and password back to the signin action, which checks them against our User model in the database:

```
def signin
  if request.post?
    user = User.find(:first, :conditions => ['username = ?', params[:username]])
    if user.blank? ||
        Digest::SHA256.hexdigest(params[:password] + user.password_salt) !=
          user.password_hash
      raise "Username or password invalid"
    end
    session[:user] = user.id
    redirect_to :action => session[:intended_action],
                :controller => session[:intended_controller]
  end
end
```

The SQL and SHA2 code in this action is unsightly and gives too much of the model's implementation away, so we can move it into the User model. While we're in there, we'll add a validator to ensure that only one User can be created with a given username:

Authentication/app/models/user.rb

```ruby
require 'digest/sha2'
class User < ActiveRecord::Base
  validates_uniqueness_of :username

  def self.authenticate(username, password)
    user = User.find(:first, :conditions => ['username = ?', username])
    if user.blank? ||
      Digest::SHA256.hexdigest(password + user.password_salt) != user.password_hash
      raise "Username or password invalid"
    end
    user
  end
end
```

We can now simplify the signin action to look like this:

```ruby
def signin
  if request.post?
    session[:user] = User.authenticate(params[:username], params[:password]).id
    redirect_to :action => session[:intended_action],
                :controller => session[:intended_controller]
  end
end
```

Finally, to top this recipe off with a little icing, we'll add the ability to sign out of the application. The signout action will simply remove the user id from session and redirect to the application's home page. The full AdminController now looks like the following:

```ruby
class AdminController < ApplicationController
  before_filter :check_authentication, :except => [:signin]

  def check_authentication
    unless session[:user]
      session[:intended_action] = action_name
      session[:intended_controller] = controller_name
      redirect_to :action => "signin"
    end
  end

  def signin
    session[:user] = User.authenticate(params[:username], params[:password]).id
    redirect_to :action => session[:intended_action],
                :controller => session[:intended_controller]
  end
```

```
  def signout
    session[:user] = nil
    redirect_to home_url
  end
  # ...the real application's actions would be here.
end
```

Note that home_url() refers to a hypothetical named route that you would need to configure. See Recipe 36, *Make Your URLs Meaningful (and Pretty)*, on page 153 to find out how.

What would we do if we needed authentication to apply to multiple controllers? Simple: move the authentication-related code, including the filter declarations, to our ApplicationController class. Since all our controllers extend ApplicationController by default, they will all inherit the filters and methods we define there.

Discussion

If you need to store extra profile information along with a user object, it may be tempting to put the entire User object in session on authentication. It's best to avoid doing this, because you'll invariably find yourself debugging your application, wondering why data changes to your user's profile don't seem to be taking effect, only to realize that you're looking at a stale copy of the data from session.

On the other end of the spectrum, sometimes you don't actually need a user object or model at all. If you don't need to track *who* is signing into your application, sometimes a simple password will do. For example, though some weblog systems support multiple authors and can display the author of each post, many do not. Simply protecting the right to post a story would be sufficient for such a system, and for that, a password (even a hard-coded password!) could meet your needs while saving you time.

One caveat to note with this approach: even though we're redirecting to the initially requested action, we'll lose any parameters passed during the initial, preauthenticated request. Using the same pattern we used to capture the intended action and controller, how could you save the request parameters and pass them along?

Also See

If you need finer-grained access control, see the next recipe.

Authorizing Users with Roles

Problem

Different parts of your application should be accessible to different people, based on who they are and what roles they play. For example, you might have built an online community recipe book for which a number of contributors have rights to add and edit the recipes in your database. These users are more privileged than those who have an account simply to post comments, but they're less privileged than you and your few chosen helpers who have administrative rights to the website. In the admin interface, you can grant permissions to other users and change the look and feel of the entire site.

Ingredients

• Completed Recipe 31, *Authenticating Your Users*, on page 135

Solution

For this recipe, we'll assume you have already set up an authentication system for your application that looks like the one described in Recipe 31, *Authenticating Your Users*, on page 135. If your authentication system is different from the one described in this book, don't worry. Essentially, we'll need two things from it: some kind of user identifier in session and an Active Record model to represent your user object. In this recipe, those will be session[:user] (containing the user's id as a number) and User, respectively.

The basic parts of our role-based authorization scheme are users, roles, and rights. A user plays many roles. Each role affords the user zero or more rights. Assuming we already have a User model created, we'll start by generating models to represent roles and rights:

```
chad> ruby script/generate model Role
chad> ruby script/generate model Right
```

Next, we'll set up the relationships between User, Role, and Right:

```
class User < ActiveRecord::Base
  has_and_belongs_to_many :roles
  # abbreviated for clarity
end
```

```
class Role < ActiveRecord::Base
  has_and_belongs_to_many :users
  has_and_belongs_to_many :rights
end

class Right < ActiveRecord::Base
  has_and_belongs_to_many :roles
end
```

This doesn't contain anything too unusual so far. Users have Roles, which give them associated Rights. Now we'll get a more concrete idea of what Roles and Rights look like by generating the supporting database tables. (If you're using Rails 1.1 or higher, the migrations were created automatically when you created the models. You'll find them in the files called ###_add_role.rb and ###_add_right.rb, respectively.)

```
chad> ruby script/generate migration add_roles_and_rights_tables
```

We'll then edit the generated migration file to look like this:

```
class AddRolesAndRightsTables < ActiveRecord::Migration
  def self.up
    create_table :roles_users, :id => false do |t|
      t.column "role_id", :integer
      t.column "user_id", :integer
    end

    create_table :roles do |t|
      t.column "name", :string
    end

    create_table :rights_roles, :id => false do |t|
      t.column "right_id", :integer
      t.column "role_id", :integer
    end

    create_table :rights do |t|
      t.column "name", :string
      t.column "controller", :string
      t.column "action", :string
    end
  end

  def self.down
    drop_table :roles_users
    drop_table :roles
    drop_table :rights
    drop_table :rights_roles
  end
end
```

The roles_users and rights_roles table definitions set :id => false to tell Rails that they are lookup tables and don't need a generated id field. The roles table acts simply as a link between users and their rights, so it has nothing but the implicit generated id field and a name.

The most notable part of our authorization scheme's data model is the rights table. A Right signifies something a user can *do*, and in the world of Rails, things are *done* via controllers and their actions. So for our model, we're going to express rights in terms of the controllers and actions that implement the actions that a Right grants a user. Using the example of an online recipe book, you might create a Right named *Create Recipe* with the controller set to "recipe" and the action set to "create". This Right would then be granted to one or more Roles that should have access to creating recipes. For example, we might have some users that play the role of *Author*. We'll look at some more specific examples shortly.

After using the migration to create our database tables, we're ready to put this new model into action. This means setting up our controllers to allow a user access only to the actions they have been granted access to. As with the authentication recipe (see Recipe 31, *Authenticating Your Users*, on page 135), we'll accomplish this using a before_filter. With the combination of the authentication and authorization code, our ApplicationController will look like the following:

```
class ApplicationController < ActionController::Base
  layout 'standard'
  before_filter :check_authentication,
                :check_authorization,
                :except => [:signin_form, :signin]

  def check_authentication
    unless session[:user]
      session[:intended_action] = action_name
      redirect_to :controller => "admin", :action => "signin_form"
      return false
    end
  end

  def check_authorization
    user = User.find(session[:user])
    unless user.roles.detect{|role|
      role.rights.detect{|right|
        right.action == action_name && right.controller == self.class.controller_path
      }
    }
      flash[:notice] = "You are not authorized to view the page you requested"
```

```
        request.env["HTTP_REFERER"] ? (redirect_to :back) : (redirect_to home_url)
        return false
      end
    end
end
```

The new method, check_authorization(), gets the User from session and searches the user's roles for a Right that matches the current controller and action names. If no matching Right is found, a message is put into flash, and the browser is redirected to either the page from which it came (if any) or the application's unprotected home page (see Recipe 36, *Make Your URLs Meaningful (and Pretty)*, on page 153). We could display such error messages by decorating our application's standard layout with a snippet like the following:

```
<% if flash[:notice] %>
  <div class="errors">
    <%= flash[:notice] %>
  </div>
<% end %>
```

```
class HomeController < ApplicationController
  skip_before_filter :check_authentication, :check_authorization
  def index
    render :text => "A page that doesn't require a signin or any rights"
  end
end
```

Notice that our filter methods return false if they fail. This is necessary to stop additional processing down the filter chain. For example, if we left out the return false in check_authentication(), check_authorization() would be executed even when no user was found in session, causing senseless errors.

Finally, with all these filters set up, we are ready to try our new authorization scheme! So far, we haven't added any roles or rights to the system, so our once-omnipotent users will now have access to nothing but the application's home page and sign-in forms. For a real application, you'll want to build an administrative interface for managing rights and roles. For our little recipe application, we'll add them manually.

```
chad> ruby script/console
Loading development environment.
>> user = User.find_by_username("chad")
=> #<User:0x230ed5c @attributes={"username"=>"chad", "id"=>"5",
   "password"=>"2034f6e32958647fdff75d265b455ebf"}>
>> role = Role.create :name => "Recipe Author"
=> #<Role:0x230bc88 @errors=#<ActiveRecord::Errors:0x230903c @errors={},
   @base=#<Role:0x230bc88 ...>>, @new_record=false,
```

```
       @new_record_before_save=false,
       @attributes={"name"=>"Recipe Author", "id"=>2}>
>> user.roles << role
=> [#<Role:0x230bc88 @errors=#<ActiveRecord::Errors:0x230903c @errors={},
       @base=#<Role:0x230bc88 ...>>, @new_record=false,
       @new_record_before_save=false,
       @attributes={"name"=>"Recipe Author", "id"=>2}>]
>> user.save
=> true
>> right = Right.create :name => "Create Recipes",
                        :controller => "recipe", :action => "create"
=> #<Right:0x22f53ac @errors=#<ActiveRecord::Errors:0x22f1d88 @errors={},
       @base=#<Right:0x22f53ac ...>>, @new_record=false,
       @new_record_before_save=false, @attributes={"name"=>"Create Recipes",
       "action"=>"create", "id"=>2, "controller"=>"recipe"}>
>> role.rights << right
=> [#<Right:0x22f53ac @errors=#<ActiveRecord::Errors:0x22f1d88 @errors={},
       @base=#<Right:0x22f53ac ...>>, @new_record=false,
       @new_record_before_save=false, @attributes={"name"=>"Create Recipes",
       "action"=>"create", "id"=>2, "controller"=>"recipe"}>]
>> role.save
=> true
```

We have created a role called *Recipe Author* and assigned it to the user named *chad*. We then created a right called *Create Recipes* and added it to the list of rights afforded to our freshly created Role. Since the *Create Recipes* right grants access to the create action of the recipe controller, the user *chad* will now be able to access that action.

Discussion

This recipe shows a simple starting point from which you could build more complex authorization schemes. Basing rights on controllers and actions doesn't allow you to, for example, protect access to specific instances of models in your database. For more complex needs, this recipe will provide a solid building point, or you can explore third-party options such as Bruce Perens's ModelSecurity,[16] which takes authorization to such an extreme level of granularity that it allows you to set rights on the individual operations of an Active Record model.

---

[16]http://perens.com/FreeSoftware/ModelSecurity/

Cleaning Up Controllers with Postback Actions

Thanks to Marcel Molina Jr. for the code example used in this recipe.

When you're first learning Rails, you start with the one-action-per-request paradigm. For every click or form submission, there is an action in a controller somewhere waiting to respond.

But sometimes the one-action-per-request convention is unnecessary and leads to code that is less clear than it could be.

For example, when you write code to edit or create new instances of an Active Record model, there will be requests for both the forms and the forms' submission. This could result in four separate actions: new object form, new object creation, edit object form, and update object. You'll end up with a bunch of ambiguously named actions such as edit(), create(), new(), and update(), which is confusing when you have to return to it later.

It turns out that all of these requests can be handled by a single action:[17]

```
def edit
  @recipe = Recipe.find_by_id(params[:id]) || Recipe.new
  if request.post?
    @recipe.attributes = params[:recipe]
    redirect_to :main_url and return if @recipe.save
  end
end
```

That's clean and DRY.

---

[17]You'll notice that we're explicitly calling return after the redirect. Although it's not necessary in this example, since the redirect is the last executable line of the method, it's important to note that a redirect does *not* result in a return in Rails. Any code after a redirect_to() call will be executed unless there is an explicit return.

Monitor Expiring Sessions

Credit

Thanks to Dave Thomas for the idea and implementation of this recipe.

Problem

Your application explicitly expires sessions after a period of inactivity (you know—like one of those online banking applications), and you'd like to help your users keep track of how long they have before the application signs them out.

Ingredients

• Rails 1.1 or higher

Solution

With a mixture of an after_filter(), a periodically_call_remote() call, and an RJS template, we can quickly whip up a nice effect. Here are the salient parts of a BankAccountController that times a session out after ten minutes of inactivity:

```
KeepAnEyeOnYourSessionExpiry/app/controllers/bank_account_controller.rb
class BankAccountController < ApplicationController
  before_filter :update_activity_time, :except => :session_expiry
  def update_activity_time
    session[:expires_at] = 10.minutes.from_now
  end
  def session_expiry
    @time_left = (session[:expires_at] - Time.now).to_i
    unless @time_left > 0
      reset_session
      render '/signin/redirect'
    end
  end
end
```

Before almost all the requests in our application, we call the filter method update_activity_time. This filter sets the time that the user's session should be expired based on the last time the user showed any activity in the application.

We don't run the update_activity_time filter for the session_expiry action. Looking at a sample view for this controller will show you why:

KeepAnEyeOnYourSessionExpiry/app/views/bank_account/index.rhtml

```
<html>
<head>
    <%= javascript_include_tag :defaults %>
</head>
<body>
    <div id='header'></div>
    <%= periodically_call_remote :url => {
                                    :action => 'session_expiry'},
                                    :update => 'header' %>
    <div id='body'>Here's where your application's real functionality goes.</div>
</body>
```

Using periodically_call_remote(), we call the session_expiry() action (every ten seconds—the default), placing the action's contents in the initially empty <*div*> tag called header. If it's not yet time for the session to be expired, the session_expiry() action renders its view:

KeepAnEyeOnYourSessionExpiry/app/views/bank_account/session_expiry.rhtml

```
<% if @time_left < 1.minute %>
<span style='color: red; font-weight: bold'>
    Your session will expire in <%= @time_left %> seconds
</span>
<% end %>
```

If the session is due to expire in less than a minute, session_expiry's view will display a warning in bold red, which will be updated every ten seconds.

If the session is due to time out, session_expiry() will reset the session and invoke an RJS template (see Recipe 6, *Update Multiple Elements with One Ajax Request*, on page 29) that redirects the browser to the application's sign-in URL:

KeepAnEyeOnYourSessionExpiry/app/views/signin/redirect.rjs

```
page << "window.location = '#{signin_url}';"
```

Why didn't we use redirect_to() in session_expiry() to handle the redirect? Why resort to JavaScript? Browsers won't do a full redirect when they receive a 302 HTTP response code via an Ajax request. So we cheat a little and use RJS to generate a client-side redirect.

Rendering Comma-Separated Values from Your Actions

Thanks to Mike Clark for his ideas on this recipe.

Sometimes the easiest and most satisfying (for you *and* your users) way to implement a reporting requirement is to simply provide your application's data in a format your users can import into their favorite reporting and analytical tools. The most common format for such a thing is CSV, or Comma-Separated Values.

Here's how you generate CSV from Rails.

Imagine you have an Order model that tracks product orders. Here's a simple controller that will export your orders to a CSV file:

`RenderCSV/app/controllers/export_controller.rb`

```ruby
class ExportController < ApplicationController
  def orders
    content_type = if request.user_agent =~ /windows/i
                     'application/vnd.ms-excel'
                   else
                     'text/csv'
                   end

    CSV::Writer.generate(output = "") do |csv|
      Order.find(:all).each do |order|
        csv << [order.id, order.price, order.purchaser, order.created_at]
      end
    end
    send_data(output,
              :type => content_type,
              :filename => "orders.csv")
  end
end
```

The first line of orders() is a fun hack. If the browser's USER_AGENT contains the string windows, we set the content type of the response to one that will cause Microsoft Excel to pop open if it's installed. Otherwise, the content type is set to the standard text/csv.

This action renders something like the following:

```
1,123.22,Kilgore Trout,Sun Apr 02 17:14:58 MDT 2006
2,44.12,John Barth,Sun Apr 02 17:14:58 MDT 2006
3,42.44,Josef K,Sun Apr 02 17:14:58 MDT 2006
```

Here we use Ruby's CSV library in its most basic incarnation. If you need more customizable output, consult the documentation for the CSV library.

Make Your URLs Meaningful (and Pretty)

You want your URLs to be meaningful and easy to remember. The popular "Web 2.0" applications of today, such as Flickr and del.icio.us, have cast aside the hideous, obfuscated, Active Server Page–generated URLs of days past in favor of clean, short URLs that users can understand. For example, popular bookmarks tagged with "rails" are accessible in del.icio.us via http://del.icio.us/popular/rails. The most interesting photographs posted to Flickr during March of 2006 are accessible via http://flickr.com/explore/interesting/2006/03/.

How do you support this style of URL in your application without having to copy and paste code into multiple controllers and views? How do you cleanly turn components of your application's URLs into parameters that will drive the application's business logic?

Action Controller ships with a powerful framework called Routes. With this framework, *routes* enable you to map incoming URLs to specific controllers, actions, and even *parameters* in your application. Unlike technologies such as Apache's mod_rewrite plugin, Action Controller's routes are written in pure Ruby.

Routes are declared in the file config/routes.rb in your application's root directory. When you generate a new application, a default set of routes is created for you. The following is the default routes.rb as of Rails 1.0 (with comments removed for brevity):

`MeaningfulURLs/config/routes.rb`

```
ActionController::Routing::Routes.draw do |map|
  map.connect ':controller/service.wsdl', :action => 'wsdl'
  map.connect ':controller/:action/:id'
end
```

Routes are created via the connect() method. The first argument to connect() is the incoming path to match. The second argument is an optional Hash of additional parameters. The first route in the default routes.rb file supports Web Services Description Language URLs. The :controller part of the first argument is special. Any path components that start with a colon are interpreted as variables. :controller is, not surprisingly, the variable where the controller should go. With this route in place, an incoming request for /photos/service.wsdl would translate into the invocation of the wsdl() action in the PhotosController class.

The second (and last) route in our default routes.rb file should be familiar to anyone who has done any Rails development. It is the heart of the Rails URL convention, supporting URLs such as /photos/show/905, which would invoke the show() action on the PhotosController class, setting the :id parameter to 905.

Now that we know where the routes go and what they generally look like, let's make some of our own. Imagine we're working on a site that lets users post and share cooking recipes. We have a controller called RecipesController that houses much of the logic for the application. The RecipesController has an action, list(), that can search for and display lists of recipes based on assorted criteria, such as the recipe's author. This controller and its associated view are generic enough to be used to display lists of recipes in any part of the application that may require a recipe list.

Let's start by making a route that will let users display all recipes created by a certain author. Since the whole site centers around recipes, having the word *recipes* in the URL would be redundant. We want to support a URL that looks like this (assuming the application is installed on railsrecipes.com): http://railsrecipes.com/chad. Accessing this URL should display a list of all recipes authored by the user *chad*.

For the purpose of learning, we'll add a temporary version of our list action that will simply raise an exception, passing any supplied parameters. This causes the application to fail and display these parameters in the web browser. We won't go into the details of performing the search, since once you know how to get the parameters, the search is nothing new. Here's what the controller should look like:

```
MeaningfulURLs/app/controllers/recipes_controller.rb
class RecipesController < ApplicationController
  def list
    raise params.inspect
  end
end
```

Now we can create our route. Open your config/routes.rb, and add the following line after all the other routes' definitions:

```
map.connect ':user', :controller => 'recipes',
                     :action => 'list',
                     :filter => 'user'
```

With your local server running on the default port of 3000, you should now be able to access http://localhost:3000/chad. You should see an error page with the heading RuntimeError in Recipes#list. This is a good thing. It means your request was routed to the list action you just created. Just below the heading, you should see a dump of the request's parameters. This dump will contain four pairs of items: the user parameter, the action, the controller, and the filter parameter, which we could use in our action to determine what we're filtering on.

Cool. Now, what if we wanted to narrow our search to recipes that were authored by a specified user *and* tagged as *appetizer*? We have multiple ways to achieve this affect, but one way would be to modify the previous route declaration to look like this:

```
map.connect ':user/:tag', :controller => 'recipes',
                          :action => 'list',
                          :filter => 'user',
                          :tag => ''
```

This route matches URLs such as http://localhost:3000/chad/appetizer, populating both the :user and :tag parameters. If no tag parameter is supplied, the route will still match, and the default value of an empty string will be placed in the :tag parameter. Default parameter values can be set to any Ruby expression, so if we wanted all searches to default to *south indian*, we could replace the last option with :tag => 'south indian'.

Now, let's create a route that will match http://localhost:3000/popular and display the site's top-ranked recipes. We'll also provide support for optionally adding a tag, like we did in our previous example. We can accomplish this with the following addition to routes.rb:

```
map.connect 'popular/:tag', :controller => 'recipes',
                            :action => 'list',
                            :tag => '',
                            :filter => 'popular'
```

There are two points of interest here. First, you'll notice that if you put this rule *under* the existing routes in routes.rb, the wrong parameters get populated. Why is that? Because the Routes engine processes routes in the order they appear in the file, and there's nothing to distinguish the word *popular* from a user's name. So what happens is our previous route matches, and *popular* gets placed in the user parameter.

Second, this example demonstrates the use of string literals as part of routes. In fact, a route can consist entirely of literals as in the following contrived example:

```
map.connect 'uta/tumba/chennaagide', :controller => 'recipes',
                           :action => 'list',
                           :filter => 'popular',
                           :tag => 'south indian'
```

The static URL, http://locahost:3000/uta/tumba/chennaagide, will always return a list of popular South Indian recipes.

Finally, let's provide support for seeing the recipes that were added on a specific day, defaulting to the current day. Put this route *before* the user route:

```
map.connect 'daily/:month/:day/:year',
          :controller => 'recipes',
          :action => 'list',
          :filter => 'daily',
          :month => Time.now.month,
          :day => Time.now.day,
          :year => Time.now.year,
          :requirements => {
            :year => /\d+/,
            ,:day => /\d+/,
            :month => /\d+/
          }
```

This is a big one. It accepts URLs that look like: http://localhost:3000/daily/09/06/1997 and populates :month, :day, and :year parameters. If the year is left off the URL, it will default to the current year. It's the same with day and month. Through the :requirements option to the connect() call, we also specify that the year, day, and month must be numeric digits for this route to match.

Finally, Routes comes with a great perk that we shouldn't leave unmentioned: *named routes*. Instead of calling connect() in your route definition, you can call a nonexistent method on the map object like this:

```
map.popular 'popular/:tag', :controller => 'recipes',
                          :action => 'list',
                          :tag => '',
                          :filter => 'popular'
```

With this in place, from your controllers, your views, and your functional and integration tests, you can construct a URL for this route using the autogenerated method popular_url(). You can even provide parameters to the generated URL by calling the generated method with a Hash, like this:

```
popular_url(:tag => 'south indian')
```

This not only saves typing but makes your applications less brittle. If for some reason you have to change the name of a controller or action, if you're using named routes, you have to change *references* to that controller or action in only one place.

Stub Out Authentication

This recipe was written by Rails core team member Marcel Molina Jr.

You know that your Rails application will include authentication eventually. Focus first on what is most important. Authentication is a requirement, but it's rarely the *core* of what your application does.

Wrap your authentication logic in a method called logged_in?. Always use this method to determine whether the user is authenticated. When you start developing your project, add a stub for logged_in? in your ApplicationController that just returns true.

```
def logged_in?
  true
end
helper_method :logged_in?
```

You can then start using the logged_in? method throughout your application as you intended to without worrying about the implementation details.

Later, when you're ready to implement an authentication scheme, you can just replace true with the actual authentication code.

If you needed to not only check whether someone had authenticated but to access their user profile, you could use a method like the following:

```
def current_user
  Struct.new("User", :name, :password).new("chad", "secret")
end
```

You could then use the current_user method throughout the application and replace its implementation when you're ready.

Convert to Active Record Sessions

By default, for ease of development, Rails stores its sessions on the file system as serialized Ruby objects. This works fine on a single computer for a developer, but it doesn't scale very well when you go to production. A much faster and more maintainable solution is to store your sessions in the database using Active Record.

Configuring something like this might sound like a daunting task, but it's actually one of the most surprisingly easy tasks you'll encounter in Rails. It takes only a minute:

1. The default config/environment.rb file ships with the necessary configuration to store your sessions in the database *in the file* but commented out by default. Find the following line in that file, and uncomment it:

   ```
   config.action_controller.session_store = :active_record_store
   ```

2. Now we need to create the table that will store our session data. Use the included Rake task to generate an Active Record migration that will create the table: rake db:sessions:create for Rails 1.1 or rake create_sessions_table for version 1.0.

3. Run the migration: rake migrate

4. Restart your server.

You can now hit any session-enabled action of your application, and you should be able to see a new row if you execute the following SQL:

```
select * from sessions;
```

Write Code That Writes Code

You notice a recurring pattern in your application. You're writing essentially the same actions over and over again in various controllers.

Looking at the declarative style of many of the Rails helpers such as in_place_edit_for() and auto_complete_for(), you want your own code to be expressed as succinctly.

How does Rails implement these so-called macros—code that writes your actions for you?

Ruby is an extremely dynamic language. We are all exposed to its dynamic typing system daily, but the dynamism doesn't end there.

Ruby, like Lisp and Smalltalk before it, allows programmers to easily write code that writes and loads code at runtime. This is a really deep topic, and we're not going to attempt to dig too far into it here. Instead, we'll focus on the details necessary to implement our own Action Controller macros.

Let's imagine we have a complex application with a large domain model for which we have many actions that implement a simple search. You have standardized the look and feel of this search across the application so that users have a consistent interface. In fact, you've made the look and feel so consistent that you are able to reuse the same view for all the search actions.

A typical instance of one of these actions might look like the following simplified example. This one is for searching through contacts in a contact database.

WriteCodeThatWritesCode/app/controllers/contacts_controller.rb

```
def search
  Contact.with_scope(:find => {
        :conditions => ['account_id = ?', current_user.account_id]}) do
    @title = "Your Contacts"
    @results = Contact.find(:all,
                            :conditions => ['name like ?', "%#{params[:term]}%"])
    @display_as = :name
```

```
    @display_action = "view"
    render :template => 'shared/search_results'
  end
end
```

Over the life of our application, because we have refactored separate actions into being able to use a single view, we ended up with this "configure by instance variable" style. We set several variables in this action that influence the behavior of the shared view. Let's look at the shared view now:

WriteCodeThatWritesCode/app/views/shared/search_results.rhtml

```
<h2 class='search_header'>
  <%= @title %>
</h2>
<ul>
  <% @results.each do |result| %>
  <li>
    <%= link_to result.send(@display_as),
              :action => @display_action,
              :id => result
    %>
  </li>
  <% end %>
</ul>
```

We see here that the view of search results is structurally the same across all search actions and uses the instance variables set in the search action to decide what heading to use, which action to link each result to, and which attribute of the returned item to use as the display value for the link. We can now easily use this same view to display search results for practically any Active Record model, provided we create a search action that follows the expected protocol.

The problem here is that although the view has been nicely cleaned up of duplication, we still have a ton of duplicated code in our controllers. In a big application, this kind of pattern might propagate itself tens of times. If we needed to change the behavior of the search results view, we would have to edit each action that references it. Bad news.

Notice also that our action uses with_scope() to limit the search to include contacts only within a certain set of criteria. In this case, we're modeling a situation wherein the system has multiple accounts (one per subscribed company), inside of which are many users. Users shouldn't be able to view data that was created by people in other companies in the context of other accounts, so we need to consistently take care to limit the scope of our queries. If we forget to do this in one of our search actions, it could be embarrassing and damaging to the application's credibility. It would be greatly preferable to automate this so we don't have to worry about remembering it each time.

What would be *great* is if we could simply do something like the following in our controllers whenever we wanted a search action:

```
search_action_for :contacts, :title => "Your Contacts"
```

In idiomatic Rails style, this would create a search action for the Contact model with a sensible set of defaults that could be overridden by an options Hash passed in as the second parameter to the method. Let's convert our existing search() action to a macro-driven implementation.

The quickest and easiest way to make this macro available from any controller in the application is to define it in ApplicationController. Here's our ApplicationController with the macro defined:

WriteCodeThatWritesCode/app/controllers/application.rb

```
Line 1    class ApplicationController < ActionController::Base
   -        def self.search_action_for(table, options = {})
   -          model_class = Object.const_get(table.classify)
   -          define_method(:search) do
   5            search_code = lambda do
   -              @title = options[:title] || "Your #{table.humanize}"
   -              search_column = options[:search_column] || 'name'
   -              @display_as = options[:display_as] || :name
   -              @display_action = options[:display_action] || "view"
   10             @results = model_class.find(:all, :conditions =>
   -                            ["#{search_column} like ?", "%#{params[:term]}%"])
   -              render :template => 'shared/search_results'
   -            end
   -            (options[:scoped] == false) ?
   15               search_code.call : scope(model_class, &search_code)
   -          end
   -        end
   -        def scope(model_class, &block)
   -          model_class.with_scope(
   20            :find => { :conditions => ['account_id = ?', current_user.account_id] },
   -              &block)
   -        end
   -      end
```

Walking through the code, you'll see that search_action_for() is defined using self.search_action_for(). This is because we're defining the method to be called on the controller class itself—not on *instances* of that class. When we call a method inside a class definition, it gets called on that class. This method uses const_get() to dynamically look up a constant by name. In Ruby, classes are constants, so in this case we're actually looking up the class using its name.

Rails actions are simply methods defined on controllers. So to write code that writes Rails actions for us, we need to be able to define methods dynamically. We can do this with Ruby's define_method() method. We name the method search(), because we want the action to be called search(). Although we're defining this code in ApplicationController, it will be run in the context of the controller from which it is called. So if we call it inside ContactsController, it will define a method called search() in that controller—not in ApplicationController.

Next we use the lambda() method to define a block of code. This is the code that makes up the search() action's real logic. We could have skipped using a lambda here and just written the code inline, but we're going to need the code in block form so that we can conditionally call with_scope() later in the method. We'll get to that in a bit, so for now just take it on faith.

The first step of the search code's logic is setting up our configuration. We support a set of sensible defaults, which users can optionally override using the options parameter. In addition to the variables we set in our contact-specific version of search(), we're also providing the ability to override which column the query will use in its WHERE condition, which we've named search_column in the options parameter.

Now that we have all of the configuration taken care of, on line 10 we actually do the find(). Notice that we're calling find() on the model_class variable. This was set *outside the scope of our dynamic method definition* to the model class for which we're creating a search action. That class, by virtue of Ruby's support for closures, gets embedded in the action and won't be looked up again when the action is invoked.

Finally, there may be some cases for which we don't want to scope on account_id for a model. In our simple example, we allow an option to turn scoping off, with scoping as the default behavior. On line 14, we conditionally apply scoping to the code by either calling it bare or passing it as a block to the scope() method. The scope() method assumes that any model it receives has an account_id column. I'll leave supporting additional methods of scoping as an exercise for you, should you need that capability.

So now we have a search() action maker that we can use in any controller we want and with any model. If we had a controller for managing

appointments and wanted to support searching them, all we'd have to
do is add something like the following to our appointments controller:

```
search_action_for :appointments,
                   :title => "Upcoming appointments",
                   :search_column => 'description',
                   :display_as => :subject
```

This is a great way to use less code for the same features, remove duplication, and make life easier. We've gone through a simple example here,
but these basic building blocks can be applied to a diverse set of problems. Now that you've seen it once, let your imagination take over, and
you're sure to find many ways this technique could help you on your
own projects.

Discussion

You can confront reuse in many ways. The two most prevalent ways are
either to generate code or to create a runtime framework. This recipe
combines those two. We generate code at runtime.

This kind of runtime code generation can be powerful. But it comes
at a price. Creating powerful abstractions such as these requires code
that is sometimes complex and uses the most advanced features of
Ruby. During development, it can be difficult to debug problems with
generated code.

Typically, though, generated code done *well* creates an expressive, productive environment. It's a balancing act and a decision you shouldn't
take lightly.

Also See

If you create something reusable in this manner, you might consider
packaging it as a plugin. See Rick Olson's Recipe 52, *Making Your Own
Rails Plugins*, on page 237, for more information.

And as an experiment, see how much of what you've learned in this
recipe could be applied to creating macros for Active Record models.
You'll be surprised by how much you can already do!

Manage a Static Site with Rails

After spending enough time in Rails, I find myself getting used to the Rails layout mechanism and seriously missing it when I'm doing static sites. Sure, other systems are specifically geared toward creating static sites. But I use Ruby and Rails, and I'd rather not learn another system that I have to use in static-site situations.

Given that Rails has a simple and robust caching mechanism, we can use Rails as a static-site management tool. Just set up a controller under which to store your static content (I called mine *pages*), and add the following line inside the controller's class definition:

```
after_filter { |c| c.cache_page }
```

This tells the controller to cache every action as it is accessed. Now, when you access this page via your browser, Rails will create a static, cached version of it that will be served directly by the web server on subsequent requests.

The generated pages will include any layouts that would normally be applied, or even partials that have been rendered within your views. This is a great way to componentize your static content. If your site displays the same contact list in several places, for example, you can create a partial view with that information and render it where appropriate.

Keep in mind that if you use this method on a page that requires authentication, the page that is cached will be the version that the first user saw. So if this page showed sensitive account information, that user's information would show up for *every* user who accessed the site. Only use this technique with content that is the same for all users!

Part IV

Testing Recipes

Creating Dynamic Test Fixtures

The Rails framework has done us all a service by building in the ability to manage test data through fixture files. These files can be either comma-separated text files or, more commonly, YAML files. You place sample data in fixtures that are then loaded before your tests run, giving you test subjects on which to ensure that your code behaves as you expect.

Even though testing is much easier in the Rails world, creating fixture data can become tedious when you're working on a big application with a rich domain. You want to make sure you have samples that represent normal application usage scenarios as well as edge cases, and creating all that data—especially when many of the attributes are often inconsequential to the test you're creating them for—can be tiring and time-consuming.

Rails development is supposed to be fun! How can we take away the tedium of creating large quantities of test fixtures?

An often-overlooked feature of the way Rails deals with fixture files is that before passing them into the YAML parser, it runs them through ERb. ERb is the same templating engine that powers our .rhtml templates. It allows you to embed arbitrary Ruby expressions into otherwise static text.

When used in YAML test fixtures, this approach can be extremely powerful. Consider the following example. This fixture data is a sample of a larger file used for testing posts to a message board application. A Post in this application can be a reply to an existing Post, which is specified by the parent_id field. Imagine how bored you'd get (and how many errors you'd probably commit) if you had to create dozens more of such posts to test various edge conditions.

```
DynamicTestFixtures/test/fixtures/posts.yml
```
```
first_post:
  id: 1
  title: First post!
  body: I got the first post!  I rule!
  created_at: 2006-01-29 20:03:56
  updated_at: 2006-01-29 21:00:00
  user_id: 1
reply_to_first_post:
  id: 2
  title: Very insightful
  body: It's people like you that make participation in
        this message board worthwhile.  Thank you.
  parent_id: 1
  created_at: 2006-01-30 08:03:56
  created_at: 2006-01-30 08:03:56
  user_id: 2
third_level_nested_child_post:
  id: 3
  title: This post is buried deep in the comments
  body: The content isn't really important.  We just want to test
        the application's threading logic.
  created_at: 2006-01-30 08:03:56
  created_at: 2006-01-30 08:03:56
  parent_id: 2
  user_id: 1
```

As I was entering this data into the posts.yml file, by the time I reached the third entry I was annoyed and starting to copy and paste data without much thought. For example, the third entry's purpose in our fictional application is to provide sample data for testing nested comments. We might need to be able to show the total nested child count of replies to a post to get a high-level idea of the activity going on in that part of the discussion.

If that were the case, the only field in the third fixture with any real meaning is the parent_id field. That's the one that associates this post with the child of the root post. I don't care what the post's title or body is or who posted it. I just need a post to be there and be counted.

Since fixtures are preprocessed through ERb, we can use embedded Ruby snippets to generate fixture data. Assuming we want to test with greater numbers of posts than three, let's generate a block of posts, randomly disbursed under the existing thread:

```
DynamicTestFixtures/test/fixtures/posts.yml
```
```
<% 1.upto(50) do |number| %>
child_post_<%= number %>:
```

```
    id: <%= number + 3 %>
    title: This is auto-generated reply number <%= number %>
    body: We're on number <%= number %>
    created_at: 2006-01-30 08:03:56
    created_at: 2006-01-30 08:03:56
    <%# Randomly choose a parent from a post we've already generated -%>
    parent_id: <%= rand(number - 1) + 1 %>
    user_id: <%= rand(5) + 1 %>
<% end %>
```

Now, if we load our fixtures, we can see that we have 53 Posts in our database:

```
chad> rake load_fixtures
(in /Users/chad/src/FR_RR/Book/code/DynamicTestFixtures)
chad> ruby script/runner 'puts Post.count'
53
chad> ruby -rpp script/runner 'pp Post.find(53)'
#<Post:0x23311e0
 @attributes=
   {"updated_at"=>nil,
    "body"=>"We're on number 50",
    "title"=>"This is autogenerated reply number 50",
    "id"=>"53",
    "user_id"=>"4",
    "parent_id"=>"36",
    "created_at"=>"2006-01-30 08:03:56"}>
```

Wonderful! Now what if we wanted to do something smart with the dates? For example, we might want to test that when a post is updated, it is sorted back to the top of the list and redisplayed as if new. Of course, we could do that by copying and pasting dates and then hand-editing them, but who wants to spend their time that way? We can save ourselves some time, some pain, and probably a few self-inflicted bugs by delegating to some helper methods.

Here's how we'd do that:

DynamicTestFixtures/test/fixtures/posts.yml

```
<%
   def today
     Time.now.to_s(:db)
   end
   def next_week
     1.week.from_now.to_s(:db)
   end
   def last_week
     1.week.ago.to_s(:db)
   end
%>
```

```
post_from_last_week:
  id: 60
  title: Pizza
  body: Last night I had pizza.  I really liked that story from AWDWR. :)
  created_at: <%= last_week %>
  updated_at: <%= last_week %>
  user_id: 1
post_created_in_future_should_not_display:
  id: 61
  title: Prognostication
  body: I predict that this post will show up next week.
  created_at: <%= next_week %>
  updated_at: <%= next_week %>
  user_id: 1
updated_post_displays_based_on_updated_time:
  id: 62
  title: This should show up as posted today.
  body: blah blah blah
  created_at: <%= last_week %>
  updated_at: <%= today %>
  user_id: 2
```

Not only does this technique save time and reduce the chance for error, but it's also a lot easier to read. The words *next week* carry a lot more semantic significance than a hard-coded date. They tell you not just *what* the data is but a little of *why* it's set the way it is. Other dated-related method names such as month_end_closing_date() or random_date_last_year() could convey significance (or *insignificance*) of a value. And, of course, there's no reason to stop with dates. This is ERb, which means it's Ruby, and anything that's possible with Ruby is possible in these fixtures.

You probably noticed the calls to, for example, 1.week.ago(). These aren't included with Ruby; also not included is the ability to format a Time object for use with a database. These methods ship with Rails. Since your fixtures are loaded in the context of a Rails application, all your model classes, helper libraries, and the Rails framework itself are available for your use.

Discussion

Though you can generate fixtures at runtime with ERb, sometimes it's easier to pregenerate your fixtures. If you just need a bunch of static data that isn't going to change much, you might consider writing a script that creates static YAML fixtures that you then just check in and manage like usual.

Another way to quickly generate fixture data is to generate scaffolding for your models, enter your data via the autogenerated forms, and then dump your live data into fixtures files. For more information about how to dump data into fixtures, see Recipe 42, *Extracting Test Fixtures from Live Data*, on page 179.

Also See

Since fixture files are usually declared in YAML format, a thorough understanding of the YAML can make for a more enjoyable experience when creating them. The YAML specification, like YAML itself, has an open license and can be downloaded at http://yaml.org/spec/.

Extracting Test Fixtures from Live Data

Credit

Thanks to Rails core developer, Jeremy Kemper (bitsweat), for the code on which this recipe is based.

Problem

You want to take advantage of the unit testing features in Rails, but your data model is complex, and manually creating all those fixtures sounds like a real drag. You've implemented enough of your application that you're able to populate its database via the application's interface—a far better interface than plain-text YAML files! Now you have a rich set of data that would be great for unit testing. How do you create fixtures from that existing data?

Solution

Active Record gives us all the ingredients we need to generate fixtures from our existing data. The basic steps are as follows:

- Establish a connection to the database.
- Query the database for the names of its tables.
- Select the data for each table in turn, and convert it into YAML.
- Generate a unique name for the data in the row.
- Write the results to a file named after the table name.

Let's use a simple database model to demonstrate. We'll create a model to represent people and the clubs they are members of. First we'll create the models. We might normally create the table definitions first, but we're going to use the models to create sample data during our migration.

`CreateFixturesFromLiveData/app/models/person.rb`

```ruby
class Person < ActiveRecord::Base
  has_and_belongs_to_many :clubs
end
```

CreateFixturesFromLiveData/app/models/club.rb

```
class Club < ActiveRecord::Base
  has_and_belongs_to_many :people
end
```

People can belong to many clubs and clubs can have many members. For the sake of demonstration, we'll generate some sample data in our migration file. In the real world, we would probably set up a simple set of scaffolds for data entry, and we could easily create a lot more sample data. The Active Record migration file should look like the following:

CreateFixturesFromLiveData/db/migrate/001_create_people_and_clubs_tables.rb

```
class CreatePeopleAndClubsTables < ActiveRecord::Migration
  def self.up
    create_table :people do |t|
      t.column :name, :string
    end

    create_table :clubs do |t|
      t.column :name, :string
    end

    create_table :clubs_people, :id => false do |t|
      t.column :person_id, :integer
      t.column :club_id, :integer
    end

    chad = Person.create(:name => "Chad")
    kelly = Person.create(:name => "Kelly")
    james = Person.create(:name => "James")

    hindi_club = Club.create(:name => "Hindi Study Group")
    snow_boarders = Club.create(:name => "Snowboarding Newbies")

    chad.clubs.concat [hindi_club, snow_boarders]
    kelly.clubs.concat [hindi_club, snow_boarders]
    james.clubs.concat [snow_boarders]
    [chad, kelly, james].each {|person| person.save}
  end

  def self.down
    drop_table :people
    drop_table :clubs
    drop_table :clubs_people
  end
end
```

After we've run this migration, we should have two Club objects and three Person objects in our database. Now let's load the Rails console and take some of the steps toward accomplishing our end goal of creating fixtures from this data:

```
chad> ruby script/console
    Loading development environment.
    >> ActiveRecord::Base.establish_connection
    => #<ActiveRecord::Base::ConnectionSpecification:0x233cd38 @config...
    >> ActiveRecord::Base.connection.tables
    => ["clubs", "clubs_people", "people", "schema_info"]
```

Based on the set of steps we laid out at the beginning of this recipe, we're almost halfway there! But there's one table in the list that we don't want to create fixtures for. The special schema_info table is used by Active Record to manage migrations, so we wouldn't want to create fixtures for that. Make a mental note, and let's continue through our checklist. We need to issue a query for each table's data and convert each row to YAML. We'll start with a single table:

```
>> ActiveRecord::Base.connection.select_all("select * from people")
=> [{"name"=>"Chad", "id"=>"1"}, {"name"=>"Kelly", "id"=>"2"},
    {"name"=>"James", "id"=>"3"}]
```

The Active Record connection adapter's select_all() method returns an array of hash objects, each containing key/value pairs of column name and value for its respective row. Not coincidentally, it's trivial to translate these hash objects into the required YAML format for a fixture:

```
>> puts ActiveRecord::Base.connection.select_all("select * from people").map do |row|
       row.to_yaml
   end
name: Chad
id: "1"
name: Kelly
id: "2"
name: James
id: "3"
=> nil
```

We're almost there! At this point, we've tackled all the hard stuff that needs to be done, so it makes sense to put this code together in a script that we can keep handy to run when needed. Since most Rails automation tasks are handled using Rake, we'll throw together a quick Rake task. You can refer to Recipe 48, *Creating Your Own Rake Tasks*, on page 213, for a full description of how to create a Rake task. We'll create a file called lib/tasks/extract_fixtures.rake and populate it with the fruits of our exploration:

CreateFixturesFromLiveData/lib/tasks/extract_fixtures.rake

```
desc 'Create YAML test fixtures from data in an existing database.
Defaults to development database.  Set RAILS_ENV to override.'

task :extract_fixtures => :environment do
  sql  = "SELECT * FROM %s"
  skip_tables = ["schema_info"]
  ActiveRecord::Base.establish_connection
  (ActiveRecord::Base.connection.tables - skip_tables).each do |table_name|
    i = "000"
    File.open("#{RAILS_ROOT}/test/fixtures/#{table_name}.yml", 'w') do |file|
      data = ActiveRecord::Base.connection.select_all(sql % table_name)
      file.write data.inject({}) { |hash, record|
        hash["#{table_name}_#{i.succ!}"] = record
        hash
      }.to_yaml
    end
  end
end
```

We can now invoke this task by typing rake extract_fixtures in the root directory of our application. The task uses the Rails environment, so by default it will dump the fixtures from your development database. To extract the fixtures from your production database, you would set the RAILS_ENV environment variable to "production".

Note that this task will overwrite any existing fixtures you may have, so be sure to back up your files before running it.

Running our new Rake task results in fixture files being created under the test/fixtures/ directory of our application as in the following people.yml file:

CreateFixturesFromLiveData/test/fixtures/people.yml

```
--
people_001:
  name: Chad
  id: "1"
people_002:
  name: Kelly
  id: "2"
people_003:
  name: James
  id: "3"
```

These fixture files are ready to be loaded using the load_fixtures Rake task or through your unit or functional tests.

Discussion

You may occasionally encounter data that, when extracted, won't load properly. Since the fixtures files are in YAML format, the extracted data must be parseable by the YAML parser. If you encounter strings that won't parse properly, you need to make sure they are being escaped when you extract them. To do that, you can override the to_yaml() method on the String class. Add the following to the top of your Rake file (before any task definitions):

```ruby
require 'yaml/encoding'
class String
  alias :old_to_yaml :to_yaml
  def to_yaml(opts = {})
    YAML.escape(self).old_to_yaml(opts)
  end
end
```

Testing Across Multiple Controllers

Credit

Rails core team member Jamis Buck wrote this recipe.

Problem

You want to write tests for a multistep process in your application that spans multiple controllers.

Ingredients

• Rails 1.1 or higher

Solution

Integration tests are a new feature of Rails 1.1 that take testing your applications to a new level. They are the next logical progression in the existing series of available tests:

• Unit tests are narrowly focused on testing a single model.

• Functional tests are focused on testing a single controller and the interactions between the models it employs.

• Integration tests are broad, story-level tests that verify the interactions between the various actions supported by the application, across all controllers.

This makes it easier to duplicate session management and routing bugs in your tests. What if you had a bug that was triggered by certain cruft accumulating in a user's session? It's hard to mimic that with functional tests.

For an example, consider a fictional financial application. We have a set of "stories" that describe how the application should function:

• Bob wants to sign up for access. He goes to the login page, clicks the "Sign Up" link, and fills out the form. After submitting the form, a new ledger is created for him, and he is automatically logged in and taken to the overview page.

- Jim, an experienced user, has received a new credit card and wants to set up a new account for it. He logs in, selects the ledger he wants to add the account to, and adds the account. He is then forwarded to the register for that account.

- Stacey's a disgruntled user who has decided to cancel her account. Logging in, she goes to the "account preferences" page and cancels her account. Her data is all deleted, and she is forwarded to a "sorry to see you go" page.

Starting with the first story, we might write something like the following. We'll create the file stories_test.rb in the test/integration directory.

IntegrationTesting/test/integration/stories_test.rb

```
require "#{File.dirname(__FILE__)}/../test_helper"

class StoriesTest < ActionController::IntegrationTest
  fixtures :accounts, :ledgers, :registers, :people

  def test_signup_new_person
    get "/login"
    assert_response :success
    assert_template "login/index"

    get "/signup"
    assert_response :success
    assert_template "signup/index"

    post "/signup", :name => "Bob", :user_name => "bob", :password => "secret"
    assert_response :redirect
    follow_redirect!
    assert_response :success
    assert_template "ledger/index"
  end
end
```

Run this by invoking the file directly via ruby or by typing the following:

chad> **rake test:integration**

The code is pretty straightforward: first, we get the /login URL and assert that the response is what we expect. Then we get the /signup URL, post the data to it, and follow the redirect through to the ledger.

However, one of the best parts of the integration framework is the ability
to extract a testing DSL[18] from your actions, making it really easy to
tell stories like this. At the simplest, we can do that by adding some
helper methods to the test. Here's a revised version of our test method
and its new helpers:

IntegrationTesting/test/integration/stories_test.rb

```ruby
def test_signup_new_person
  go_to_login
  go_to_signup
  signup :name => "Bob", :user_name => "bob", :password => "secret"
end

private
def go_to_login
  get "/login"
  assert_response :success
  assert_template "login/index"
end

def go_to_signup
  get "/signup"
  assert_response :success
  assert_template "signup/index"
end

def signup(options)
  post "/signup", options
  assert_response :redirect
  follow_redirect!
  assert_response :success
  assert_template "ledger/index"
end
```

Now, you can reuse those actions in other tests, making your tests very
readable and easy to build. But it can be even neater! Taking advantage
of ActionController::IntegrationTest's open_session() method, you can create
your own session instances and decorate them with custom methods.
Think of a session as a single user's experience with your site. Consider
this example:

---

[18]Domain-Specific Language

```
                  IntegrationTesting/test/integration/stories_test.rb
class StoriesTest < ActionController::IntegrationTest
  fixtures :accounts, :ledgers, :registers, :people

  def test_signup_new_person
    new_session do |bob|
      bob.goes_to_login
      bob.goes_to_signup
      bob.signs_up_with :name => "Bob", :user_name => "bob", :password => "secret"
    end
  end

  private

  module MyTestingDSL
    def goes_to_login
      get "/login"
      assert_response :success
      assert_template "login/index"
    end

    def goes_to_signup
      get "/signup"
      assert_response :success
      assert_template "signup/index"
    end

    def signs_up_with(options)
      post "/signup", options
      assert_response :redirect
      follow_redirect!
      assert_response :success
      assert_template "ledger/index"
    end
  end

  def new_session
    open_session do |sess|
      sess.extend(MyTestingDSL)
      yield sess if block_given?
    end
  end
end
```

The new_session() method at the bottom simply uses open_session() to create a new session and decorate it by mixing in our DSL module. By adding more methods to the MyTestingDSL module, you build up your DSL and make your tests richer and more expressive. You can even use named routes in your tests (see Recipe 36, *Make Your URLs Meaningful (and Pretty)*, on page 153) to ensure consistency between what your application is expecting and what your tests are asserting! For example:

```
def goes_to_login
  get login_url
  ...
end
```

Note that the new_session() method will actually return the new session as well. This means you could define a test that mimicked the behavior of two or more users interacting with your system at the same time:

IntegrationTesting/test/integration/stories_test.rb

```
class StoriesTest < ActionController::IntegrationTest
  fixtures :accounts, :ledgers, :registers, :people

    def test_multiple_users
      jim = new_session_as(:jim)
      bob = new_session_as(:bob)
      stacey = new_session_as(:stacey)

      jim.selects_ledger(:jims)
      jim.adds_account(:name => "checking")
      bob.goes_to_preferences
      stacey.cancels_account
    end

    private

    module MyTestingDSL
      attr_reader :person
      def logs_in_as(person)
        @person = people(person)
        post authenticate_url, :user_name => @person.user_name, :password => @person.password
        is_redirected_to "ledger/list"
      end
      def goes_to_preferences
        # ...
      end
      def cancels_account
        # ...
      end
    end

    def new_session_as(person)
      new_session do |sess|
        sess.goes_to_login
        sess.logs_in_as(person)
        yield sess if block_given?
      end
    end
end
```

To further demonstrate how these DSLs can be built, let's implement the second of the three stories described at the beginning of this article: Jim adding a credit-card account:

IntegrationTesting/test/integration/stories_test.rb

```ruby
def test_add_new_account
  new_session_as(:jim) do |jim|
    jim.selects_ledger(:jims)
    jim.adds_account(:name => "credit card")
  end
end

private

module MyTestingDSL
  attr_accessor :ledger

  def is_redirected_to(template)
    assert_response :redirect
    follow_redirect!
    assert_response :success
    assert_template(template)
  end

  def selects_ledger(ledger)
    @ledger = ledgers(ledger)
    get ledger_url(:id => @ledger.id)
    assert_response :success
    assert_template "ledger/index"
  end

  def adds_account(options)
    post new_account_url(:id => @ledger.id), options
    is_redirected_to "register/index"
  end
end
```

Integration tests with DSLs make your code more readable and make testing more fun. And, if testing is fun, you're more likely to do it.

Discussion

You may notice that individual integration tests run slower than individual unit or functional tests. That's because they test so much more. Each of the tests shown in this recipe tests multiple requests. Most functional tests test only one. Also, integration tests run through the entire stack—from the dispatcher, through the routes, into the controller, and back. Functional tests skip straight to the controller.

Write Tests for Your Helpers

Thanks to Rails core team member Scott Barron for the idea for this recipe.

You have been extracting your view logic into nice, clean helpers. Since these helpers are used throughout your application, you want to make sure they're well tested. But how do you write unit tests for your helpers?

Let's say we're developing an online recipe book, and we have a helper that looks like this:

`WriteTestsForHelpers/app/helpers/application_helper.rb`

```ruby
# Methods added to this helper will be available to all templates in the application.
module ApplicationHelper
  def recipe_link(recipe)
    link_to "#{recipe.name} (#{recipe.comments.count})",
            { :controller => 'recipes',
              :action => 'show',
              :id => recipe},
            :class => "recipe-link#{recipe.comments.count > 0 ? '-with-comments' : ''}"
  end
end
```

The helper allows us to easily link to specific recipes from throughout the site, adjusting the CSS class depending on whether any users have commented on the recipe, without having to type all the same code in over and over again. Now we want to write automated tests for this functionality.

Helpers aren't usually accessible from unit tests, so unlike most things in Rails, it's not immediately obvious how to get access to them. First we'll need to create a Ruby source file under our test/unit/ directory to house the test. Let's call it recipe_link_helper_test.rb. In the file, in addition to the usual Test::Unit boilerplate code, we'll include our Application-Helper and the Rails helpers on which it depends. Here's the beginning of the file, test/unit/recipe_link_helper_test.rb:

`WriteTestsForHelpers/test/unit/recipe_link_helper_test.rb`

```ruby
require File.dirname(__FILE__) + '/../test_helper'
class RecipeLinkHelperTest < Test::Unit::TestCase
  include ActionView::Helpers::UrlHelper
  include ActionView::Helpers::TextHelper
  include ActionView::Helpers::TagHelper
  include ApplicationHelper
```

Now we can write a test that exercises our helper:

WriteTestsForHelpers/test/unit/recipe_link_helper_test.rb

```ruby
def test_link_to_recipe_with_comments_shows_count
  r = Recipe.create(:name => "test")
  3.times {r.comments.create}
  assert_match(/\(3\)/, recipe_link(r))
end
```

Unfortunately, running this test results in an ugly error complaining about url_for() being called on nil. Following that error into the Rails source will lead to a series of patches and errors. I'll save you the trouble by giving you the following setup() method you can add to your test, which sets things up to sufficiently test helpers:

WriteTestsForHelpers/test/unit/recipe_link_helper_test.rb

```ruby
def setup
  @controller = RecipesController.new
  request     = ActionController::TestRequest.new
  @controller.instance_eval { @params = {}, @request = request }
  @controller.send(:initialize_current_url)
end
```

If you needed this functionality (or more) throughout your tests, you could define this setup() method in a module and include it in the tests that needed it.

Part V

Big-Picture Recipes

Automating Development with Your Own Generators

You find yourself repeating the same set of steps to create pieces of an application. Perhaps you've created a framework or a pattern that you use consistently throughout your code. As a result, every time you create a new application or a new widget within your application, you find yourself robotically applying the pattern.

Rails generators. If you're using Rails, you've seen them. You probably at the least use them to create the initial structure of your application, to create new controllers and views, to add new models, and to generate new migrations. And, of course, the most infamous Rails generator is the Scaffolding generator, which creates code to implement the CRUD elements of a given model. Thankfully, instead of just creating a one-off hack to implement these generators, the Rails developers came up with a reusable framework for template-driven code generation.

This makes it easy to create your own generators and install them so that they're first-class citizens in the eyes of the generate script.

Generators can come in handy either for repeating a pattern across multiple applications or for creating a similar structure for multiple elements in a single application. For a concrete example, imagine you've created a Tumblelog,[19] which is like a weblog but with many small posts of different types. You may, for example, post pictures, quotes, links, or sound clips, and each type of post would have its own input form and its own specialized view. A picture might need a form with a title and a URL, while a quote would require fields for a body and an attribution. For every type, you would also need to create model files, and you've decided it would be easiest to separate specialized behavior into one controller per post type. With just a few post types implemented, you end up with a structure that looks something like this:

---

[19]For an example, see http://project.ioni.st.

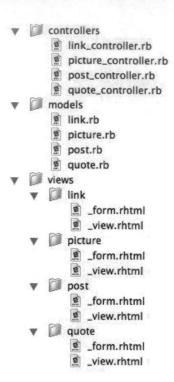

In this structure, each model class inherits from Post to take advantage of Rails' single-table inheritance model. All the controllers inherit from PostController to get access to functionality that is common to all types of posts. And to get up and running quickly when you add a new type of post, it's convenient to have _view.rhtml and _form.rhtml partials that include every possible field for a Post so you can immediately add posts of the new type and then incrementally modify the views to be appropriate to that type.

If you had an active imagination, you could concoct an unending list of post types to add to your new Tumblelog system. Even using the built-in generators for models and controllers that come with Rails, adding new post types would quickly become a burden. This is a perfect opportunity to whip up your very own generator.

The first step in creating your generator is to set up the generator's directory structure in one of the places the Rails framework is expecting it. Rails looks for user-defined generators in the following locations when the script/generate command is invoked (where *RAILS_ROOT* is the root directory of your application and ~ is your home directory):

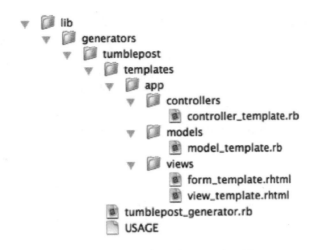

Figure 45.5: DIRECTORY LAYOUT FOR GENERATORS

- *RAILS_ROOT*/lib/generators
- *RAILS_ROOT*/vendor/generators
- *RAILS_ROOT*/vendor/plugins/*any subdirectory*/generators
- ~/.rails/generators

In addition to these paths, the script/generate command will look for installed gems whose names end in *_generator*.

Typically, the vendor directory is used to store third-party software—stuff developed by someone else. And, since this generator is tightly linked to our Tumblelog application, we'd like to keep it in the same directory structure as our application instead of putting it in our home directory. So by process of elimination, we'll create our generator under lib/generators in our application's root directory.

By convention, a generator is laid out as shown in Figure 45.5. You should name the generator's directory whatever you want to call the generator. In the example here, the generator would be called tumblepost and would be invoked by calling this:

```
ruby script/generate tumblepost
```

The file tumblepost_generator.rb in the tumblepost directory holds our generator's main logic. USAGE is a text file containing usage instructions that will be displayed when invoking our generator without any arguments, and templates is a directory where we'll put the source templates from which our code will be generated. For our Tumblelog Post generator, we'll create one template for every file the generator should create.

The heart of the generator is the Manifest, which is defined in tumble-post_generator.rb. Let's look at that file:

```
class TumblepostGenerator < Rails::Generator::NamedBase
  def manifest
    record do |m|
      m.class_collisions class_name

      m.template "app/controllers/controller_template.rb",
                 "app/controllers/#{file_name}_controller.rb"

      m.template "app/models/model_template.rb",
                 "app/models/#{file_name}.rb"

      m.directory File.join('app/views', file_name)
      m.template "app/views/form_template.rhtml",
                 "app/views/#{file_name}/_form.rhtml"
      m.template "app/views/view_template.rhtml",
                 "app/views/#{file_name}/_view.rhtml"

      m.readme "POST_GENERATION_REMINDER"
    end
  end
end
```

Rails ships with two classes from which you can extend your generators: Rails::Generator::Base and Rails::Generator::NamedBase. NamedBase is an extension of the bare-bones Base generator, providing a lot of helpful functionality for dealing with a single named argument on the command line (for example, the name of a controller or model you want to create). Unless you're doing something *extremely* simple with generators, you probably want to use NamedBase.

A generator's primary job is to create a Manifest, which Rails expects to be accessible via a method called manifest(). The record() method provides an easy way to create a new manifest, which it yields (as the variable m in this case) to the block it is called with. The manifest's job is to hold the information about what a generator should do. This includes actions such as copying files, creating directories, and checking for naming collisions. When you make a generator, you write a list of actions into a manifest that will then be executed by the script/generate command. Because the manifest doesn't actually *do* the requested actions, Rails can do helpful things by using them as the list of files to remove via the script/destroy command.

Our manifest is pretty simple. First it checks, using the class_name() method of class NamedBase, to make sure that the requested class name isn't yet taken by Ruby or Rails. This prevents you from doing something like this:

```
chad> ruby script/generate tumblepost File
```

A *File* Post type in a Tumblelog might seem like a good idea for creating a post that consists of nothing but an attached file, but naming the class File might result in some unexpected behavior since it overlaps with Ruby's core File class. class_name will help you catch oddities like that before they occur.

Next in the manifest, we have two calls to template(). Each tells the generator to use the first argument as a template from which to generate the second argument. By convention, your template files should live in a directory called templates, while the generated files will be placed in the relative path from the root of your application's directory. Here, we use NamedBase's file_name() method to generate the properly inflected version of the generated object's name for a file name. Because we've used the template() method, the source file will be run through eRB before being written to the destination. This allows us to programatically construct the contents of the generated files. For example, the beginning of our controller_template.rb might look like this:

```
class <%= class_name %>Controller < TumblepostController
  def new
    @thing = <%= class_name %>.new
  end
end
```

If we had instead used NamedBase's file() method, the generator would have done a simple copy from the source to the destination. file() and template() both support options for setting file permissions on the generated files as well as autocreating the generated file's *shebang* line (the magic first line of a UNIX shell script, which tells the operating system which program to execute the script with). So, for a script that is meant to be executable, you might do something like this:

```
m.file "bin/source_script",
      "scripts/generated_script",
      :chmod => 0755,
      :shebang => '/some/weird/path/to/ruby'
```

This would set the script's permissions to be readable and executable by everyone and would set its first line to look like this:

```
#!/some/weird/path/to/ruby
```

In addition to these options, the template() method can accept a hash of local *assigns*, just like regular Action View ERb templates. So, for example, the following:

```
m.template "source_file.rb",
          "destination_file.rb",
            :assigns => {:name_for_class => "HelloWorld"}
```

binds the local variable name_for_class to the value "HelloWorld" for use within the template file.

Since templates are evaluated by ERb, we could run into problems if our source files are ERb templates that have dynamic snippets to be called at runtime by our application. For example, the inclusion of <%= flash[:notice] %> in a source .rhtml file would cause the generator to substitute the value in flash[:notice] while it generates the destination files, which is obviously not what we want. To prevent that from happening, .rhtml templates can escape these tags by using two percent signs, such as <%%= flash[:notice] %>. These tags will be replaced by their single-percent sign equivalents in the generated .rhtml files.

Finishing our walk through the manifest, we see calls to directory() and readme(). The call to directory() tells the generator to create a directory in the destination with the given relative path. In our case, we need to create directories for our view templates before we can write them into their respective homes. The readme() method allows generator creators to specify one or more text files to be displayed during code generation. If, for example, there are postgeneration steps that should be taken manually to create a post in the Tumblelog of the new type, we could display a message (stored in templates/POST_GENERATION_REMINDER) that would be displayed at the end of our generator's run.

Now that we have our generator set up, we can call it from our application's root directory. If we wanted to create a new Post type that would allow us to upload sound files, we could generate the structure for that type with the following:

```
chad> ruby script/generate tumblepost SoundClip
      create  app/controllers/sound_clip_controller.rb
      create  app/models/sound_clip.rb
      create  app/views/sound_clip
      create  app/views/sound_clip/_form.rhtml
      create  app/views/sound_clip/_view.rhtml
      readme  POST_GENERATION_REMINDER
Don't forget to customize the auto-generated views!
```

Code generation is a contentious topic. If a code generator is buggy, it will propagate bugs in such a way that they are hard to fix when they're discovered. You may think you've fixed a bug to find that you have fixed only one of many occurrences of the bug. There is a fine line between when it's the right choice to use a code generator and when the same thing could be accomplished more cleanly with runtime framework code.

What if your generator needs to create database tables? Rails generators support the creation of Active Record migrations. If you use the migration_template() method, the generator is smart enough to find the last migration number available and to name the new file appropriately. The call looks like this:

```
m.migration_template "db/migrations/migration_template.rb", "db/migrate"
```

Unlike template(), with migration_template() you don't specify the full destination file's path in the second parameter. You specify only the destination directory, and migration_template() will create the file name for you.

If you have RubyGems installed, try running the following command:

```
gem search -r generator
```

You'll see a listing of many Rails generators that have been created and deployed as gems. This is not only a great source of examples from which to learn more about how to implement your own generators, but you may even find that the generator you thought you needed to create already exists in some shape or form. Install a few and play around with them. Some great stuff has already been done for you.

Continuously Integrate Your Code Base

You and your team members occasionally forget to make sure all of your tests run properly before checking in your code. Occasionally, you even forget to add a critical file to source control, rendering the "golden" copy of your application unusable.

- The continuous_builder plugin, installable from the root of your Rails application with the following:

```
chad> ruby script/plugin install continuous_builder
      + ./continuous_builder/README.txt
      + ./continuous_builder/lib/continuous_builder.rb
      + ./continuous_builder/tasks/test_build.rake
```

- This recipe requires that you manage your source code with the Subversion (http://subversion.tigris.org) version control system. If you need to support other version control systems, try Damage Control (http://dev.buildpatterns.com/trac/wiki/DamageControl).

Hidden in the Rails plugin repository is a charming little program that will allow you to watch your Subversion repository and to run your application's unit and functional tests every time anyone commits anything. Continuous integration systems like this are nothing new, but this one takes the cake in terms of simplicity. Created by Rails core developers David Heinemeier Hansson and Tobias Lütke, the Continuous Builder plugin is a simple Rake task that gets executed with each commit to your source repository and then emails any exceptional results to the destination of your choice.

With the proper guidance (this recipe, of course), the plugin is easy to set up. Assuming you already have it installed and checked into your application's vendor/plugins directory, the first step is to set up your Subversion server.

The Continuous Builder must be installed as a commit hook into the Subversion server. To install it, you'll need to have permissions to the actual repository where your application resides. If you don't know the location of your repository, ask the person who set it up to help you. In your repository's directory, you will find a subdirectory called hooks. Look for a file named post-commit. If the file does not exist, you can create it with your text editor of choice.

A fresh file should look something like this:

```
#!/bin/sh
DEVELOPERS=chad@chadfowler.com
BUILDER="'Continuous Builder' <cb@chadfowler.com>"
BUILD_DIRECTORY=/path/to/build_directory
APP_NAME=MyApp
RAKE=/usr/local/bin/rake

cd $BUILD_DIRECTORY/my_app_under_svn && \
    $RAKE -t test_latest_revision NAME="$APP_NAME" \
                                  RECIPIENTS="$DEVELOPERS" \
                                  SENDER="$BUILDER" &
```

You should, of course, tweak the settings to match your application and environment. DEVELOPERS should be set to a comma-separated list of email addresses that will receive messages when a build fails.

Each time you commit your code, Continuous Builder will go to your BUILD_DIRECTORY, run a Subversion update, and then execute your tests. Once you've decided where that directory will be, create the directory and svn co your code to it. You should *not* use your BUILD_DIRECTORY for development.

APP_NAME gives your application a unique name that will identify it in the emails Continuous Builder sends when there's a problem. And finally, RAKE should specify the full path to your Rake executable. For security reasons, Subversion executes its hooks with an empty environment, so you'll need to specify an absolute path here.

After you've saved the file, make sure it is set to be executable by the process Subversion runs as. If you're running Subversion as a module inside Apache, that will be the user the Apache server is running as (ps aux|grep httpd will probably show you that if you're not immediately sure how to find out). You'll also need to make sure your specified BUILD_DIRECTORY is both readable and writable by the same user.

In case you skipped the previous paragraph, go back and read it. Subversion is not very nice about reporting errors in its hooks. If you commit a change to your application and nothing at all seems to happen on the Subversion server, it's probably a permissions problem.

Now go to your BUILD_DIRECTORY, and ensure that you can successfully run your tests. Unless you've made some serious modifications to your default Rakefile, issuing a bare rake command should run the tests. Keep in mind that if your application uses one, you'll need to have access to your database (along with the proper database.yml configuration) for your tests to run. If all goes well with the test run, let's test the commit hook.

Go back to your development environment and make a change to your tests that deliberately breaks one. Instead of changing an existing test method, I would just add a new one like this:

```
def test_check_to_see_if_the_post_commit_hook_is_listening
  assert false
end
```

Run your tests, and witness the failure. Now check in your code. Within a minute or two, you should receive an email from the address you configured as BUILDER telling you the build is broken, as shown in Figure 46.6, on the next page. Once you've received the email, remove the failing test and commit your change. You should now receive an email saying that you have fixed the build.

If you want to monitor multiple applications in this way, you can add a line to the end of your post-commit file for each application you want to autobuild, like this:

```
cd $BUILD_DIRECTORY/my_other_app_under_svn &&
    $RAKE -t test_latest_revision NAME="Other Application Name" \
                                  RECIPIENTS="$DEVELOPERS" \
                                  SENDER="$BUILDER" &
```

Now that you have this running, you and your teammates can leave the office in peace, without that nagging feeling that you've forgotten to check something in.

Discussion

What if no email shows up when you intentionally break the build? Unfortunately, Subversion post-commit hooks are not very friendly when things go wrong. They just sit there quietly, leaving you to wonder what happened.

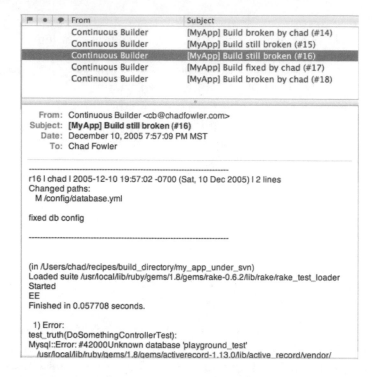

Figure 46.6: THE CONTINUOUS INTEGRATION PHONES HOME

If this happens to you, first check permissions on the post-commit hook itself. Make sure it's executable by the user who Subversion runs as. Then try running it manually just to make sure there are no obvious errors:

```
chad> ./post-commit
```

Next, look in your checked-out application directory on the Subversion server, and see whether there is a file called log/last_build.log. If the file does not exist, it means Continuous Builder was probably never invoked or there was a problem early in the process. If the file *does* exist and contains text such as failed, you know the post-commit hook is running but there's a problem with email delivery. In either case, if you can, log in as (or use sudo to become) the user who Subversion runs as, and try running the rake command manually:

```
rake -t test_latest_revision NAME=MyApp \
        RECIPIENTS=youremail@example.com \
        SENDER=youremail@example.com
```

If that doesn't shed any light, check your spam filters to make sure the email isn't being filtered out.

If the problem appears to be in the post-commit hook, the only way to get error messages is to redirect your process's output to a log file. You can change the last line of your post-commit hook to look like this:

```
cd $BUILD_DIRECTORY/my_app_under_svn &&
    $RAKE -t test_latest_revision NAME="$APP_NAME" \
                                  RECIPIENTS="$DEVELOPERS" \
                                  SENDER="$BUILDER" 2> /tmp/post-commit.log
```

This will direct the error output to the file /tmp/post-commit.log on your next commit. If you still can't find the problem, the Subversion FAQ[20] has a section on debugging post-commit hooks that might be helpful.

---

[20]http://subversion.tigris.org/faq.html#hook-debugging

Getting Notified of Unhandled Exceptions

Problem

You've reached what you think is a pragmatic balance between action-specific exception handling and letting your application's errors bubble up to the top of the framework. You *believe* that most of the critical errors are accounted for and unhandled exceptions will be rare in production.

However, you'd like to be sure that's the case, and you'd like to know about any exceptions you haven't caught, just in case there are any lingering showstoppers after you go live.

Ingredients

- The exception_notification plugin, installable from the root of your Rails application with:

  chad> **ruby script/plugin install exception_notification**

- Rails 1.1 or higher

Solution

When an action results in an unhandled exception, Action Controller calls its rescue_action_in_public() method. In Rails 1.0, the implementation of that method looks like this:

```
def rescue_action_in_public(exception)
  case exception
  when RoutingError, UnknownAction then
    render_text(IO.read(File.join(RAILS_ROOT, 'public', '404.html')),
                "404 Not Found")
  else
    render_text "<html><body><h1>Application error (Rails)</h1></body></html>"
  end
end
```

If you've ever fat-fingered a URL for your application or written code that generates an unhandled exception, you've seen the output of this method. It's not very friendly, and it doesn't provide you with much information about what went wrong. The good news is that you can override this method's behavior in your own application. This is a great place to add code that will notify you when something goes wrong. You can customize it to your heart's content.

Let's drop our own version in as an experiment, just to see it work. Since we're doing this in development, the first thing we need to do is set the application up to *not* treat all requests as "local." Rails differentiates between local and nonlocal requests, so it can spill its guts to programmers during application development (usually on the loopback IP address of 127.0.0.1) while keeping its dirty laundry out of sight when deployed for the public.

What we want in our experimentation is for Rails to behave in development as it would in production. So, we want none of our requests to appear to be local. First, open config/environments/development.rb and look for the line that starts with this:

```
config.action_controller.consider_all_requests_local
```

Make sure that variable is set to false.

Next, we can go into the controller of our choice and add the following code:

```
def local_request?
  false
end
```

This overrides the local_request? method in ActionController::Base, in a hackish but adequate way. We're going to remove this code when we're done, so a hack is OK.

Next, in the same file, add the following method definition:

```
def rescue_action_in_public(exception)
  render :text => "Something bad happened."
end
```

Finally, we need to write some bad code that will demonstrate the error handler. The following action will do the trick:

```
def boom
  raise "boom!"
end
```

You can now start your application and visit the boom action via the appropriate URL. You should see an otherwise blank page with the text "Something bad happened."

So now, you can imagine enhancing this method to bundle all manner of diagnostic information and ship it to you in an email. You would probably want to include all the parameters that were sent to the action, anything in session, detailed information about your current environment, and any relevant backtrace, all nicely formatted so that it's easy to read when trouble strikes.

As if reading your mind, it turns out that Rails core contributor Jamis Buck has already done all this work for you. In the central Rails plugin repository, you'll find the Exception Notifier plugin. If you haven't already installed it, do that now.

First we'll need to remove the experimental code from our controller. Leave the boom() method in for now (we'll use that to demonstrate the Exception Notifier), but remove your rescue_action_in_public() and local_request?() methods. Now, in the same controller, after the class definition line, add the following two lines of code:

```
include ExceptionNotifiable
local_addresses.clear
```

The Rails plugin loader finds the plugin and loads it for us. So, these two lines are all you need to tell the Exception Notifier to start handling exceptions for your controller. The call to local_addresses.clear is equivalent in purpose to our previously overridden local_request? method. We will remove the local_addresses.clear call once we have the notifier working.

One last bit of configuration, and we can give this a try. Edit your application's config/environment.rb and add the following to the bottom:

```
ExceptionNotifier.exception_recipients = %w(you@yourdomain.com)
ExceptionNotifier.sender_address =
        %("Application Error" <notifier@yourdomain.com>)
ExceptionNotifier.email_prefix = "[Your Application Name]"
```

This code sets who receives the error notifications, who the messages appear to be sent from, and what the beginning of the email Subject line will look like, respectively. Be sure to change these values to fit your own email address and application name. If you don't know what to set the sender_address to, you can set it to your own email address. After making these changes, restart your Rails application for the changes to take effect.

```
 _____
| 0 0 0            [Rails Recipes] home#boom (RuntimeError) "boom!" — Inbox |
|_____|
| ( ⊘ )  ( 📄 )    ( ← )  ( ↞ )  ( → )    ( 🖨 )                        |
|  Delete  Junk     Reply  Reply All Forward   Print                   |
|_____|
```

From: Application Error <chad@chadfowler.com>
Subject: **[Rails Recipes] home#boom (RuntimeError) "boom!"**
Date: December 12, 2005 8:28:00 AM MST
To: Chad Fowler

A RuntimeError occurred in home#boom:

boom!
[RAILS_ROOT]/app/controllers/home_controller.rb:13:in `boom'

Request:
----

* URL: http://localhost:3000/home/boom
* Parameters: {"action"=>"boom", "controller"=>"home"}
* Rails root: .

Session:
----

* @data:{:intended_action=>"new", :user=>5, "flash"=>{}}
* @new_session: false
* @session_id: "06cbfd196c7161589d00c764ad786726"

Environment:
----

* GATEWAY_INTERFACE : CGI/1.1
* HTTP_ACCEPT   : */*
* HTTP_ACCEPT_ENCODING: gzip, deflate
* HTTP_ACCEPT_LANGUAGE: en
* HTTP_CONNECTION   : keep-alive
* HTTP_COOKIE   : _session_id=06cbfd196c7161589d00c764ad786726
* HTTP_HOST   : localhost:3000
* HTTP_USER_AGENT   : Mozilla/5.0 (Macintosh; U; PPC Mac OS X; en) AppleWebKit/416.12 (KHTML, like Gecko) Safari/416.13
* PATH_INFO   : /home/boom

Figure 47.7: MAIL NOTIFYING US OF AN EXCEPTION IN OUR APPLICATION

Now, if you visit your boom action, you should see your application's public/500.html page, and in the background an email like the one in Figure 47.7 should be in transit to your inbox.

Discussion

If for some reason you don't get an email, tell Rails to be noisy about mail delivery failures. Edit your config/environments/development.rb file, and look for the line that sets config.action_mailer.raise_delivery_errors. Set this to true, and restart your application. Next time you reload the boom action, you should see any mail delivery errors reported in your browser.

Creating Your Own Rake Tasks

Software development is full of repetitive, boring, and therefore error-prone tasks. Even in the ultraproductive Rails environment, any complex application development will result in at least *some* work that would be better automated. And if you're after automation, the Rails Way to do it is with Jim Weirich's Rake.

Rails comes with its own set of helpful Rake tasks. How do you add your own?

Rake, like make before it, is a tool whose primary purpose is to automate software builds. Unlike make, Rake is written in Ruby, and its command language is also pure Ruby. As a brief introduction to Rake, we'll start by looking at a couple of simple, non-Rails-dependent Rake tasks that will demonstrate the basics of how Rake works.

Imagine you're maintaining a website that keeps a catalog of jazz musicians, categorized by musical instrument and genre, so users of the site can browse through and discover musicians that they might not know. You accept submissions to the site as comma-separated text files that you review, then convert to XML, and upload to your web server for further processing. This is a perfect candidate for automation.

Commands for Rake should be specified in a Rakefile. By convention, Rake will automatically look in the current directory for a file called Rakefile if you don't specify a file name when invoking the rake command. Otherwise, you can tell rake which file to load by passing the file name to its -f parameter. Here's what a simple Rakefile for processing our musician list would look like:

CreatingYourOwnRakeTasks/SimpleRakefile

```
Line 1   desc "Convert musicians.csv to musicians.xml if the CSV file has changed."
   -     file 'musicians.xml' => 'musicians.csv' do |t|
   -        convert_to_xml(t.prerequisites.first, t.name)
   -     end
```

```
 5
   require 'rake/contrib/sshpublisher'
   desc "Upload Musicians list XML file to web server for processing."
   task :upload => 'musicians.xml' do |t|
     puts "Transferring #{t.prerequisites.last}..."
10   publisher = Rake::SshFilePublisher.new(
                          "www.chadfowler.com",
                          "/var/www/html/jazz_people",
                          File.dirname(__FILE__),
                          t.prerequisites.first)
15   publisher.upload
   end

   task :default => :upload
```

In a nutshell, this Rakefile will look for changes to the file musicians.csv and, if it's changed, will convert that file into XML. Then it will transfer the new musicians.xml file to a server. Assuming you've saved this in a file named Rakefile, you can invoke all this logic by typing rake.

And now for how it works. On line 8 we define a Rake task called upload. This name is what we use to tell the rake command what to do when it runs. When defining a Rake task, after the name you can optionally define one or more dependencies. In this case, we've declared a dependency on the file musicians.xml. This is the file that our program will upload to the web server. On line 9 we see a reference to the task's prerequisites() method. Not surprisingly, this is a list of the prerequisites that were specified in the task's definition—in this case, the musicians.xml file.

Tasks and dependencies are what makes Rake tick. The dependency on line 8 is more than just a static reference to a file name. Because we declared a file task on line 2, our musicians.xml now depends on another file named musicians.csv. In English, what we've declared in our Rakefile is that before we perform the upload, we need to make sure musicians.xml is up-to-date. musicians.xml is up-to-date only if it was last processed *after* musicians.csv's last update. Rake's file() method handles the automatic creation of a task that checks these time stamps for us. If musicians.csv is more recent than its XML sibling, line 3 will cause a new musicians.xml file to be created from its contents. (The convert_to_xml() method is defined elsewhere in the Rakefile but left out of the example for the sake of brevity.)

The last line declares the upload() task to be the default task, meaning a bare invocation of the rake command will execute the upload() task.

The calls to desc, such as the one on line 1, describe the purpose of each task. They have two functions: they're a static code comment for when you're reading the Rakefile, and they provide a description when the rake command needs to list its available tasks:

```
chad> rake --tasks
rake musicians.xml  # Convert musicians.csv to musicians.xml if the CSV file has changed.
rake upload         # Upload Musicians list XML file to web server for processing.
```

If we were to create a musicians.csv file that looks like this:

CreatingYourOwnRakeTasks/musicians.csv

```
Albert, Ayler, Saxophone
Dave, Douglas, Trumpet
Bill, Frisell, Guitar
Matthew, Shipp, Piano
Rashid, Ali, Drums
William, Parker, Bass
```

invoking our upload task would result in the following output:

```
chad> rake
(in /Users/chad/src/FR_RR/Book/code/CreatingYourOwnRakeTasks)
Converting musicians.csv to musicians.xml
Transferring musicians.xml...
scp -q ./musicians.xml www.chadfowler.com:/var/www/html/jazz_people
```

But if we immediately run it again, we see this:

```
chad> rake
(in /Users/chad/src/FR_RR/Book/code/CreatingYourOwnRakeTasks)
Transferring musicians.xml...
scp -q ./musicians.xml www.chadfowler.com:/var/www/html/jazz_people
```

Since musicians.xml was already up-to-date, Rake skipped its generation and continued with the upload.

So now we know how to define Rake tasks that depend on other Rake tasks and how to set up file generation that depends on other files. Though we obviously haven't touched every detail of Rake, since its command language is Ruby, we know enough to be productive immediately.

Suppose we decide to rewrite our jazz musician database using Rails, and instead of generating and transferring an XML file, we want to simply insert the records from our CSV files into a database. We have a Musician model with string attributes for given_name, surname, and instrument. Let's take our previous example and make it work with Rails.

The first thought you might have is to edit the Rails-generated Rakefile in your application's root directory and add your tasks there. However, to avoid code duplication, the Rails developers have separated their Rake tasks into external files that are distributed with the Rails framework. On opening the generated Rakefile, you'll see that it's all but empty with a friendly comment at the top instructing you to put your own tasks in the lib/tasks directory under your application root. When you invoke the Rails-generated Rakefile, the Rails framework will automatically load any files in that directory with the file extension .rake. This way, upgrading the core Rails Rake tasks is easier and less likely to result in a file conflict.

So let's create our own tasks in a file called lib/tasks/load_musicians.rake under our application's root directory:

```
CreatingYourOwnRakeTasks/lib/tasks/load_musicians.rake.first_attempt
```

```
desc "Load musicians and the instruments they play into the database."
task :load_musicians => 'musicians.csv' do |t|
  before_count = Musician.count
  File.read(t.prerequisites.first).each do |line|
    given_name, surname, instrument = line.split(/,/)
    Musician.create(:given_name => given_name,
                    :surname => surname,
                    :instrument => instrument)
  end
  puts "Loaded #{Musician.count - before_count} musicians."
end
```

This task is relatively simple. It depends on the existence of the musicians.csv file, which it naively reads, creating a new Musician entry for each line read. It concludes with an announcement of how many records were loaded.

Unfortunately, running this task as is doesn't result in the desired behavior:

```
chad> rake load_musicians
(in /Users/chad/src/FR_RR/Book/code/CreatingYourOwnRakeTasks)
rake aborted!
ActiveRecord::ConnectionNotEstablished
```

Hmm. We're apparently not connected to our database. And, come to think of it, we haven't told the Rake task which of our databases to connect to. In a typical Rails application, this is all handled for us implicitly via the environment. Fortunately, the Rails developers have provided a way for us to write Rake tasks that are dependent on the Rails envi-

ronment. Intuitively, this is implemented via a Rake dependency called
:environment. Let's add :environment to our task's dependency list:

CreatingYourOwnRakeTasks/lib/tasks/load_musicians.rake

```
desc "Load musicians and the instruments they play into the database."
task :load_musicians => ['musicians.csv', :environment] do |t|
  before_count - Musician.count
  File.read(t.prerequisites.first).each do |line|
    given_name, surname, instrument = line.split(/,/)
    Musician.create(:given_name => given_name,
                    :surname => surname,
                    :instrument => instrument)
  end
  puts "Loaded #{Musician.count - before_count} musicians."
end
```

With a musicians.csv file in place, the task now works as expected:

```
chad> rake load_musicians
(in /Users/chad/src/FR_RR/Book/code/CreatingYourOwnRakeTasks)
Loaded 6 musicians.
```

Lovely. But our application is really simple right now, and we're planning to evolve it. What do we do if our data model changes fairly often?
First, we can make our parsing and loading logic a little smarter. Here's
an enhanced version of the task that will adapt to change a little better.
It assumes that the first line of the file contains the column names for
the data values in the rest of the file.

CreatingYourOwnRakeTasks/lib/tasks/load_musicians.rake

```
desc "Load musicians and the instruments they play into the database."
task :load_musicians_enhanced =>
         ['musicians_with_column_names.csv', :migrate] do |t|
  before_count = Musician.count
  lines = File.read(t.prerequisites.first).split("\n")
  # Strip white space
  attributes = lines.shift.split(/,/).collect{|name| name.strip}
  lines.each do |line|
    values = line.split(/,/)
    data = attributes.inject({}) do |hash,attribute|
      hash[attribute] = values.shift
      hash
    end
    Musician.create(data)
  end
  puts "Loaded #{Musician.count - before_count} musicians."
end
```

Now, we can lay the files out more flexibly and even add columns to
the files. Of course, if we add columns to the file, we'll need to add

them to the database as well. If we're managing our data model via Active Record migrations, we can save ourselves the trouble of trying to remember to keep it updated by adding the :migrate task to the dependency list for our task. Since the :migrate task already initializes the Rails environment, we can replace the :environment dependency with :migrate. Now whenever we run the :load_musicians_enhanced task, our database schema will be automatically updated first!

Also See

Martin Fowler has written an excellent introduction to Rake, which is freely available from his website at http://www.martinfowler.com/articles/rake.html.

Dealing with Time Zones

Credit

Thanks to Rails core developers Jamis Buck and Scott Barron for their input and ideas on this recipe.

Problem

Web applications, centrally hosted as they are, often cater to users all over the globe. The way you consume and display dates in a desktop application or a small, wholly co-located company's intranet isn't sufficient for a globally distributed user base.

How do you store, retrieve, and display dates in a Rails application in such a way that it honors the users' time zones?

Solution

You can implement time zone support in two main ways. You can store dates in the user's time zone and translate them behind the scenes in case you need to do calculations against other users' dates or the system time (both of which may be in other time zone). Or you can store all dates assuming the same time zone and translate all date-related user interactions to the appropriate time zone on a per-user basis.

Though we in different time zone have many ideas of how we should express what time it is *locally*, barring deep metaphysical arguments, time really is a centralized concept here on planet Earth. There is only one current time. The only variance is in how we express it relative to where we are. You can think of time zone, then, as analogous to symbolic links on a file system or normalized data structures in a database. There is only one time, but the time zones provide a symbolic, localized representation of that time.

So, we'll choose to store our times in this manner. Specifically, we'll store times in coordinated universal time, known more popularly by its abbreviated form, UTC.

Since we're storing the time as UTC, we need two things: some way of knowing what our users' time zones are and some way of translating those local times to and from UTC as our users interact with the application.

To demonstrate, let's create a simple application for tracking reminders for tasks. We'll need a model to represent users and another for their tasks. Starting with the database schema, here's a migration to implement a simple version of the application:

DealingWithTimeZones/db/migrate/001_add_users_and_task_reminders_tables.rb

```
class AddUsersAndTaskRemindersTables < ActiveRecord::Migration
  def self.up
    create_table :users do |t|
      t.column :name, :string
      t.column :time_zone, :string
    end
    create_table :task_reminders do |t|
      t.column :user_id, :integer
      t.column :due_at, :datetime
      t.column :description, :text
    end
  end

  def self.down
    drop_table :users
    drop_table :task_reminders
  end
end
```

As you can see in the migration, users have a name and a time zone. And as you can probably tell by the column names, we'll also set up a has_many() relationship between users and task reminders. Here are the associated model files:

DealingWithTimeZones/app/models/user.rb

```
class User < ActiveRecord::Base
  has_many :task_reminders, :order => "due_at"
end
```

DealingWithTimeZones/app/models/task_reminder.rb

```
class TaskReminder < ActiveRecord::Base
  belongs_to :user
end
```

Now that we have our model set up, let's look more closely at the time_zone attribute of the users table. What should we store there? Since we're going to be thinking of local times as relative to UTC and we're going to be making conversions (read doing *math*) to and from UTC, it would be really helpful to store the time zone's offset from UTC so we can just add or subtract when we need to convert.

It's tempting to set the type of the time_zone column to :integer and to store the offset directly in the users table in seconds. The problem is that just the offset isn't enough information. To illustrate, take the USA's Mountain Time and Arizona Time and Mexico's Chihuahua. These three time zone all share the same offset (-7 hours from UTC). But they are three distinct time zones. You don't want your Mexican users to have to select "Mountain Time" for their time zone. They won't recognize it.

Worse, Arizona, unlike Mountain Time and Chihuahua, doesn't observe daylight saving time. This means that during the summer months, their translations are in fact different.

So instead, we'll store the name of the time zone and we'll map that to the right offset from UTC. For example, Mountain Time in the USA will be referred to as "Mountain Time (US & Canada)." Now we just have to figure out where to get and store all these mappings.

It turns out that if you have Rails installed, you already have these mappings. The ActiveSupport framework provides a class called Time-Zone, which stores a big list of virtually all the world's time zones and can translate time for a given zone to and from UTC.

Let's take TimeZone for a test drive in the Rails console:

```
chad> ruby script/console
>> TimeZone.all.size
=> 142
>> TimeZone['Wellington']
=> #<TimeZone:0x22df354 @name="Wellington", @utc_offset=43200>
>> now = Time.now
=> Thu Feb 09 09:13:11 MST 2006
>> time_in_wellington = TimeZone['Wellington'].adjust(now)
=> Fri Feb 10 04:13:11 MST 2006
>> TimeZone['Wellington'].unadjust(time_in_wellington)
=> Thu Feb 09 09:13:11 MST 2006
```

So as we can see by the sample, if we know that a user is in the Wellington time zone, we can get a reference to the matching TimeZone instance and easily adjust to and from Wellington time. With this knowledge, we can put together the model facing ingredients of the recipe. Imagine we have a Time object, due_date, that was created in a user's configured time zone (in this case we'll say New Delhi). Before creating a new

TaskReminder with this time, we'll need to convert it to UTC. And if we wanted to retrieve and display the time to the user, we would need to convert it back. Here's how we could do that:

```
chad> ruby script/console
>> u = User.create(:name => "Chad", :time_zone => "New Delhi")
=> #<User:0x22dbb28 @attributes={"name"=>"Chad", "id"=>1,
   "time_zone"=>"New Delhi"},
   ... @base=#<User:0x22dbb28 ...>, @errors={}>>
>> due_date # (imagine this was supplied by the user)
=> Sun Feb 19 10:30:15 MST 2006
>> utc_due_date = TimeZone[u.time_zone].unadjust(due_date)
=> Sat Feb 18 22:00:15 MST 2006
>> reminder = u.task_reminders.create(:due_at => utc_due_date,
      :description => "Return library books")
=> #<TaskReminder:0x227fb84 @attributes={"id"=>1,
     "description"=>"Return library books",
     "due_at"=>Sat Feb 18 22:00:15 MST 2006, "user_id"=>1}, ... @errors={}>>
>> # Then, to display to the user:
?> puts "Task '#{reminder.description}' due at \
               #{TimeZone[u.time_zone].adjust(reminder.due_at)}"
Task 'Return library books' due at Sun Feb 19 10:30:15 MST 2006
```

That was not so difficult, eh? But it's kind of ugly with all that TimeZone lookup code. We can significantly clean it up using the Active Record's composed_of() macro. Here's the new User class definition:

DealingWithTimeZones/app/models/user.rb

```
class User < ActiveRecord::Base
  has_many :task_reminders, :order => "due_at"
  composed_of :tz,
              :class_name => 'TimeZone',
              :mapping => %w(time_zone name)
end
```

And now we can access it like this:

```
chad> ruby script/console
>> u = User.find(:first)
=> #<User:0x2255dd4 @attributes={"name"=>"Chad", "id"=>"1",
     "time_zone"=>"New Delhi"}>
>> u.tz
=> #<TimeZone:0x22abba8 @name="New Delhi", @utc_offset=19800>
>> u.tz = TimeZone['Wellington']
=> #<TimeZone:0x22ab770 @name="Wellington", @utc_offset=43200>
>> u.tz.adjust(Time.now)
=> Fri Feb 10 05:43:51 MST 2006
```

Now we just need a way to allow each user to select their time zone. We could use the TimeZone.all() method and build a list to select from. Thankfully, though, Rails lends another hand with the built-in helper time_zone_select(). Here's a sample view that allows the user to select his or her time zone to be saved with the user profile:

DealingWithTimeZones/app/views/user/time_zone.rhtml

```
<% form_for :user, @user, :url => {:action => "update_time_zone"} do |f| %>
    <label for="time_zone">
        Select your time zone:
    </label>
    <%= f.time_zone_select :time_zone %><br />
    <%= submit_tag %>
<% end%>
```

Note that we've used form_for() for this example, which requires Rails 1.1.

Using time_zone_select(), the form we've generated will look like:

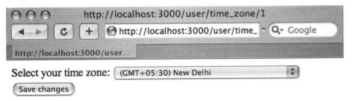

After you've added time zone support to your application, you'll quickly notice that it results in a lot of conversion code in both your controllers and your views. Duplication, being the root of all evil and all that, can be removed pretty simply with the following inclusions in your ApplicationController class (assuming that you're storing the user id in session):

DealingWithTimeZones/app/controllers/application.rb

```
class ApplicationController < ActionController::Base
  def user2utc(time)
    current_user.tz.unadjust(time)
  end

  def utc2user(time)
    current_user.tz.adjust(time)
  end

  def current_user
    User.find(session[:user])
  end
end
```

These methods simplify your controllers and views, allowing you to convert times based on the currently logged in user's time zone.

Discussion

The current implementation of TimeZone doesn't yet take daylight saving time into account. If you need to support daylight saving time, Philip Ross's TZInfo gem should do the trick for you. You can install it with (sudo) gem install tzinfo. The TZInfo gem is considerably slower to use than the Rails built-in TimeZone class, so use it only if you need daylight saving time support.

Jamis Buck has also created a plugin that can be used to bridge the Rails built-in time zone functionality and the TZInfo gem. You can install it with the command ruby script/plugin install tzinfo_timezone. The overridden TimeZone functionality works like the Rails built-in TimeZone class, except that instead of calling adjust() and unadjust(), you should call local_to_utc() and utc_to_local(), respectively.

Living on the Edge (of Rails Development)

Problem

One of the exciting things about a young, innovative framework like Rails is that it's in a constant state of change. New features are added and bugs are fixed on a daily basis.

How can your application take advantage of the newest Rails features as they happen?

Solution

You've got three major ways to keep your application in sync with the latest in Rails development.

The Rails Way to stay on the bleeding edge assumes that your application is being managed by the Subversion version control system. It involves using the Subversion property svn:externals to set up the Rails Subversion repository as an external module. The svn:externals property is set on a directory in your repository, telling Subversion that when it updates that directory, it should retrieve the named subdirectories from an external Subversion repository. It's kind of like a symbolic link for your version control system.

To set your application up this way (the Rails core team calls this Edge Rails), go into your Rails application's vendor/ directory, and execute the following command:

```
chad> svn propset svn:externals \
    "rails http://dev.rubyonrails.org/svn/rails/trunk" .
```

Now you've told Subversion that it should check out the Rails repository's trunk under vendor/rails the next time you update your working copy. A simple Subversion update in your application's root directory will install Edge Rails, meaning that your Rails installation will be up-to-date as of the last time you updated your application's source tree.

```
chad> svn up
Fetching external item into 'rails'
A    vendor/rails/cleanlogs.sh
```

```
A    vendor/rails/release.rb
A    vendor/rails/actionmailer
A    vendor/rails/actionmailer/test
A    vendor/rails/actionmailer/test/mail_helper_test.rb
...
```

The directory vendor/rails is special in the Rails environment. When your application boots, the config/boot.rb file checks for the existence of this directory and, if it exists, loads Rails from it instead of any installed gems. Under the vendor/rails directory, you'll find subdirectories for all the major Rails components: actionmailer, activerecord, actionpack, activesupport, railties, and actionwebservice.

So, what if you're not using Subversion to manage your application's code? No problem. We've got two more ways for you to stay on the Edge.

If you have the Subversion client installed, you can check the Rails repository's trunk out into your vendor/rails directory. Remember that if you have a properly structured vendor/rails directory, your application will load it instead of any installed gems—regardless of where it originated.

From your vendor/ directory, run the following command:

```
chad> svn co http://dev.rubyonrails.org/svn/rails/trunk rails
A    rails/cleanlogs.sh
A    rails/release.rb
A    rails/actionmailer
A    rails/actionmailer/test
A    rails/actionmailer/test/mail_helper_test.rb
...
```

The disadvantage of running it this way is that if you want your Rails installation to stay truly at the Edge, you'll need to explicitly svn up the vendor/rails directory. This method is also not as portable between development environments, since the checkout will have to be replicated on every new computer and in every new checked-out copy of your application.

True to the opinionated nature of Rails, the path of least resistance is clearly to use Subversion to manage not just Rails but your application's source code as well.

Now that you're running Edge Rails, you may occasionally need the stability that a specific release brings. For example, you might have a schedule demo of your application for which you need bleeding-edge features, but you can't risk messing up with an unknown incompatibility introduced in the Rails trunk. If you're running a version of Edge Rails that *works*, you can freeze your application to that specific version with the following command:

```
chad> rake freeze_edge
(in /Users/chad/src/FR_RR/Book/code/LivingOnTheEdge)
rm -rf vendor/rails
mkdir -p vendor/rails
mkdir -p vendor/rails/railties
A     vendor/rails/railties/lib
A     vendor/rails/railties/lib/rails_generator
A     vendor/rails/railties/lib/rails_generator/commands.rb
...
```

When you're ready to go back to the bleeding edge, you can do so with rake unfreeze_rails.

If for some reason you can't even *install* Subversion (much less manage your code with it), you have one more option for staying on the leading edge of Rails development: beta gems. The Rails team releases periodic gem updates to a special beta server, and you can install these Beta releases using the usual RubyGems install method:

```
chad> sudo gem install rails -s http://gems.rubyonrails.org
```

This won't get you onto the true *edge* of Rails development, but it's an easy alternative for those that want to move a little faster than the stable releases while sticking with their usual RubyGems-based installation procedures.

Discussion

Living on the edge is not without its risks. Bugs are fixed but also *injected* into the source tree as development progresses. Needless to say, it's best to deploy your application against a stable Rails release.

If you're running Edge or Beta Rails in your development environment, you may occasionally experience unusual behavior that's hard to track down. To avoid long, fruitless application debugging sessions, you would be well served to place some kind of reminder at your workstation that says, "Are you sure it's not a Rails bug?" It's rare that the Rails trunk is *seriously* broken, but speaking from experience, it's frustrating to burn an hour looking for your *own* bug only to find that the framework is at fault.

That being said, one of the benefits of running Edge Rails is that you can more easily contribute to Rails itself. If you were to run into a legitimate Rails bug while working on your own application, an Edge Rails installation puts you in a prime position to both fix the bug and submit your changes. Since you're running against the latest Rails version, submitting your changes as a patch is as simple as doing this:

```
chad> cd vendor/rails
chad> svn diff > descriptive_patch_name.diff
```

You can then submit this patch (including automated tests!) with a description of the problem it solves at http://dev.rubyonrails.org/newticket. Be sure to start the ticket's summary field with the string [PATCH] to alert the Rails core team that you are not just reporting an issue but also including a fix.

It's satisfying to see your changes trickle back down to you when your fix is added to the core framework.

Syndicate Your Site with RSS

Problem

RSS and Atom feeds are ubiquitous. Although they were originally created to track news stories, it's now common for an application to offer a feed for just about anything that might update over time. Applications offer RSS and Atom feeds to allow their users to track comments, new product releases, version control commits, and pretty much anything you can imagine.

With syndication becoming more and more common, your users are going to start to expect it of you. How do you add syndication to your Rails applications?

Solution

Two major syndication formats[21] are in play today: RSS (Really Simple Syndication) and Atom. Although there are some technical differences between these formats, the end-user experience is the same: RSS and Atom provide the ability to syndicate chronologically sensitive site updates via XML feeds.

Plenty of Web resources are available[22] that detail these formats and how they work architecturally, so we won't belabor the points here. Suffice it to say that RSS and Atom both involve the production of an XML file by a server of some sort and the consumption and display of the contents of this file (usually in reverse chronological order) by one or more clients, known as news *aggregators*. These aggregators allow a simple, unified view of what has changed across a potentially large number of websites.

So, if you want your site to produce a feed that one of these aggregators is capable of displaying, you need to publish with the aggregator in mind. All the major news aggregators these days support both RSS and Atom, so for this recipe we'll focus on just one of the formats: RSS.

---

[21] Actually, RSS is the subject of a huge amount of political tension on the Web, so it has splintered into at least three separate flavors. Save yourself a headache, and don't worry about any of those flavors except for RSS 2.0.

[22] http://en.wikipedia.org/wiki/Web_feed

The concepts involved in producing an RSS feed are nearly identical to those of producing an Atom feed, so with a little research, you can easily produce either. So let's stop talking and start cooking up a feed!

As an example, we'll create a feed to syndicate new recipes added to an online cookbook application. Whenever a recipe is added or updated, users should be able to receive updates in their news aggregators. Let's create a simple model to represent users and recipes in the cookbook. We'll start with a migration to define the database schema:

`SyndicateYourSite/db/migrate/001_add_users_and_recipes.rb`

```ruby
class AddUsersAndRecipes < ActiveRecord::Migration
  def self.up
    create_table :recipes do |t|
      t.column :title, :string
      t.column :instructions, :text
      t.column :author_id, :integer
      t.column :created_at, :datetime
      t.column :updated_at, :datetime
    end

    create_table :ingredients do |t|
      t.column :recipe_id, :integer
      t.column :name, :string
      t.column :unit, :string
      t.column :amount, :float
    end

    create_table :users do |t|
      t.column :name, :string
      t.column :password, :string
    end
  end

  def self.down
    drop_table :recipes
    drop_table :ingredients
    drop_table :users
  end
end
```

The basic story with our schema is that we have users who author many recipes, and the recipes have zero or more ingredients. It's a simplistic schema, but it works. Here are the associated models:

`SyndicateYourSite/app/models/recipe.rb`

```ruby
class Recipe < ActiveRecord::Base
  has_many :ingredients
  belongs_to :author, :foreign_key => 'author_id', :class_name => 'User'
end
```

```
class Ingredient < ActiveRecord::Base
  belongs_to :recipe
end
```

```
class User < ActiveRecord::Base
  has_many :recipes, :foreign_key => 'author_id'
end
```

What do we want to accomplish with our RSS feed? If the core functionality of the application is to allow users to share recipes, we would like to add a feed to the application that will enable our users to subscribe to the running stream of new and updated recipes. With information overload plaguing so many of us these days, the ability to let the system keep track of what's new for you can make a huge difference.

We'll start by creating a separate controller for the feed. You don't *have* to serve feeds through a separate controller, but you'll frequently find that in a complex application, the behavior of the typical action doesn't apply to an RSS feed. You won't want to apply the same authentication or authorization rules to an RSS feed (more on this later). You won't want to run an RSS feed through the same kinds of filters that you might run an HTML action through. It just tends to be cleaner and easier to keep things separate.

This being a food-related website, we'll give the controller a name with two meanings: FeedController:

```
chad> ruby script/generate controller Feed
exists  app/controllers/
   :            :
```

Let's create a simple action that grabs the 15 latest recipes from the database. We'll call it recipes(). This leaves the FeedController open to serve other feeds, should we eventually have the need.

```
def recipes
  @recipes = Recipe.find(:all, :order => "updated_at, created_at", :limit => 15)
  @headers["Content-Type"] = "application/rss+xml"
end
```

Now we've done the easy part. Our FeedController has selected the latest recipes to be added to the feed. Note that we set the content type of the action to "application/rss+xml". This lets HTTP clients know that we're feeding them RSS, so they can respond appropriately. Nowadays, even some web browsers can support RSS, so you'll see nicer behavior from the clients if you tell them what you're giving them.

Now it's time to generate the feed itself. And now we have a decision to make: how should we create the feed's XML?

We have three fairly good ways to create the feed file. We could use Ruby's built-in RSS library. This library provides a nice, clean API for both generating and consuming RSS. Alternatively, we could create an ERb template (an .rhtml file) that is preformatted as an RSS feed and uses dynamically inserted Ruby snippets to generate the recipe's content. Finally, we could use the XML Builder library to generate the RSS feed via an .rxml template.

Each possible approach has its merits. Since we want to keep this recipe as Atom-compatible as possible, we'll rule out using Ruby's built-in RSS library. That leaves us with either ERb or XML Builder. This being an XML feed, we're likely to have a cleaner experience with XML Builder, so we'll go with that.

Just as with ERb templates, XML Builder templates should be named after the actions they provide a view for. Here's what our recipes.rxml template looks like:

SyndicateYourSite/app/views/feed/recipes.rxml

```
xml.instruct!
xml.rss "version" => "2.0", "xmlns:dc" => "http://purl.org/dc/elements/1.1/" do
  xml.channel do
    xml.title 'Recipes on Rails'
    xml.link url_for(:only_path => false,
                     :controller => 'recipes',
                     :action => 'list')
    xml.pubDate CGI.rfc1123_date(@recipes.first.updated_at)
    xml.description h("Recipes created for and by guys who shouldn't be cooking.")
    @recipes.each do |recipe|
      xml.item do
        xml.title recipe.title
        xml.link url_for(:only_path => false,
                         :controller => 'recipes',
                         :action => 'show',
                         :id => recipe)

        xml.description h(recipe.instructions.to_s)
        xml.pubDate CGI.rfc1123_date(recipe.updated_at)
        xml.guid url_for(:only_path => false,
                         :controller => 'recipes',
                         :action => 'show',
                         :id => recipe)
```

```
        xml.author h(recipe.author.name)
      end
    end
  end
end
```

In case you've never seen a XML Builder template before, here's XML Builder in the shell of a really, really small nut: all those method calls on the implicitly available object, xml, end up generating XML tags of the same name. The tags get whatever value you pass into the method calls, and if you pass in a block, all the nested calls create nested tags.

XML Builder templates are Ruby code, and they run as Rails views, which means you can call all those wonderful helpers you normally use in your .rhtml files. In this example, we use the Action View method url_for(). We could have just as easily used any other built-in Rails helpers or even custom helpers defined in our application.

We won't go into too much detail on the RSS specification and what each element in this feed means. You can read the full RSS 2.0 specification at http://blogs.law.harvard.edu/tech/rss if you're into that kind of thing. This is the high-level overview.

RSS feeds have channels. Channels are named and have URLs, titles, and descriptions. More important, channels have items in them that also have URLs, titles, and descriptions as well as authors and the time stamp of when they were created. In our case, as you can see, these items are going to be recipes.

With this overview of XML Builder and RSS, the workings of recipes.rxml become self-apparent. The one little critical nugget you may not have noticed is the use of the :only_path option to url_for(). This one is easy to forget, because it's seldom necessary in everyday Rails development. It tells Rails to generate a URL with the full protocol and host name as opposed to just the relative path to the URL. Since these feeds will be consumed outside our application, a relative path won't do.

Here's an abbreviated example of the RSS feed we generate:

SyndicateYourSite/sample.xml

```xml
<?xml version="1.0" encoding="UTF-8"?>
<rss version="2.0" xmlns:dc="http://purl.org/dc/elements/1.1/">
  <channel>
    <title>Recipes on Rails</title>
    <link>http://myserver:2003/recipes/list</link>
    <pubDate>Fri, 03 Mar 2006 04:53:50 GMT</pubDate>
```

```
    <description>
        Recipes created for and by guys who shouldn't be cooking.
    </description>
    <item>
      <title>Canned Fish and Chips</title>
      <link>http://myserver:2003/recipes/show/6</link>
      <description>
          1. Open can. 2. Empty contents into bowl. 3. Serve.
      </description>
      <pubDate>Fri, 03 Mar 2006 04:58:42 GMT</pubDate>
      <guid>http://:2003/recipes/show/6</guid>
      <author>David</author>
    </item>
  </channel>
</rss>
```

And here's what a full feed would look like in an RSS aggregator:

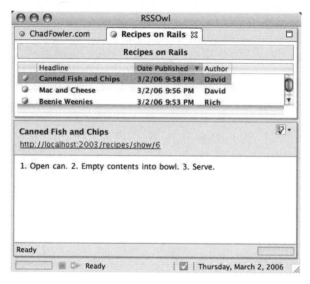

Now that we have a feed available, we naturally want the world to know about it. Of course, there's always the tried-and-true method of putting a big RSS button on your website with a link to the feed. But there's also a trick for helping web browsers and aggregators automatically discover available feeds. Although it's not a published, official standard, a de facto standard for RSS autodiscovery has emerged using the HTML *<link>* tag. The tag goes in your page's *<head>* element and looks like this (from my website):

```
<link href="http://www.chadfowler.com/index.cgi?rss"
      rel="alternate"
      title="RSS"
      type="application/rss+xml" />
```

Browsers and aggregators know how to extract these tags from web pages to find the feed links. This is a really good thing to put in your layouts. It's much easier for your users to remember mycooldomain.com when they're trying to subscribe to your feed than some technical URL. Thankfully, Rails makes adding an autodiscovery link trivial. Inside the <*head*> of your page template, insert the following:

```
<%= auto_discovery_link_tag(:rss, {:controller => 'feed', :action => 'recipes'}) %>
```

If you had created an Atom feed, you could replace :rss with :atom. Rails will generate the <*link*> code for you, so you don't have to remember the syntax.

Finally, as an optimization measure, since we've put our RSS code in a separate controller, we can add the following to the top of the feed controller, just below the class definition:

```
session :off
```

RSS requests are stateless, so there's no need to generate a session for every request. Since aggregators generally won't send any cookies with their requests, leaving session enabled for a feed could translate into hundreds of thousands of sessions needlessly created in a short span of time.

Discussion

RSS feeds are a great way to keep track of a large amount of time-sensitive data. They're good for tracking public sites, but they're also good for keeping track of your private information. For example, an RSS aggregator is a powerful tool for managing a software project when attached to a bug tracker, source control repository, and a discussion forum.

The problem is that this kind of data is private and usually requires authentication. RSS aggregators are hit or miss when it comes to supporting authentication schemes, so it will probably be necessary to work around the problem. One way to do that is by using obfuscated, resource-specific URLs. You can read more about how to do that in Recipe 53, *Secret URLs*, on page 241.

Also See

Another point to consider when you start serving feeds is that they can result in a lot of site traffic. Since feed aggregators poll the server at fixed intervals, you may find your site experiencing an exponential jump in hits.

To reduce the amount of actual traffic this translates into, you can set up your actions to respond to the If-Modified-Since HTTP header. Most feed aggregators will send this header with each request, indicating the last time they received a content update. Your application can use the date sent in this header field to determine whether there are any new feed items and, if not, return an HTTP response code of 304, which means "not modified."

For more information about the If-Modified-Since header, see the HTTP 1.1 specification.[23] For an example of how to support this header in Rails, see the discussion of HTTP caching in the online Rails Cookbook at http://manuals.rubyonrails.com/read/chapter/62.

---

[23]http://www.w3.org/Protocols/rfc2616/rfc2616-sec14.html#sec14.25

Making Your Own Rails Plugins

Credit

Rails plugin guru and core team member Rick Olson (a.k.a. technoweenie) wrote this recipe.

Problem

You've developed a few applications already, and you're getting ready to start on a new application. You noticed that you've implemented a handy search method in a previous project that would be helpful for the new application's models. It would be nice if you could extract this into a common library for not only your applications but also the rest of the Rails community's applications.

Solution

Plugins are a simple way to extend the Rails framework. They let you implement slices of functionality by adding new or reopening existing classes in Ruby or Rails. This functionality can solve more specific problems that may not have common use cases for most applications. Or, it could simply fix a bug by *monkey patching*[24] specific methods.

Plugins usually begin life as integral parts of real applications. The best reusable code comes from real, concrete need. With this in mind, let's walk through the process of extracting code from an existing application into a reusable plugin.

Imagine you have created a weblog application that implements a simple interface to search multiple fields of a model (in this case, Post) for a given string. With this code, it is easy to search your weblog's posts for any post whose title, body, or short description matches the given string. The following is what this might look like in your Post model:

---

[24]A term coined by Python programmers to describe the use of a language's dynamism to patch core language features at runtime. The term has a derogatory flavor in the Python community but is used by Rubyists with pride.

```
class Post < ActiveRecord::Base
  has_many :comments

  def self.search(query, fields, options = {})
    find :all,
          options.merge(:conditions => [[fields].flatten.map { |f|
              "LOWER(#{f}) LIKE :query"}.join(' OR '),
                {:query => "%#{query.to_s.downcase}%"}])
  end
end
```

As you move on to develop new applications, you realize that this functionality comes up again and again, and it would be a great candidate for extraction into a plugin. Let's do that.

First, we'll create the stub plugin files with the plugin generator. Rails comes with a convenient generator to make this easy for you. Enter ruby script/generate plugin to see the included documentation:

```
rick> script/generate plugin active_record_search
create   vendor/plugins/active_record_search/lib
   ;                  :                :
```

Now, let's extract the method from the Post model to an ActiveRecord-Search module. Make these changes to the file active_record_search.rb in the directory vendor/plugins/active_record_search/lib/.

```
# Adds a search method to query your ActiveRecord models
module ActiveRecordSearch
  # Query your ActiveRecord models.
  #
  #   Post.search 'foo', [:title, :summary]
  #   => [#<Post>, #<Post>, #<Post>]
  #
  def search(query, fields, options = {})
    find :all, options.merge(:conditions => [[fields].flatten.map { |f|
        "#{f} LIKE :query"}.join(' OR '), {:query => "%#{query}%"}])
  end
end
```

Now that you've created your library, you need to write the code Rails uses to bootstrap the plugin. Your plugin's init.rb files are always run as the final step of the initialization process of your Rails application. It is at this point that you can perform the steps to load the plugin. Not only will we need to load the ActiveRecordSearch module, but we need to extend ActiveRecord::Base with it. extend() is used here instead of include() because the search() method needs to be a class method on your model (as opposed to an instance method that can be invoked on the *instances* of your model).

Special init.rb Variables

init.rb has access to some variables set up by Rails Initializer:

- directory is the full path on your system to the plugin.
- name stores the plugin's name, which is taken from its directory name.
- loaded_plugins is a set of the plugins that have been currently loaded.
- config contains a reference to the current configuration object.

install.rb is another special plugin file. It is run immediately after the plugin is installed. I like to print the contents of the README file with this:

```
puts IO.read(File.join(directory, 'README'))
```

Note: The install.rb functionality currently requires Rails 1.1.

```
require 'active_record_search'
ActiveRecord::Base.extend ActiveRecordSearch
```

Now that this plugin exists, every model of every application into which it is installed will magically have a search() method that can match against one or many fields in the model.

Discussion

Plugins are rapidly gaining traction in the Rails community. They provide a convenient platform for developers to distribute functionality that may not be appropriate in Rails for one reason or another. Here are some common examples:

- Custom Active Record functionality provided through Acts (such as the built-in acts_as_list()).
- New Action View template alternatives to RHTML.
- Controller filters providing features such as output compression, request filtering, etc.
- Helpers that integrate with external products or services.

Also See

The best way to learn how to create a plugin is to look at existing plug-ins. The Rails wiki lists plugins,[25] and plugins by the core developers are also available.[26]

---

[25]http://wiki.rubyonrails.org/rails/pages/Plugins
[26]http://dev.rubyonrails.org/svn/rails/plugins/

Secret URLs

Sometimes, you need to restrict access to a resource—be it a URL, an email address, or an instant messaging destination—and it's inconvenient or impractical to use a normal username/password authentication mechanism. A commonly occurring example of this is RSS feeds. You don't want to require a username and password, because your aggregator may not support that kind of authentication. Or you may be using a public RSS aggregation service such My Yahoo or Bloglines and (understandably) unwilling to type in your username and password.

Another common example is that of an account activation link. A user signs up for your site, and you send them an email confirmation to ensure that they can at least be traced back to that email address. You want to give them an easy way to get back from the email to the site, so you give them an easy activation link.

So how do you protect these resources while eliminating the need for a username and password?

A common solution to this problem is to generate an obfuscated URL that will sign someone directly into an account or allow them to gain access to a protected resource.

Let's walk through a simple example. Imagine we are developing a simple messaging module for a larger application. The application gives each user an inbox. Application users can then send and receive simple messages within the context of our larger application.

It's a nice feature that our users have been asking for, but in practice, it's yet another place (in addition to their email and other websites) that users have to go to keep up with the flow of information. To counteract this problem, we decide to set up a simple RSS feed to allow each user to track his or her inbox.

We can easily create a feed for each inbox using the instructions found in Recipe 51, *Syndicate Your Site with RSS*, on page 229. The problem now is that these messages are private, so they need to be protected.

But we may not be able to get our RSS aggregator to work with a username and password. So, we'll generate an obfuscated URL through which to access these feeds.

First let's look at the schema describing users, their inboxes, and the messages in those inboxes. Here's the migration file that defines it:

SecretURLs/db/migrate/001_add_users_inboxes_messages.rb

```
class AddUsersInboxesMessages < ActiveRecord::Migration
  def self.up
    create_table :users do |t|
      t.column :name, :string
      t.column :password, :string
    end
    create_table :inboxes do |t|
      t.column :user_id, :integer
      t.column :access_key, :string
    end
    create_table :messages do |t|
      t.column :inbox_id, :integer
      t.column :sender_id, :integer
      t.column :title, :string
      t.column :body, :text
      t.column :created_at, :datetime
    end
  end

  def self.down
    drop_table :users
    drop_table :inboxes
    drop_table :messages
  end
end
```

This is a simple model. Users have inboxes, and inboxes have messages. The only unusual part of the model is on line 9 where the access_key column is defined for the inboxes table. This is the magic key we'll use to let our users into select parts of the application without a username and password.

Next we'll use the standard Rails model generators to create User, Inbox, and Message models. Here are the models and their associations.

SecretURLs/app/models/user.rb

```
class User < ActiveRecord::Base
  has_one :inbox
end
```

SecretURLs/app/models/inbox.rb

```
class Inbox < ActiveRecord::Base
  has_many :messages
end
```

SecretURLs/app/models/message.rb

```
class Message < ActiveRecord::Base
  belongs_to :inbox
end
```

Now how do we populate the inbox's access_key? Since every inbox is going to need one, we can populate it at the time of the inbox's creation. The most reliable way to make sure this happens is to define it in the model's before_create() method. This way, we can set the access_key whenever an Inbox is created without having to remember to set it in our calling code. Here's the new inbox.rb:

SecretURLs/app/models/inbox.rb

```
class Inbox < ActiveRecord::Base
  has_many :messages
  before_create :generate_access_key
  def generate_access_key
    @attributes['access_key'] = MD5.hexdigest((object_id + rand(255)).to_s)
  end
end
```

In Inbox's before_create() callback, we create a random access key and assign the attribute. Then Active Record's instance creation life cycle runs its course, and the Inbox is saved—access key and all.

For this example, we've created a random access key using the Ruby-assigned object id and a random number. The access key is not guaranteed to be unique, which could theoretically be a problem. For a more reliably unique id, see Bob Aman's UUIDTools library.[27]

Now each Inbox has its own obfuscated access key. All that's left is to set up access control for the Inbox's RSS feed, allowing passage to those with the proper key.

We'll assume that the feed is set up in a separate FeedController with no authentication or authorization applied (those should be applied to, for example, the InboxesController, which is one good reason for putting RSS feeds in their own controller). We can set up a security check on the Inbox feed with a before_filter. Here's the (abbreviated) FeedController:

---

[27]http://rubyforge.org/projects/uuidtools/

```
SecretURLs/app/controllers/feed_controller.rb
```

```ruby
class FeedController < ApplicationController
  before_filter :authenticate_access_key, :only => [:inbox]
  def authenticate_access_key
    inbox = Inbox.find_by_access_key(params[:access_key])
    if inbox.blank? || inbox.id != params[:id].to_i
      raise "Unauthorized"
    end
  end
  def inbox
    @inbox = Inbox.find(params[:id])
  end
end
```

The before_filter() tells Action Controller to run authenticate_access_key() whenever the inbox action is requested. authenticate_access_key() looks for an Inbox with a matching access key and then validates that the returned Inbox is the one the user requested. If no Inbox matches, an error is raised. Otherwise, the request continues, and the RSS feed is rendered.

The URL for the feed for inbox number 5 would look something like this: http://localhost/feed/inbox/5?access_key=b6da56...92f98287b12c04d47. We can generate the URL for this feed (so our users can subscribe) in our views with the following code (assuming we have an @inbox instance variable available):

```erb
<%= url_for :controller => 'feed',
            :action => 'inbox',
            :id => @inbox,
            :access_key => @inbox.access_key
%>
```

Also See

To make the obfuscated URLs a little easier on the eyes, see Recipe 36, *Make Your URLs Meaningful (and Pretty)*, on page 153.

Quickly Inspect Your Sessions' Contents

Sometimes weird things happen with session data during development. And, unfortunately, when things go wrong with session data in Rails, it's pretty easy to get stuck. At times like these, it's helpful to be able to inspect the contents of your sessions from the console.

By default, Rails sessions are stored as marshaled Ruby objects on the file system. In Rails 1.0, their default location is /tmp, though as of Rails 1.1 are stored in a tmp directory under your application's root (if one exists).

I use the following script to print the contents of all the session files in my /tmp directory. When things start going crazy and I don't know why, I know it's time to run the script.

`DumpingSessionContentsDuringDevelopment/script/dump_sessions`

```ruby
#!/usr/bin/env ruby
require 'pp'
require File.dirname(__FILE__) + '/../config/environment'
Dir['app/models/**/*rb'].each{|f| require f}
pp Dir['/tmp/ruby_sess*'].collect {|file|
  [file, Marshal.load(File.read(file))]
}
```

You can call it like this:

```
chad> ruby script/dump_sessions
[["/tmp/ruby_sess.073009d69aa82787", {"hash"=>{"flash"=>{}}}],
 ["/tmp/ruby_sess.122c36ca72886f45", {"hash"=>{"flash"=>{}}}],
 ["/tmp/ruby_sess.122f4cb99733ef40", {"hash"=>
   {:user=>#<User:0x24ad71c @attributes={"name"=>"Chad", "id"=>"1"}>,
   "flash"=>{}}}
 ]
]
```

Mike Clark suggests that you can also dump sessions from an Active Record session store. He supplied the Rake task listed on the following page that does it for you:

```ruby
namespace :db do
  namespace :sessions do
    desc "Dumps the database-backed session data"
    task :dump => [:environment] do |t|
    require 'pp'
    Dir['app/models/**/*rb'].each{ |f| require f}
    sessions = CGI::Session::ActiveRecordStore::Session.find_all
    sessions.each do |session|
      pp session.data
    end
  end
  end
end
```

Sharing Models between Your Applications

You have a single set of models that you need to use from multiple Rails applications. The Rails applications have different functionality but use the same database and the same model logic.

You can, of course, install your models as regular Ruby libraries or RubyGems. This would involve placing them somewhere in Ruby's $LOAD_PATH, where they would be accessible via normal require calls. You could add the require calls to your config/environment.rb file, and your application would have access to the models.

But this isn't a very usable solution for development. Rails plays a lot of fancy games to make sure you don't have to stop and start your development web server every time you change a piece of code. You would find that using the require method would result in your code not reloading properly. But switching to the load method, which reloads the files every time, would be inefficient in production.

You also don't want to have to reinstall your models every time you change them. It would be most convenient if the place where you develop your models is the same place your applications' development environments look for them.

The simplest solution to this problem, if you're on a system that supports the facility, is to use symbolic links. Say you had your models in the directory ~/development/rails/shared_models/ and your applications in the directories ~/development/rails/app1 and ~/development/rails/app2. Create a symbolic link from ~/development/rails/app1/app/models to the directory ../../../shared_models. Then, if ~/development were the root of your source control tree, checking out all three projects would always result in a correct path to the models, since we used a relative path name in the link.

A cleaner and more cross-platform approach, if you're using Subversion for version control, would be to use the svn:externals property of Subversion to point your app/models directory to an external repository path. For example, if your models were managed in the repository at http://railsrecipes.com/svn/shared_models, you could change your application's models directory to reference it by changing to your app directory and typing the following:

```
svn propset svn:externals "models http://railsrecipes.com/svn/shared_models" .
```

Future updates of your application's code (via svn up) would pull any updates to the shared models code as well. Additionally, if you changed the code under app/models, you could actually commit it directly from there and it would update your shared repository.

Finally, you could install your models as a Rails plugin. You would initially generate the plugin structure with the Rails generator:

```
chad> ruby script/generate plugin shared_models
    :           :            :
create  vendor/plugins/shared_models/init.rb
create  vendor/plugins/shared_models/lib/shared_models.rb
create  vendor/plugins/shared_models/tasks/shared_models_tasks.rake
create  vendor/plugins/shared_models/test/shared_models_test.rb
```

You would then place your model files directly under the directory vendor/plugins/shared_models/lib. Code distributed as a plugin is automatically reloaded by the usual Rails reloading mechanism.

Installing your shared models as a plugin is a really good choice when the shared models represent only a subset of the models required by each application. For example, if you had specialized models for an administrative application and for a consumer-facing application that both manipulated the same core data, you could distribute those core models as a plugin while allowing each specializing application to have its own app/models directory with its own application-specific models.

To enable easy installation of these models, you could use the built-in Rails plugin installer and house your models either in a Subversion repository or in an HTTP-accessible directory.

Also See

For further information about making Rails plugins, see Recipe 52, *Making Your Own Rails Plugins*, on page 237.

Generate Documentation for Your Application

Ruby comes with a powerful documentation system called RDoc. How do you use RDoc to generate and browse documentation for your application and its dependencies?

The first thing you'll probably want to have documentation for is Rails itself. If you've installed Rails using RubyGems, you can always get to the documentation for all your installed Rails versions (and every other gem on your system!) using the gem_server command.

Just run gem_server, and direct your web browser to http://localhost:8808. If you need to run it on a different port, you can set the port with the -p option: gem_server -p 2600. You'll see a list of all your installed gems, and you can click the gem to browse its documentation.

If you are running Edge Rails (see Recipe 50, *Living on the Edge (of Rails Development)*, on page 225), you can use the built-in Rake task doc:rails to generate documentation. The generated HTML will go into doc/api. This is especially helpful since the main site doesn't maintain current documentation for the evolving world of the Rails trunk. If you like, you can change the RDoc template used by setting the template environment variable to the name of the template in question.

If you're using one or more plugins, you can generate HTML documentation for them with rake doc:plugins, which will deposit the docs in doc/plugins/each_plugin_name (one directory for each plugin you have installed).

Finally, you can generate documentation for your *own* application with rake doc:app. This will, predictably, store its generated documents in doc/app.

Processing Uploaded Images

Credit

Bruce Williams wrote this recipe.

Problem

You're planning an image upload feature, and you'd like your application to resize large images into thumbnails for viewing.

Ingredients

For this recipe you'll need RMagick, the Ruby API to ImageMagick and GraphicsMagick. Once you have ImageMagick and GraphicsMagick (and their headers), just install the gem:

```
bruce> sudo gem install rmagick
```

Solution

Let's say we're implementing a small personal gallery application to store family pictures. We're not planning to store a lot of information here—just a name, a description, and the image files themselves.

Let's get right into the code. Here is the upload form:

```
<% form_for :image,
            @image,
            :url  => { :action => 'create'},
            :html => { :multipart=>true }    do |f| %>
  <label for='image_name'>Name:</label>
  <%= f.text_field :name %><br/>
  <label for='image_file_data'>Image File:</label>
  <%= f.file_field :file_data %><br/>
  <label for='image_description'>Description:</label><br/>
  <%= f.text_area :description, :cols => 80, :rows => 5 %><br/>
  <%= submit_tag "Save" %>
<% end %>
```

> Don't forget to use the :multipart => true option in your forms, or nothing will be uploaded at all.

Notice we're not using file_field_tag(); the file_data parameter will end up being accessible via params(:image)(:file_data) and won't get any special treatment from the controller:

```
def create
  @image = Image.create params[:image]
end
```

The controller code is dead simple. The details of image storage and processing are tucked away in the Image model where they belong:

ProcessingImages/app/models/image.rb

```
Line 1   require 'RMagick'
   -
   -     class Image < ActiveRecord::Base
   -
   5       DIRECTORY = 'public/uploaded_images'
   -       THUMB_MAX_SIZE = [125,125]
   -
   -       after_save :process
   -       after_destroy :cleanup
  10
   -       def file_data=(file_data)
   -         @file_data = file_data
   -         write_attribute 'extension',
   -                         file_data.original_filename.split('.').last.downcase
  15       end
   -
   -       def url
   -         path.sub(/^public/,'')
   -       end
  20
   -       def thumbnail_url
   -         thumbnail_path.sub(/^public/,'')
   -       end
   -
  25       def path
   -         File.join(DIRECTORY, "#{self.id}-full.#{extension}")
   -       end
   -
   -       def thumbnail_path
  30         File.join(DIRECTORY, "#{self.id}-thumb.#{extension}")
   -       end
   -
   -       #######
   -       private
  35       #######
   -
   -       def process
   -         if @file_data
   -           create_directory
  40           cleanup
   -           save_fullsize
   -           create_thumbnail
   -           @file_data = nil
```

```
            end
45      end

        def save_fullsize
          File.open(path, 'wb') do |file|
            file.puts @file_data.read
50        end
        end

        def create_thumbnail
          img = Magick::Image.read(path).first
55        thumbnail = img.thumbnail(*THUMB_MAX_SIZE)
          thumbnail.write thumbnail_path
        end

        def create_directory
60        FileUtils.mkdir_p DIRECTORY
        end

        def cleanup
          Dir[File.join(DIRECTORY, "#{self.id}-*")].each do |filename|
65          File.unlink(filename) rescue nil
          end
        end

    end
```

The basic idea is that Image.create() calls file_data= and sets @file_data
and the extension attribute (that we save for later). The image object is
saved to the database, and process() is called afterward. The process()
method does a bit of housekeeping first, making sure our image storage
directory exists and removing any old files for this image object that
may already exist (in the case of an update). Once that's done, process()
answers its true calling and saves the full-size image and the related
thumbnail.

The rest of the model is for convenience—methods to find file paths
and URLs of images for use in views. The important remaining piece
of code is the cleanup() method, which is called if the model instance
is destroyed. When an image record is destroyed, we presumably won't
need its associated files any longer.

Discussion

This is only one way to do it. The main point to remember is that
the model (not the controller) should be handling the details of saving,
processing, and removing its related files.

The basic concept of processing files in an after_save lends itself to a lot of other applications. You could use the same type of hook to handle document conversion or any number of other model housekeeping chores.

We've barely scratched the surface of what RMagick can do in this recipe. For more information about RMagick, check out the RMagick web page at http://rmagick.rubyforge.org.

Also See

You might want to look at Sebastian Kanthak's file_column plugin,[28] which wraps up this type of functionality with some template helpers and a small framework. We chose to implement our own recipe from scratch to demonstrate the concepts. If you need something more advanced than what's presented here, file_column might be a good starting point.

---

[28]http://www.kanthak.net/opensource/file_column/.

Easily Group Lists of Things

Rails 1.1 includes two new small but powerful methods to make dealing with lists easier. Enumerable#group_by() and Array#in_groups_of() solve two problems that often arise during web development.

Here is Enumerable#group_by():

```
<%
employees = Employee.find(:all).group_by {|employee|
  employee.title
}
%>
<% employees.each do |title, people| %>
  <h2><%= title %></h2>
  <ul>
    <% people.each do |person| %>
      <li><%= person.name %></li>
    <% end %>
  </ul>
<% end %>
```

The group_by() accepts a block that returns a grouping value, and returns a hash with all the items in the initial list grouped under keys that are set to the values returned by the group_by() block.

Then, if you're trying to build a grid of values where the number of items in the grid is variable, the new Array#in_groups_of() method will make life much easier for you:

```
<table class="calendar">
<% (1..DAYS_IN_MARCH).to_a.in_groups_of(7) do |group| %>
  <tr>
    <% group.each do |day| %>
      <td><%= day %></td>
    <% end %>
  </tr>
<% end %>
</table>
```

Array#in_groups_of() divides an array into groups of the size specified by its first parameter and yields those groups to a block for processing. By default, in_groups_of() pads empty cells in the groups with nil. You can optionally add a second parameter to the call, which will cause the method to pad with the argument supplied instead.

Keeping Track of Who Did What

Credit

Thanks to Dave Thomas for the idea for this recipe.

Problem

Your application contains sensitive information, and for auditing purposes you need to keep track of who changes that information and when it is changed. Whether it's whiny users complaining (incorrectly) that your application is changing their data or compliance with a government regulation, there are many times when you might need an audit trail.

How do you create this audit trail without cluttering up your application's *real* code with logging statements?

Solution

If you want to observe updates to a model in a decoupled way, Active Record observers are a great choice. However, if you need access to session state or other controller-level data elements at the time of an update, observers are (rightly) unable to access that information.

That's the dilemma with application auditing. The "who" of a web application is usually stored in session. And session is not something you should couple with your model layer if you want to keep your application clean.

Enter Action Controller's Cache::Sweeper objects. These beauties are intended to be used for clearing an application's page cache when the cached pages' underlying data are updated. But if you take a step back and look at them with an open mind, they're really just loosely coupled observers that bridge the model and controller layers of your application.

Cache sweepers can observe your Active Record models in the same way that Active Record observers do. But when their callbacks are invoked, they have access to the instantiated controller that is handling the request as it happens!

Let's demonstrate with a simple example. We'll create a simple system for managing the results of people's IQ tests. To secure the system, we'll use the authentication implementation from Recipe 31, *Authenticating Your Users*, on page 135. Here's a migration implementing a simplified schema for the application:

```ruby
KeepingTrackOfWhoDidWhat/db/migrate/001_add_people_table.rb
class AddPeopleTable < ActiveRecord::Migration
  def self.up
    create_table :people do |t|
      t.column :name, :string
      t.column :age, :integer
      t.column :iq, :integer
    end
  end

  def self.down
    drop_table :people
  end
end
```

For the sake of demonstration, after applying this migration, let's generate a scaffolding for objects of type Person:

```
chad> ruby script/generate scaffold Person
      exists  app/controllers/
        :              :
```

Now we have a simple model and a set of actions for managing the model. Following the instructions in Recipe 31, *Authenticating Your Users*, on page 135, we will simply add authentication to the application in app/controllers/application.rb. Now we can not only restrict access to certain individuals, but we can find out *who* is performing an action.

Now we'll create a simple Cache::Sweeper that will observe changes to Person instances and log those changes to the database. We'll name the class AuditSweeper and will put it in app/models/. Here's what it looks like:

```ruby
KeepingTrackOfWhoDidWhat/app/models/audit_sweeper.rb
class AuditSweeper < ActionController::Caching::Sweeper
  observe Person
  def after_destroy(record)
    log(record, "DESTROY")
  end
```

```
  def after_update(record)
    log(record, "UPDATE")
  end

  def after_create(record)
    log(record, "CREATE")
  end

  def log(record, event, user = controller.session[:user])
    AuditTrail.create(:record_id => record.id, :record_type => record.type.name,
                      :event => event, :user_id => user)
  end
end
```

If you've worked at all with Active Record callbacks, you'll recognize the three methods starting with after_. They are called after each of the three named events on the models this sweeper observes. Note that we need to use *after* filters and not *before* filters so we'll have access to freshly created records' Ids, which don't get set until after an initial save. As you can see on line 2, this sweeper observes the Person model.

The real work of this sweeper takes place in the log() method. For each change to any Person, the log() method creates an AuditTrail record, noting who performed the change, which record was modified, and what action (update, create, or destroy) was taken. Note that we access the user from session via Cache::Sweeper's controller attribute, which returns the instance of the current controller that is processing the request.

You're probably wondering where this AuditTrail model came from and where it's storing its data. Rightly so, because we haven't created it yet. Let's do that.

Here's the migration that defines this schema (if you're using Rails 1.1 or later, the migration file will be created automatically when you create the AuditTrail model in the next step):

KeepingTrackOfWhoDidWhat/db/migrate/002_add_audit_trails_table.rb

```
class AddAuditTrailsTable < ActiveRecord::Migration
  def self.up
    create_table :audit_trails do |t|
      t.column :record_id, :integer
      t.column :record_type, :string
      t.column :event, :string
      t.column :user_id, :integer
      t.column :created_at, :datetime
    end
  end
```

```
def self.down
  drop_table :audit_trails
end
end
```

We then generate an Active Record model for this schema. The generated class is good enough to suit our needs.

```
chad> ruby script/generate model AuditTrail
   :              :              :
```

After applying the new migration, we're ready to create AuditTrail records with our sweeper. But our PeopleController doesn't yet know about the sweeper, so left as is, it will never be invoked. To tell PeopleController to enable the sweeper, we can add the following line to the top of our scaffolding-generated app/controllers/people_controller.rb file:

> KeepingTrackOfWhoDidWhat/app/controllers/people_controller.rb

```
cache_sweeper :audit_sweeper
```

Finally, to try this, we'll need to make sure we have caching enabled. Even though we're not technically *doing* any caching, our auditing mechanism relies on Rails' caching code, and the default setting for Rails in development is to turn caching off. To turn it on, edit your config/environments/development.rb file, and look for the line that starts with config.action_controller.perform_caching. Set its value to true, and restart your local server if it's already running.

> Because we're using the Rails caching mechanism for our auditing code, we may end up turning on *actual* caching in development. This could lead to confusing application behavior if you forget that it is enabled. After you have your cache sweeper working, turn it off in development, and use your unit and functional tests to ensure that it's working properly as you evolve your application.

Now if we create, modify, or delete Person records via our PeopleController, new AuditTrail records will be created, detailing what change was made, who made it, and when it happened. For example, if I created a new Person named Barney via the generated scaffolding, I would see something like the following in the Rails console:

```
chad> ruby script/console
Loading development environment.
>> AuditTrail.find(:all)
=> [#<AuditTrail:0x26b6a60 @attributes={"record_type"=>"Person",
"event"=>"CREATE", "id"=>"1", "user_id"=>"2", "record_id"=>"1",
"created_at"=>"2006-03-12 12:31:02"}>]
```

Discussion

What we've created so far tells us *who* performed *what action* and *when* they did it. But, in the case of a create or update, it doesn't tell us what the record's attributes were set to.

If we wanted that kind of verbose logging, we would have a number of ways to accomplish it. Since the audit_trails table is meant to be usable to track changes to any type of model, we could add a text field for the model's data and set it to be serializable (into YAML) by Active Record.

Distributing Your Application As One Directory Tree

Credit

Thanks to Tim Case for the idea for this recipe.

Problem

Your application depends on third-party libraries. Although you can install and manage those libraries with RubyGems, you prefer to distribute your entire application as one, self-contained bundle. This means the root of your application should contain Rails and all its components plus any of other dependencies your application may have.

Solution

First we'll take care of Rails, because the Rails team has taken care of this one for us. If you're running from RubyGems, Rails ships with a Rake task to pull all the gems into your application's root in such a way that they will be automatically used when your application is initialized.

```
chad> rake freeze_gems
(in /Users/chadfowler/topsecretapp)
Freezing to the gems for Rails 1.0.0
rm -rf vendor/rails
mkdir -p vendor/rails
Unpacked gem: 'activesupport-1.2.5'
Unpacked gem: 'activerecord-1.13.2'
Unpacked gem: 'actionpack-1.11.2'
Unpacked gem: 'actionmailer-1.1.5'
Unpacked gem: 'actionwebservice-1.0.0'
Unpacked gem: 'rails-1.0.0'
```

The freeze_gems Rake task grabs the Rails gems and unpacks them under the application root's vendor directory. Whatever version your application would have used is the version that will be unpacked and frozen. This is typically the latest version available on your system, though it can be hard-coded to any version you like in your environment.rb file.

After freezing the gems, your vendor directory will look something like this:

If you ever want to switch back to the RubyGems version (perhaps you want to upgrade the version you have frozen, for example), you can easily do it with another supplied Rake task:

```
chad> rake unfreeze_rails
(in /Users/chadfowler/topsecretapp)
rm -rf vendor/rails
```

This task simply removes the rails directory from vendor. That's all Rails needs to know to return to using the system-installed gems.

What about non-Rails libraries? Perhaps you rely on Mike Granger's BlueCloth library for transforming Markdown text into HTML.[29] How could you include that in your application's root directory to avoid having to install it on every system on which you might want to run your application?

Rails is a Ruby framework, so there are as many ways to accomplish this as Ruby allows. But, as with most Rails tasks, there is a convention. The convention is to put third-party libraries into the vendor directory. That's why it's called vendor.

Before Rails plugins (see Recipe 50, *Living on the Edge (of Rails Development)*, on page 225), the best way to freeze external libraries into your Rails application would have have been to unpack them into your application's vendor directory and edit your config/environment.rb to add that directory to Ruby's $LOAD_PATH. So for BlueCloth, you would run the following from your application's vendor directory:

```
chad > gem unpack BlueCloth
Unpacked gem: 'BlueCloth-1.0.0'
```

---

[29]http://daringfireball.net/projects/markdown/

This creates a directory called BlueCloth-1.0.0, which you can add to your application's $LOAD_PATH by adding the following to the end of your config/environment.rb:

```
$LOAD_PATH.unshift "#{RAILS_ROOT}/vendor/BlueCloth-1.0.0/lib"
```

This makes the files in BlueCloth's lib directory available to Ruby's require() method.

But most applications follow a convention for their directory layouts. And that convention happens to be compatible with the Rails plugin system. The convention is that they all tend to have a lib subdirectory that should be added to the load path. The Rails plugin system automatically adds all such directories to Ruby's load path when it starts.

So if the library you want to install follows this convention (as Blue-Cloth does), you can run the gem unpack from your application's vendor/plugins directory instead of its vendor directory and skip the modification to config/environment.rb.

Now you can check all this structure into your source control repository or include it in the application archive in which you distribute your application, and the application will be runnable without having to set up a bunch of dependencies.

Adding Support for Localization

Credit

Long-time Ruby programmer and designer Bruce Williams (who, in a past life, worked as an Arabic translator) wrote this recipe.

Problem

Your application is (or will be) used all over the world. You'd like it to support multiple languages and format information such as times and currency specifically for each user's locale.

Ingredients

Josh Harvey and Jeremy Voorhis's Globalize plugin, installable from the root of your Rails application with the following:

```
bruce> ruby script/plugin install \
  http://svn.globalize-rails.org/svn/globalize/globalize/trunk
```

Solution

For this recipe, we're going to model a small online store that specializes in Middle Eastern and Asian food imports. The store's customer base is made up primarily of non-English-speaking Middle Eastern and Asian people, so localization is a must.

Assuming you have the Globalize plugin installed, the first thing you'll need to do is to set up its required tables and data:

```
bruce> rake globalize:setup
```

Next, you'll need to set your base language and default locale in config/environment.rb. You can add this anywhere at the end of the file. For an English speaker in the United States, it would be:

```
include Globalize
Locale.set_base_language 'en-US'
Locale.set 'en-US'
```

International Characters

By default, Rails isn't set up to handle non-English characters. Here's what you'll need to do to make it work:

1. Add the following to your config/environment.rb file:

```
$KCODE = 'u'
require 'jcode'
```

This sets Ruby's character encoding to UTF-8.

2. Next you need to set your database connection to transfer using UTF-8. For MySQL and PostgreSQL, you can do this by adding a line to your database's configuration in your config/database.yml file. For MySQL it would be this:

```
encoding: utf8
```

And for PostgreSQL:

```
encoding: unicode
```

For SQLite, simply compiling UTF-8 support in is all you need to do. For other database systems, consult the system's documentation on how to set character encoding for connections.

3. Set the character encoding and collation for the database and/or tables you'll be accessing. *Collation* refers to the method that will be used for sorting. If you change your character set to Unicode but leave your database's collation untouched, you may end up with some unexpected results coming from ORDER BY clauses. For details on how to set character set and collation for your database, check your database software's manual.

4. Set encoding information in the content type your application returns for each request. The easiest way to do this is to put an after_filter() in your ApplicationController. Here's an example filter that will work in most cases (including RJS templates):

```
after_filter :set_charset
def set_charset
  unless @headers["Content-Type"] =~ /charset/i
    @headers["Content-Type"] ||= ""
    @headers["Content-Type"] += "; charset=utf-8"
  end
end
```

> ### International Characters (continued)
>
> 5. Add encoding information to your templates. Even if you are transferring documents using Unicode, if a user saves them to his or her local hard disk, there needs to be some way of identifying the encoding. Prepend the following inside your layout's *<head>* section:
>
> ```
> <![[CDATA
> <meta http-equiv="Content-Type"
>     content="text/html; charset=utf-8">
> ]]>
> ```
>
> As long and drawn out as this procedure may seem, it's still not a total solution. There are major fixes in the works for Ruby 2.0, but for now internationalization is a difficult area for Ruby. There are several efforts underway to work around this. At the time of this writing they are all still experimental. Watch the Rails mailing list for announcements.

Congratulations, you're ready to start translating!

مبروك! أنت مستعد!

Now, digging into our little grocery store application, we'll turn our attention to setting the user's language/locale. We'll allow the user to do this in two ways:

- Set it when the user logs in (for users who log in before browsing our products)

- Allow users who are not logged in to manually set it (for users who want to browse first, creating or logging into an account right before checking out)

We'll use these two techniques to set a session variable and have a before_filter() that will call Locale.set() for each request. This will involve adding code to AccountsController (our controller that handles authentication) to set the session variable and adding a before_filter in ApplicationController to use Locale.set() to set the locale for each request.

Here's AccountsController; all we do here is set the session variable in login and the manual change_locale actions:

```
Globalize/app/controllers/accounts_controller.rb

class AccountsController < ApplicationController

  def login
    case request.method
    when :post
      begin
        user = User.authenticate(@params[:email], @params[:password])
        session[:user] = user.id
        session[:locale] = user.locale
        go_to = session[:destination]
        session[:destination] = nil
        redirect_to (go_to || home_url) unless performed?
      rescue User::InvalidLoginException => e
        flash[:notice] = e.message
        redirect_to login_url unless performed?
      end
    when :get
    end
  end

  def logout
    @session[:user] = nil
    redirect_to home_url
  end

  def change_locale
    session[:locale] = params[:locale] unless params[:locale].blank?
    redirect_to :back
  end

end
```

Nothing special appears there. In login we just use the stored locale value for the user, and in change_locale we use a CGI parameter. Now let's look at our before_filter in ApplicationController that will handle actually setting the locale during each request:

```
before_filter :set_locale

def set_locale
  Locale.set session[:locale] unless session[:locale].blank?
  true
end
```

So, we have a working system that can handle the selection of a locale. This is where things start to get fun.

Probably the easiest way to preview the usefulness of localization is in views; we'll get into models a bit later.

Globalize gives you a few easy-to-use string methods to handle view translations; translate() and t() (which is just an alias) are for simple translations, and /() is for printf-looking functionality. Here are a few examples from our application:

```
<% unless params[:search].blank? %>
  <p><%= "Found %d products." / @products.size %></p>
<% end %>
```

For quick, easy, little bits of translation, use the t() method. We use that on the page where customers can manage their order:

```
<%= link_to "Remove".t, :action => 'remove', :id => item.product_id %>
```

It turns out String#/() is really just syntactic sugar for String#translate() with a few arguments preset. Refer to Globalize's core_ext.rb for details.

Offering locale-friendly versions of dates and currency is also simply done, courtesy of the loc() (localize()) method:

```
<%= Time.now.loc "%H:%M %Z" %>
```

So, it turns out translating views is really easy. Since the translations themselves are stored in globalize_translations, it's just a matter of throwing up some scaffolding to edit them.

Now, in our little grocery app, the majority of what we're going to be displaying will be model data: our products. For this to really work as a truly international app, we'll have to be able to translate attributes on the model as well. It won't do to have "Place Order" in 25 languages if the only way to figure out what you're buying is by looking at pictures.

Good news—this is where Globalize really shines. Let's take a quick look at our Product model for an example:

```
class Product < ActiveRecord::Base
  translates :name, :description
end
```

The translates() method call lets Globalize know it will be handling translation of the name() and description() attributes. Now let's look at how you save a model with multiple translations by adding a new product:

```
Locale.set 'en-US'
prod = Product.create(:name => "Yemenese Coffee",
                      :description => "Coffee from the South of Yemen")
Locale.set 'ar-LB'
prod.name = "قهوة يمنية"
prod.description = "قهوة من جنوب اليمن"

prod.save
```

As you can see, Locale.set is very important. When a model's attributes are handled by Globalize, Globalize interprets any assignments to those attributes as their translation in the current locale. Globalize makes the process easy by handling the details behind the scenes using the globalize_translations table and some creative overriding of some of ActiveRecord::Base's internals (such as find()); this is a detail that you'll need to keep in mind if you're using find_by_sql(), which it doesn't override.

> The locale name given to Locale.set consists of a language code (from globalize_languages) and a country code (from globalize_countries). This is nice, but as translations are stored by language, not locale, if we wanted a specific translation for Canadian English, for instance, a new language row would need to be added to the globalize_languages table.

Localization is fun stuff—it can seem a little complex, but with Globalize, it's easily manageable and simple to get running.

Discussion

Not all languages are read from left to right! Be kind to languages such as Arabic and Hebrew and support right-handed page layouts (hint: load another style sheet by checking Locale.active.language.direction() to change text alignment, and maybe even place labels for form fields on the left or right hand side depending on direction).

We certainly haven't touched on everything relating to Globalize; it has features such as support for pluralization, routing to locale-specific templates, and the Currency class that we haven't even looked at here. Globalize is just chock-full of goodies, so check it out—this was just an appetizer!

Also See

The Globalize website[30] has more background on the plugin, including a FAQ, examples, and information on more complex topics.

---

[30]http://www.globalize-rails.org

The Console Is Your Friend

One of the best things about switching to Rails from another platform is the script/console command. It's good to quickly develop the habit of always leaving a console window open when you're working on a Rails application. It's a great tool for both exploration during development and administration in production.

```
chad> ruby script/console
Loading development environment.
>>
```

Instead of going directly to your database when you need to query for application data, use your models directly from the console instead of typing SQL into your database server's monitor console. The behavior you experience in the Rails console is a closer match to what your end users will experience, since you're using the same code:

```
>> Person.find_by_first_name("Chad").email
=> "chad@chadfowler.com"
```

Always forgetting the column names for your tables? Just ask for them:

```
>> Calendar.column_names
=> ["id", "creator_id", "description", "org_id"]
```

If your Ruby is compiled with readline support,[31] you can autocomplete class and method names using the Tab key. Type part of a method name, press Tab, and you'll see a list of all matching method names. Who needs an IDE?!

If you're working repeatedly on the same class or object, you can change your session's scope to that object so all method calls are sent to it:

```
>> me = Person.find_by_first_name("Chad")
...
>> irb me
>> name
=> "Chad Fowler"
>> email
=> "chad@chadfowler.com"
```

Just type exit to shift to the original context.

---

[31]To find out, type ruby -rreadline -e 'p Readline'. If Ruby echoes Readline back to you, you have it!

If you make changes to your models or supporting classes and want those changes to be reflected in your running console, you don't have to exit and restart it. In Rails 1.0, Dispatcher.reset_application!() will cause a class reload. Rails 1.1 makes it even simpler with reload!().

Speaking of Rails 1.1, the console now gives you an implicit variable, app, which is an instance of ActionController::Integration::Session. You can directly call methods on it as if you were inside a live integration test.[32]

```
>> app.get "/"
=> 302
>> app.follow_redirect!
=> 200
```

---

[32]See Recipe 43, *Testing Across Multiple Controllers*, on page 185.

Automatically Save a Draft of a Form

Credit

Thanks to reader David Vincelli for the idea for this recipe.

Problem

Some forms take a long time to complete. As application developers, we try to minimize this where possible by making more user-friendly choices in our designs, but sometimes there's nothing we can do. For example, email systems, message boards, and weblogs are all systems that inherently involve a lot of data entry before a form is submitted. When I'm typing a post for the whole world to see, I want to make sure it's just right before I click `Submit`.

But all that typing in between saves makes me really nervous. And it makes your users nervous too. What if your browser crashes or the power goes out and your computer shuts off? You'll lose your work. I don't know about you, but after I've spent ten minutes typing something only to lose it, I don't want to do it again. It's frustrating and demotivating.

That's not the kind of negative experience we want our users to have. How can we give them the ability to save a quick, unpublished draft of their work on a form before fully submitting it? Better yet, how can we do it for them so they don't even have to remember to click `Save Draft`?

Solution

For this recipe, we'll create a quick-and-dirty model to represent a weblog system. Weblog posts have an author, a title, a body, and a time stamp showing the date on which they were created. Here's the Active Record migration defining the schema. (If you're using Rails 1.1 or higher, the migration file will be created automatically when you create the Post model in the next step.)

```
AutomaticallySaveADraft/db/migrate/001_add_posts_table.rb
```

```ruby
def self.up
  create_table :posts do |t|
    t.column :author, :string
    t.column :title, :string
    t.column :body, :text
    t.column :created_at, :datetime
  end
end
```

We'll use the default generated model to support this schema:

```
chad> ruby script/generate model Post
   exists   app/models/
   exists   test/unit/
   exists   test/fixtures/
   create   app/models/post.rb
   create   test/unit/post_test.rb
      :             :
```

To make this as painless for the user as possible, we're going to save our drafts asynchronously using Ajax. So, remember to include the built-in Rails JavaScript files. I usually put them in the *<head>* tag in my application's layout:

```erb
<%= javascript_include_tag :defaults %>
```

We'll generate a controller called PostsController to handle our weblog's posts. Then we'll create a simple action and form for making a new message. Here's the action, that will handle both the new Post form and the form's callback, which saves the Post to the database:

```
AutomaticallySaveADraft/app/controllers/posts_controller.rb
```

```ruby
def new
  if request.get?
    @post = session[:post_draft] || Post.new
  else
    @post = Post.create(params[:post])
    session[:post_draft] = nil
    redirect_to :action => 'list'
  end
end
```

This should be a pretty familiar pattern, with the exception of the session(:post_draft) session variable. We'll get to that in a minute, but you can probably begin to guess what's happening.

Here's the associated view. This view uses the new Rails 1.1 form_for() method. If you're not using Rails 1.1 or higher, you'll need to adjust it to use the old-style Rails form helpers.

AutomaticallySaveADraft/app/views/posts/new.rhtml

```
<% form_for :post, @post,
            :url => { :action => "new" },
            :html => {:id => 'post_form'} do |f| %>
  Title: <%= f.text_field :title %><br/>
  Body: <%= f.text_area :body %><br/>
  <%= submit_tag "Save Post" %>
<% end %>
<div id='draft-message' style='color:red;'>
</div>
<%= observe_form 'post_form',
                 :url => {:action => 'save_draft'},
                 :update => 'draft-message',
                 :frequency => 30  %>
```

This is not a remarkable form. What *is* interesting is the code that follows the form definition. We have an empty *<div>* tag named draft-message and a form observer that updates this *<div>* with its results. Every 30 seconds, the contents of the form get sent to this action:

AutomaticallySaveADraft/app/controllers/posts_controller.rb

```
def save_draft
  session[:post_draft] = Post.new(params[:post])
  render :text => "<i>draft saved at #{Time.now}</i>"
end
```

Simple but effective. The save_draft() action saves the form's contents in session as a Post object and then renders a message (which fills our previously empty draft-message HTML *<div>*) alerting the user that a draft has been saved.

Looking back at our new() action, we can see that the following line uses this Post object from session if it exists, otherwise instantiating a new one:

```
@post = session[:post_draft] || Post.new
```

When the Post is finally submitted, the new() action clears it from session.

Now you can load the form, type some thoughts into it, and wait for the draft message to appear. It's now safe to go surf the Web before submitting the form. You can return to it, and all your musings will still be there, ready to unleash on the world.

Validating Non–Active Record Objects

You have non-database-backed model objects that require validations. You'd like to reuse the Active Record validation framework to declare how these objects should be validated. You also want to use the helpers error_messages_on() and error_messages_for() in your views.

How do you make your custom model objects work with Active Record validations?

The Active Record validations framework is implemented inside a module that is mixed into ActiveRecord::Base. The module contains all the code required to declare validations, actually validate, and manage and report validation error messages. In an ideal world, reusing this functionality would be as simple as this:

```
class MySpecialModel < SomeOtherInfrastructure
  include ActiveRecord::Validations
end
```

Sadly, this world isn't ideal, and we can't reuse Active Record's validation framework *quite* so easily. If you were to try to use the code as is, you would see that when ActiveRecord::Validations is mixed into MySpecialModel, it tries to alias a few save-related methods that we haven't defined. It will also fail when we call the valid?() method because of an attempt to call one or more dynamically generated missing methods.

If you were to follow this trail of errors, patching as you go, you might come up with the following module:

`ValidatingNonARObjects/lib/validateable.rb`

```
module Validateable
  [:save, :save!, :update_attribute].each{|attr| define_method(attr){}}
  def method_missing(symbol, *params)
    if(symbol.to_s =~ /(.*)_before_type_cast$/)
      send($1)
    end
  end
end
```

```
    def self.append_features(base)
      super
      base.send(:include, ActiveRecord::Validations)
    end
  end
```

Place this module in lib/validateable.rb, and you can mix it into your own non–Active Record models as needed. Now, in terms of validation and error reporting, your model is virtually indistinguishable from a real Active Record model.

Here's an example of a non–Active Record model that supports Active Record validations:

ValidatingNonARObjects/app/models/person.rb

```
class Person
  include Validateable
  attr_accessor :age
  validates_numericality_of :age
end
```

To trigger the validations, just call the model's valid?() method in your controllers. This will both return true or false depending on whether the object passes validations and will populate the model's errors() so that they can be accessed from the Active Record view helpers.

Here's an example of how you can interact with the validations from the Rails console:

```
chad> ruby script/console
>> person = Person.new
=> #<Person:0x236e180>
>> person.age = "NOT A NUMBER"
=> "NOT A NUMBER"
>> person.valid?
=> false
>> person.errors
=> #<ActiveRecord::Errors:0x236b430 ...@age="NOT A NUMBER",
@errors=#<ActiveRecord::Errors:0x236b430 ...>>,
@errors={"age"=>["is not a number"]}>
>> person.age = 30
=> 30
>> person.valid?
=> true
>> person.errors
=> #<ActiveRecord::Errors:0x236b430 @base=#<Person:0x236e180 @age=30..>
```

Ruby, being as dynamic as it is, lets us do a lot of tricks to let our objects behave however we like. This is both powerful and dangerous. In this case, we're relying on intimate knowledge of the internals of Active Record's validation support to make things work. The problem with this approach is that if the internal behavior of Active Record changes in an incompatible way, our validation shim will stop working. That's OK if you're expecting it and you know how to fix it. If not, you might want to make your own validator.

Easy HTML Whitelists

Credit

This recipe was written by beta book reader Sean Mountcastle based on an idea posted in the book's forum by Koen Eijsvogels.

Problem

You want to allow your users to use certain HTML tags in their input while restricting all other HTML tags. This can help combat problems such as users creating accidental formatting problems on your site or more malicious issues such as comment spam.

Solution

You can go about implementing whitelist functionality in two ways. You can filter a user's input as it is collected, saving your filtered version to the database. Or you can filter user-entered text only when it's being displayed. We'll choose the latter, because when things go wrong it's much better to have a record of what the user actually entered as you attempt to troubleshoot.

We'll accomplish this task by creating a helper to be used from our views. We'll call it whitelist(). Create a new file called text_helper.rb in the directory lib/rails_patch/text_helper.rb, and add the following code:

EasyHTMLWhitelists/lib/rails_patch/text_helper.rb

```ruby
module ActionView
  module Helpers
    module TextHelper
      ALLOWED_TAGS = %w(a img) unless defined?(ALLOWED_TAGS)

      def whitelist(html)
        # only do this if absolutely necessary
        if html.index("<")
          tokenizer = HTML::Tokenizer.new(html)
          new_text = ""

          while token = tokenizer.next
            node = HTML::Node.parse(nil, 0, 0, token, false)
            new_text << if node === HTML::Tag && ALLOWED_TAGS.include?(node.name)
                          node.to_s
```

```
                    else
                      node.to_s.gsub(/</,  "&amp;LT;")
                    end
            end

            html = new_text
          end
          html
        end
      end
    end
end
```

This code adds the helper directly to the ActionView::Helpers::TextHelper module, which is where the other similar helpers that come with Rails are defined. This makes the helper available to any view in our application. You'll notice that this helper uses the HTML::Tokenizer class. This is a simple HTML parser that ships with Rails. The basic flow is that we parse a chunk of text (but only if it appears to have any HTML tags in it), and we replace the opening < symbol of any nonlisted HTML tag with the string &LT;.

Now we need to make this helper available to our application. The easiest way to accomplish this is to add the following line to the end of your config/environment.rb:

```
require_dependency 'rails_patch/text_helper'
```

After restarting your application, the whitelist() method should be available from all your views. Anywhere you want to whitelist data from a user, you can call:

```
<%= whitelist(@the_data) %>
```

Discussion

In this recipe we are taking advantage of the fact that classes (and modules, in this case) in Ruby are open by patching our own method into Rail's TextHelper module. This is a technique known as *monkey patching*. Alternatively, we could have defined this helper in our application's application_helper.rb file. Either way works, but doing it this way enables us to simply lift and drop the single file to use it in another application.

If you want to allow more tags than just anchors and images, add the additional tags to %w() in following line:

```
ALLOWED_TAGS = %w(a img) unless defined?(ALLOWED_TAGS)
```

Also See

You can see further examples of monkey patching in the source code for the Typo weblog where it patches ActiveRecord::Base and also Action-Controller::Components.

Adding Simple Web Services to Your Actions

You need to access the same business logic via a web browser from posts, an XML service, and Ajax requests. How do you cleanly support multiple sets of view logic within the same action?

* Rails 1.1 or higher

The following simple action creates a new Contact row in the database. It follows the fairly typical pattern of saving the contact and then redirecting to a page that lists all contacts.

AddDeadSimpleWebServiceSupportToExistingActions/app/controllers/contacts_controller.rb

```ruby
def create
  @contact = Contact.new(params[:contact])
  if @contact.save
    flash[:notice] = 'Contact was successfully created.'
    redirect_to :action => 'list'
  else
    render :action => 'new'
  end
end
```

What if the client were posting XML instead of the usual encoded data? And now what if we wanted to change the output based on what kind of client was accessing the action?

We'll start with the first question, because it's the easiest. How could we modify this action to accept XML? What if we had, say, the following Java program making a post from a legacy system to a new Rails application?

AddDeadSimpleWebServiceSupportToExistingActions/CommandLinePost.java

```java
import java.io.BufferedReader;
import java.net.URLConnection;
import java.net.URL;
import java.io.InputStreamReader;
import java.io.OutputStreamWriter;
public class CommandLinePost {

  private static void usage()
  {
    System.err.println("usage: java CommandLinePost <url>");
    System.exit(1);
  }

  public static void main(String args[])
  {
    if(args.length > 2)
        usage();
    String endPoint = args[0];
    try {
        String data = "<contact>" +
                      "<name>Kurt Weill</name>" +
                      "<phone>501-555-2222</phone>" +
                      "</contact>";

        URL url = new URL(endPoint);
        URLConnection conn = url.openConnection();
        conn.setRequestProperty("Content-Type", "application/xml");
        conn.setDoOutput(true);
        OutputStreamWriter wr =
                new OutputStreamWriter(conn.getOutputStream());
        wr.write(data);
        wr.flush();

        BufferedReader rd =
            new BufferedReader(new InputStreamReader(conn.getInputStream()));
        String line;
        while ((line = rd.readLine()) != null) {
            // Imagine this was putting the data back into a legacy
            // Java system.  For simplicity's sake, we'll just print
            // it here.
            System.out.println(line);
        }
        wr.close();
        rd.close();
    } catch (Exception e) {
        e.printStackTrace();
    }
  }
}
```

How do we modify our action to accept XML input like this and parse it into a form that we can work with? We don't.

By default, any POST made with a content type of application/xml will be parsed by the Rails built-in XmlSimple class and converted into a familiar hash of parameters that will be available, as always, via the params method in your controller. Rails uses simple but effective rules for translating the XML into a hash. If your root element is (as it is in this case) *<contact>*, a parameter will be available via params(:contact). If the *<contact>* tag contains a set of children, it will be converted into an array in the params list. Otherwise, as in this case, it will be converted into a hash with its child element names as keys.

So if you construct your XML the way Rails expects it to be constructed, the parameters will be populated exactly as if they had been submitted via an HTML form.

Let's move on to the second question we started with: how do we render a different response depending on what kind of client is accessing our action? We could hack something together where different clients pass a special parameter. Or we could inspect the HTTP USER_AGENT field if it's set. We could make our judgment based on the content type of the input to our action.

But there's a cleaner way. The HTTP specification supports a header field called *Accept*. In this field, a client can list all of the MIME types (technically called *media ranges* in this context) it is capable of accepting. So, to cook up a simple example, a browser might pass something like text/html,text/plain to indicate that either of these formats is OK.

Clients can also pass wildcards such as text/* or even */*. The server should then deliver content of the *most specific* type requested (that the server is capable of returning). It's also possible for clients to include a parameter, q, appended to each content type and connected by a semicolon. This is called the *quality* parameter and can be used to further specify an order of preference for the media ranges reported.

The advantage of this approach is that it uses the HTTP standard in the way it was intended. Many HTTP clients support this behavior, and it's easy to code an Accept header into your web service clients. The disadvantage here is that, as many standards can be, the logic to implement this would be far more complex than our initial simple hack ideas.

Thankfully, as of Rails 1.1, this logic is already integrated into the framework. Via a new method, respond_to(), it's trivial to set up a single action to respond to various media ranges and, therefore, client types. Here's a revised version of our create() action from before:

AddDeadSimpleWebServiceSupportToExistingActions/app/controllers/contacts_controller.rb

```ruby
def create
  @contact = Contact.create(params[:contact])
  respond_to do |wants|
    wants.html do
      flash[:notice] = 'Contact was successfully created.'
      redirect_to :action => 'list'
    end
    wants.xml  do
      render(:xml => @contact.to_xml, :status => "201 Created")
    end
    wants.js
  end
end
```

The new version of our action behaves similarly to the last one if the client expects HTML. However, if the client expects XML, it sets the HTTP status code to 201 (which means, appropriately, *created*) and then uses the new to_xml() method on our model to render XML to the client. The to_xml() method renders XML that follows the same basic convention that the XML input mechanism expects. Since we used the :xml option when we called render(), the content type of the response is automatically set to application/xml for us.

Finally, if the client expects JavaScript (as would be the case with an asynchronous request generated by the Rails built-in Prototype library), no special code is invoked, which means the default Rails behavior is in effect, and the action will fall through to render a template called create. This would be useful for Ajax actions for which you would like to use RJS[33] templates.

Note that for this behavior to be enabled for our client, we'd have to add the Accept header to our client program. Here's the Java code to set the client from our earlier example to accept XML:

```java
conn.setRequestProperty("Accept", "application/xml");
```

That's it! If we recompile our Java code and run it against our create() action, we should receive a nice, usable XML response.

---

[33]For more information on RJS, see Recipe 6, *Update Multiple Elements with One Ajax Request*, on page 29.

If the default parameter parsing rules aren't sufficient for your needs, you can define your own. For example, if we wanted to parse RSS documents differently than other XML document types, we could define our own parameter parser in our config/environment.rb like this (borrowed and corrected from the Rails API docs):

```
mime_type = Mime::Type.lookup('application/rss+xml')
ActionController::Base.param_parsers[mime_type] = Proc.new do
  |data|
    node = REXML::Document.new(data)
    { node.root.name => node.root }
end
```

Part VI

Email Recipes

Send Gracefully Degrading Rich-Content Emails

Despite the historic hoopla over the World Wide Web, the real killer app of the Internet has always been email. Even in the ultrahip Web 2.0 world, email is taking on an ever-increasing role in information dissemination. Web 2.0 applications are about making things easier for the user. And with the Web's information fire hose showing no sign of letting up, receiving information by email makes it easier for the user to keep up with what's happening in each of many web applications that he or she may be subscribed to.

That said, the Web has spoiled all of us email users. We're so used to the rich experience of using a well-designed HTML-based application that the plain-text emails that suited us in the past look dull by comparison. It's so much harder to make out what's important in a plain-text message. So email gets richer and richer as time goes by.

But, then again, the growth in cell phone use is staggering. And, with email and SMS capabilities, cell phones have become first-class citizens in the world of Internet applications. And the easiest, most ubiquitous way to get a message to a cell phone? That's right. Email.

So we have these finicky users with their rich mail clients and their cell phones with bare-bones text interfaces. How do we build our applications so that we can send one mail without having to know whether it's going to a cell phone or the Apple Mail client?

The Internet Engineering Task Force (IETF) has defined a standard MIME type called multipart/alternative that is designed to solve this problem. Messages with the multipart/alternative MIME type are structured exactly like messages of type multipart/mixed, which is the typical MIME type of a mail message with one or more attachments. But, though structurally identical, multipart/alternative messages are *interpreted* differently by their receivers.

Each part of a multipart/alternative-encoded message is assumed to be an alternative rendering of the same information. Upon receiving a message in the multipart/alternative format, a mail client can then choose which format suits it best.

We have two main ways to send multipart/alternative messages with Rails. Let's explore them.

Assuming we've already generated an application to work with, we'll generate a new mailer class to hold our code:

```
chad> ruby script/generate mailer Notifier multipart_alternative
exists  app/models/
   :              :
```

We also asked the generator to set up multipart_alternative() as a mail method for us. We'll edit this method to add our own logic. The multipart_alternative() method should look like the following:

GracefullyDegradingRichTextEmails/app/models/notifier.rb

```
Line 1  def multipart_alternative(recipient, name, sent_at = Time.now)
   -       subject      "Something for everyone."
   -       recipients   recipient
   -       from         'barnam@chadfowler.com'
   5       sent_on      sent_at
   -       content_type "multipart/alternative"
   -
   -       part :content_type => "text/plain",
   -         :body => render_message("multipart_alternative_plain", :name => name)
   10
   -       part :content_type => "text/html",
   -         :body => render_message("multipart_alternative", :name => name)
   -     end
```

Line 6 sets the MIME type of the message to multipart/alternative. Then, on lines 8 and 11, just as we would in a message of MIME type multipart/mixed, we add additional parts to the message, setting the content type of each. The calls to render_message() specify the extensionless names of view templates stored under app/views/notifier.

The plain-text version of the view looks like this:

GracefullyDegradingRichTextEmails/app/views/notifier/multipart_alternative_plain.rhtml

```
Hi <%= @name %>!

This is a plain-text message.  Enjoy!
```

And, true to the intention of the word *alternative*, the HTML version looks like this:

GracefullyDegradingRichTextEmails/app/views/notifier/multipart_alternative.rhtml

```
<html>
  <body>
        <h1>Hi <%= @name %>!</h1>
        This is a rich-text message.  Enjoy!
  </body>
</html>
```

That's all there is to it! We can now deliver a message and see how it looks:

```
chad> ruby script/runner 'Notifier.deliver_multipart_alternative( \
        "Chad Fowler <chad@chadfowler.com>", \
        "Chad")'
```

On my Macintosh, this message looks like this:

On the console-based mutt email client (http://www.mutt.org/), the same message looks like this:

Now that we've gotten it to work, let's make it easier. I don't know about you, but when I see all those calls to the part() method, explicitly setting up the pieces of this message, it just doesn't look very Rails-like. Why can't it be like the rest of Rails and just *know* what I'm trying to do?

It can. Let's create another method in the Notifier class to demonstrate:

GracefullyDegradingRichTextEmails/app/models/notifier.rb

```
def implicit_multipart(recipient, name, sent_at = Time.now)
  subject      "Something for everyone."
  recipients   recipient
  from         'barnam@chadfowler.com'
  sent_on      sent_at
  body(:name => name)
end
```

Where did all the code go? The answer to that question lies in the names of the corresponding view files. The same views from the previous example have been stored in the directory app/views/notifier/ as implicit_multipart.text.html.rhtml and implicit_multipart.text.plain.rhtml, respectively. Action Mailer sees these templates, recognizes the pattern in their file names, automatically sets the MIME type of the message to multipart/alternative, and adds each rendered view with the content type in its file name.

> As I write this, there are known incompatibilities between Rails and the Localization Plugin. Until these are sorted out, the implicit, filename-based multipart/alternative technique will not work correctly. You'll need to do things explicitly as in the first example.

Since Rails makes it so easy to send multipart/alternative-formatted messages, don't risk sending HTML to a cell phone again.

Discussion

Reader Peter Michaux points out that, going beyond the simple HTML example here, you might want to use images and CSS in your HTML-formatted mails. You need to consider a number of issues when doing this. CampaignMonitor has an excellent write-up available at http://www.campaignmonitor.com/blog/archives/2006/03/a_guide_to_css_1.html.

Testing Incoming Email

You are developing an application that processes incoming email messages. Your development process is too slow and complicated if you have to send an email and wait every time you make a change to the email processor. Some of your team's developers don't have the ability to easily start up an email server on their development computers, so until now, development of the email-processing component has been limited to developers whose computers have a working email server. You need a working test harness that will let you test your email-processing code.

Support for testing incoming email with Action Mailer isn't as explicit as it is with outgoing email. There are test harnesses in place to access all the mail you've sent with Action Mailer, but there are no such explicit clues as to how to test *incoming* mail processing.

Fortunately, though not quite as obvious as testing outgoing email, it's not any more difficult to test incoming email. To understand it, let's quickly review how to set up an incoming email processor. For the sake of a brief discussion, we'll assume we're using sendmail and procmail. For detailed information on setting up your system to process mail with Rails, see Chapter 19 of *Agile Web Development with Rails* [TH05] or http://wiki.rubyonrails.com/rails/pages/HowToReceiveEmailsWithActionMailer.

On a typical sendmail system, you can set up a .forward file in your home directory, specifying an email address to which to forward your incoming mail. If, instead of an email address, you specify a pipe symbol (|) followed by the name of a program, incoming email will be *piped* to that program's standard input for processing. A simple example .forward file might look like the following.

```
"|procmail"
```

The procmail program will then look in the user's home directory for a file called .procmailrc, which will tell procmail how to process incoming mail based on a configurable set of rules. We won't go into what those rules mean here, but suffice it to say that the following .procmailrc file tells procmail to pipe all incoming email to a Rails application called mail_receiver—specifically to its Receiver class. (We've split the command onto multiple lines to make it fit the page.)

```
:0 c
*
| cd /home/listener/mail_receiver && \
    /usr/bin/ruby script/runner 'Receiver.receive(STDIN.read)'
```

This is where it gets interesting from the perspective of writing tests:

```
Receiver.receive(STDIN.read)
```

The Action Mailer mail receiver simply accepts a raw email message, which in this case we've configured to come in via the application's standard input. What this means is that to run the mail receiver in a test, all we have to do is get the raw text of an email message and pass it into our mail receiver's receive() method.

Let's stop talking about it and start cookin'!

If you're like me, your email inbox is flooded with not-to-miss business opportunities every day. Whether it's a sweet deal on a miracle diet pill or the chance to make millions of dollars just by helping someone transfer some money from one bank account to another, I'm constantly worried that I get too many emails from friends and family, and I might not notice one of these gems as a result. So to demonstrate how to test incoming email processors in Rails, we'll start on a little application to help us sort through all of these incoming opportunities to make sure we don't miss any of them.

First we'll set up a mailer using the script/generate command:

```
chad> ruby script/generate mailer Receiver
   :              :
create  app/models/receiver.rb
create  test/unit/receiver_test.rb
```

As is typical in Rails Land, the generator not only created a skeleton for our mail receiver implementation, but it set up a unit test file for us as well. Let's look at the file in its pristine form before we start spicing it up:

TestingIncomingEmail/test/unit/receiver_test_pristine.rb

```
require File.dirname(__FILE__) + '/../test_helper'
require 'receiver'
```

```
class ReceiverTest < Test::Unit::TestCase
  FIXTURES_PATH = File.dirname(__FILE__) + '/../fixtures'
  CHARSET = "utf-8"

  include ActionMailer::Quoting

  def setup
    ActionMailer::Base.delivery_method = :test
    ActionMailer::Base.perform_deliveries = true
    ActionMailer::Base.deliveries = []

    @expected = TMail::Mail.new
    @expected.set_content_type "text", "plain", { "charset" => CHARSET }
  end

  private
    def read_fixture(action)
      IO.readlines("#{FIXTURES_PATH}/receiver/#{action}")
    end

    def encode(subject)
      quoted_printable(subject, CHARSET)
    end
end
```

Most of this structure is there to support testing of outgoing email. Other than the standard Test::Unit scaffolding, the part that is most applicable to us is the read_fixture() method. It's not magic, but it gives us a clue as to how we should manage the raw email text we're going to be stuffing into our mail receiver. Namely, we can store each message in a text file under our application's test/fixtures/receiver directory. If we do that, we need call only the generated read_fixture() method and pass the returned data into our Receiver class's receive() method.

So all we need is some raw email text. Since it's just text, we could construct it by hand, but we've got spam to read, and time is money! It turns out that though most of us don't need to use it much, most email clients have the ability to show you the raw source of an email message. If you can do this with your email client, you can send yourself test emails with the desired characteristics or pull existing email from your inbox and then just copy and paste their raw source into a text file to save into your fixtures directory.

Since we're going to be writing code to help us sort through the many money-making opportunities in our inboxes, I'll pull out a relevant email. The text of the raw email is as follows:

> ### Thunderbird
>
> If your client doesn't give you the option of viewing a message's source, try Thunderbird (http://www.mozilla.com). It's free and cross-platform and has the the ability to show you a message's raw source. Look in the View menu for Message Source.

```
Return-Path: <webmaster@elboniabank.com>
Received: from [192.168.0.100] (c-192-168-0-1.sd.o.nonex.net [192.168.0.100])
        by rasp.chadfowler.com (8.12.10/8.12.10) with ESMTP id jBLUc021232
        for <chad@chadfowler.com>; Wed, 21 Dec 2005 11:19:40 -0500
Mime-Version: 1.0 (Apple Message framework v746.2)
Content-Transfer-Encoding: 7bit
Message-Id: <E75372B2-32AD-402B-B930-5421238557921@chadfowler.com>
Content-Type: text/plain; charset=US-ASCII; format=flowed
To: chad@chadfowler.com
From: N'Dugu Wanaskamya <webmaster@elboniabank.com>
Subject: CONFIDENTIAL OPPORTUNITY
Date: Wed, 21 Dec 2005 04:19:00 -0700


Bulwayo, Republic of Elbonia.

MY PLEASURE,

This is a proposal in context but actually an appeal soliciting for your
unreserved assistance in consummating an urgent transaction requiring
maximum confidence. Though this approach appears desperate,I can assure
you that whatever questions you would need to ask or any other thing you
will need to know regarding this proposal, will be adequately answered
to give you a clearer understanding of it so as to arrive at a
successful conclusion.

No doubt this proposal will make you apprehensive, please i employ you
to observe utmost confidentiality and rest assured that this transaction
would be most profitable for both of us. Note also that we shall require
your assistance to invest our share in your country.

Thanks and Regards,
Mr. N'Dugu Wanaskamya
First Bank of Elbonia
```

We'll save this text in a file called confidential_opportunity in the directory test/fixtures/receiver under our application's root directory. We can now write a simple test to make sure things are working as expected. Add the following to your receiver_test.rb file (above the methods that are declared private):

TestingIncomingEmail/test/unit/receiver_test.rb

```
def test_fixtures_are_working
  email_text = read_fixture("confidential_opportunity").join
  assert_match(/opportunity/i, email_text)
end
```

This is just a smoke test to make sure we can get to the fixture and that it produces a String that can be fed into our mail receiver. Run the test. It should work. If it doesn't, you probably have a file in the wrong place. If you retrace your steps, you'll find it in a jiffy:

```
chad> ruby test/unit/receiver_test.rb
Loaded suite test/unit/receiver_test
Started
.
Finished in 0.068315 seconds.

1 tests, 1 assertions, 0 failures, 0 errors
```

Now that we have the safety net set up, we can start actually writing some code. The goal of our application is to somehow separate the emails we care about from the ones that just clutter up our mailboxes. To that end, we'll create a simple model to store messages and to rate them numerically. The higher the rating, the more "interesting" the message is. We won't look at the details of the data model here, but just keep in mind that we have a model named Mail (with a corresponding mails table) that has the expected subject, body, sender, etc., attributes as well as a numeric rating attribute.

We'll start small and test the simple processing of a message to make sure it gets added to the database. Let's write the test first:

TestingIncomingEmail/test/unit/receiver_test.rb

```
def test_incoming_email_gets_added_to_database
  count_before = Mail.count
  email_text = read_fixture("confidential_opportunity").join
  Receiver.receive(email_text)
  assert_equal(count_before + 1, Mail.count)
  assert_equal("CONFIDENTIAL OPPORTUNITY", Mail.find(:all).last.subject)
end
```

This test will fail, since our mail receiver is unimplemented. Go ahead and run it. Watch it fail now, and it'll feel better when it passes.

```
chad> rake test_units
(in /Users/chad/src/FR_RR/Book/code/TestingIncomingEmail)
/usr/local/bin/ruby -Ilib:test
"/usr/local/lib/ruby/.../rake_test_loader.rb" "test/unit/mail_test.rb"
 "test/unit/receiver_test.rb"
```

```
Loaded suite /usr/local/lib/ruby/.../rake_test_loader
Started
..F
Finished in 0.157008 seconds.

  1) Failure: test_incoming_email_gets_added_to_database(ReceiverTest)
     [./test/unit/receiver_test.rb:31]:
<3> expected but was <2>.

3 tests, 3 assertions, 1 failures, 0 errors
```

Now we'll make it pass. Let's implement the mail receiver. Edit your app/models/receiver.rb to look like this:

TestingIncomingEmail/app/models/receiver_2.rb

```ruby
class Receiver < ActionMailer::Base
  def receive(email)
    Mail.create(:subject => email.subject, :body    => email.body,
                :sender  => email.from,    :rating  => 0)
  end
end
```

We simply create a new instance of the Mail class and populate it with the contents of the incoming email. But we have the rating() set to 0. Let's put in a simple rule to increase the rating of any email that contains the word *opportunity*. Again we'll start with the test:

TestingIncomingEmail/test/unit/receiver_test.rb

```ruby
def test_email_containing_opportunity_rates_higher
  email_text = read_fixture("confidential_opportunity").join
  Receiver.receive(email_text)
  assert(Mail.find_by_subject("CONFIDENTIAL OPPORTUNITY").rating > 0)
end
```

And the simplest possible implementation would look like some variation of this:

TestingIncomingEmail/app/models/receiver_2a.rb

```ruby
class Receiver < ActionMailer::Base
  def receive(email)
    rating = 0
    if(email.subject + email.body =~ /opportunity/i)
      rating += 1
    end

    Mail.create(:subject => email.subject, :body    => email.body,
                :sender  => email.from,    :rating  => rating)
  end
end
```

It's easy to see how you could continue to iterate this way, decreasing a message's rating if it's from a friend or family member or increasing the rating if the mail's origin is the Republic of Elbonia (known to be a hotbed of high-return financial opportunities for the open-minded entrepreneur). We'll leave you to season to taste in this regard. But what if you need to check a message's attachments? How do you test that?

Mail attachments, though usually made of nontextual materials, are encoded as text for transfer over the Internet. This is lucky for us, because it means we don't have to change our approach at all. The following is what the raw text of an email with an attachment would look like:

```
TestingIncomingEmail/test/fixtures/receiver/latest_screensaver
```

```
Return-Path: <chad@chadfowler.com>
Received: from [192.168.0.100] (c-24-8-92-53.hsd1.co.comcast.net [24.8.92.53])
        by ns1.chadfowler.com (8.12.10/8.12.10) with ESMTP id jBN2fhUc007473
        for <chad@chadfowler.com>; Thu, 22 Dec 2005 21:41:43 -0500
Mime-Version: 1.0 (Apple Message framework v746.2)
To: chad@chadfowler.com
Message-Id: <689771CD-862F-49CB-B0E8-94C1517EB5C5@chadfowler.com>
Content-Type: multipart/mixed; boundary=Apple-Mail-1-231420468
From: Chad Fowler <chad@chadfowler.com>
Subject: The latest new screensaver!
Date: Thu, 22 Dec 2005 19:28:46 -0700
X-Mailer: Apple Mail (2.746.2)
X-Spam-Checker-Version: SpamAssassin 2.63 (2004-01-11) on ns1.chadfowler.com
X-Spam-Level: *
X-Spam-Status: No, hits=1.2 required=5.0 tests=BAYES_01,RCVD_IN_DYNABLOCK,
        RCVD_IN_SORBS autolearn=no version=2.63


-Apple-Mail-1-231420468
Content-Transfer-Encoding: 7bit
Content-Type: text/plain;
        charset=US-ASCII;
        delsp=yes;
        format=flowed

Hey bro, I thought you would like to see this. It's the latest new
screensaver. Everyone at the office loves it!


-Apple-Mail-1-231420468
Content-Transfer-Encoding: base64
Content-Type: application/zip;
        x-unix-mode=0644;
        name="screensaver.zip"
```

```
Content-Disposition: attachment;
        filename=screensaver.zip
```

iVBORw0KGgoAAAANSUhEUgAAABAAAAFTCAIAAAC/KhtAAAAB6GlDQ1BJQOMgUHJvZmlsZQAAeJyV
kbFrFrE3EUxz+/O7UVS9QapEOHHyjSQlJCglC7mJigrUQINWqS7Xo5k4O7y4+7S2vAVaSrQv8BQcS1
QkUHMzroIKIWHV3EOUIXCedwDR1KKD548HlfeLz3vg/OmqGUowGuF/qrN67JWr0hJ74wxU10sOTa
...
4Bv4JE4RyYntVaLtouSfBg28b6Dgse+7vFJvL6V/J+g+lnVdl2XZtu2eGIZhmqaU0umGlJLW+ulI
rfWRPj2ptWatvaStta21rzufwHsfY7yAGKP3/jkQkVKKMeZojTGllMuiE+j7fp7no53nue/774CI
5JydcyLinMs5y62uQClVa+26rtaqlPoZiEgIYRzHEML9SEQe//G3AgAAAAAAAAAAAAAAAAAAAAAA
AAAAAAAAAAAAAAAAAAAAAAAAAAAAAAAAAAAAAAAMBfAe8r3B9sCnIPeQAAAABJRU5ErkJg
gg==

```
-Apple-Mail-1-231420468-
```

If we were interested in tracking screensavers and other similar attachments that were sent to us at random, we could add another rule and assert in our tests that an attached zip file increases the rating() of an email:

`TestingIncomingEmail/test/unit/receiver_test.rb`

```ruby
def test_zip_file_increases_rating
  email_text = read_fixture("latest_screensaver").join
  Receiver.receive(email_text)
  assert(Mail.find_by_subject("The latest new screensaver!").rating > 0)
end
```

We could then add the code to our mail receiver to check for zip files, and the test would run:

`TestingIncomingEmail/app/models/receiver_3.rb`

```ruby
class Receiver < ActionMailer::Base
  def receive(email)
    rating = 0
    if(email.subject + email.body =~ /opportunity/i)
      rating += 1
    end
    if email.has_attachments?
      email.attachments.each do |attachment|
        rating += 1 if attachment.original_filename =~ /zip$/i
      end
    end
    Mail.create(:subject => email.subject, :body    => email.body,
                :sender  => email.from,    :rating  => rating)
  end
end
```

As we continued to expand this application, we would want to refactor it into a more flexible set of rules, and with our tests in place, we would be in great shape to do just that.

Sending Email with Attachments

You need to send emails with attachments from your Rails application.

Action Mailer makes it easy to send rich email with attachments. Let's walk through a simple example.

First we'll generate a controller to provide an interface to the user. Let's call it SpamController:

```
chad> ruby script/generate controller Spam
exists  app/controllers/
   :          :
```

Next we'll generate a mailer. We'll call our mailer Spammer and have the generator create a single mail method called spam_with_attachment():

```
chad> ruby script/generate mailer Spammer spam_with_attachment
   :          :
create  app/views/spammer/spam_with_attachment.rhtml
create  test/fixtures/spammer/spam_with_attachment
```

We'll look at the implementation of the mailer shortly. First let's focus on the user interface.

We'll start with a mail form. We'll put it in the file index.rhtml in the app/views/spam/ directory. The form accepts a name, a recipient email address, and a file upload. Notice that the call to form_tag() declares the form to be multipart. This is necessary in order to submit both the normal form data and the uploaded files. Here's the code for the form:

SendingEmailsWithAttachments/app/views/spam/index.rhtml

```
<%= form_tag( {:action => "spam"}, :multipart => true) %>
  <label for="name">Name of recipient:</label>
  <%= text_field_tag "name" %><br />
  <label for="email">Email address to send to:</label>
  <%= text_field_tag "email" %><br />
  <label for="file">File to upload:</label>
```

```
<%= file_field_tag "file" %><br />
<%= submit_tag "Spam!" %>
<%= end_form_tag %>
```

As you can see, the form submits to an action called spam(). The spam() action's primary job is to delegate to an Action Mailer class. We'll do that and just redirect back to the form. After all, we've called this thing Spammer so it's safe to assume that its users will want to send one mail after another.

Here's the entire SpamController class:

SendingEmailsWithAttachments/app/controllers/spam_controller.rb

```
class SpamController < ApplicationController
  def spam
    Spammer.deliver_spam_with_attachment(params[:name],
                                         params[:email],
                                         params[:file])

    redirect_to :action => "index"
  end
end
```

We're almost there. All that's left is to implement the actual mailer. The mailer is implemented as a pair of files: the mailer itself and the template it uses to render a message body. The view is a dead-simple ERb template, named after the send method on the mailer class, in this case spam_with_attachment.rhtml.

SendingEmailsWithAttachments/app/views/spammer/spam_with_attachment.rhtml

```
Hey <%= @name %>,

I thought you'd appreciate this file.

Regards,
Chad
```

The real work happens in the mailer class. Here's what ours looks like:

SendingEmailsWithAttachments/app/models/spammer.rb

```
Line 1  class Spammer < ActionMailer::Base
    -     def spam_with_attachment(name, email, file)
    -       @subject    = 'Have a Can of Spam!'
    -       @body       = {:name => name}
    5       @recipients = email
    -       @from       = 'spam@chadfowler.com'
    -       unless file.blank?
    -         attachment :body => file.read, :filename => file.original_filename
    -       end
    10    end
    -   end
```

The method starts by setting instance variables that Action Mailer uses to determine things like who it should send a message to and what the subject should be. The @body variable contains a hash of values that will be visible as local variable to our view template.

Line 8 and its surrounding unless() block contain the code for adding the attachment. The :body parameter contains the actual attachment data, which in this case is read from the multipart form submission from the user's browser. We could have also included an optional :content_type parameter, which would have set the MIME type for the attachment in the mail message. Without an explicit :content_type, Rails will default to sending a MIME type of text/plain. Most modern mail clients will make a best guess of MIME type based on file name, so though it's certainly cleaner to send the MIME type, it's not always necessary.

If we needed to, we could have attached multiple files here. Each successive call to the attachment() method creates another attachment in the message.

Discussion

Rails 1.0 shipped with a bug, affecting mail with both an attachment and a message body. The inclusion of an attachment in a message would cause the message's template not to be loaded, resulting in an empty message body. If you encounter this problem, you need to either upgrade to an official post-1.0 release of Rails or use Edge Rails.

Also See

Austin Ziegler's MIME::Types library[34] makes it extremely easy to find the correct MIME type for a given file name. MIME::Types is installable via RubyGems:

```
chad> gem install mime-types
```

---

[34]http://mime-types.rubyforge.org/

Handling Bounced Email

Thanks to Shaun Fanning for the idea for this recipe.

Problem

Your web application, as most do these days, occasionally sends email to its users. Since you are sending the mail programmatically, probably from a system account, it's difficult to know whether the invitations, reminders, or various other notifications they've sent have actually arrived at their intended destinations. A mistyped email address or a network issue could result in your users *thinking* they've caused the system to send a message when in fact the message is never delivered.

Although it's not always possible to track the *successful* delivery of an email, we can usually tell when one has *failed* to be delivered. Mail servers send bounce messages when they cannot deliver a message they receive.

How can we programmatically use these bounce messages to notify our systems and our users of delivery failures?

Solution

Not surprisingly, the Internet Powers That Be already thought of this scenario and helped to address it back in 1996 with the introduction of the Internet Engineering Task Force RFC documents numbered 1891[35] and 1892.[36] Don't be alarmed if this sounds like a form you'd have to fill out at tax time. We won't make you read the RFCs.

In a nutshell, RFC 1892 defines a MIME type called multipart/report for sending reports that are relevant to a mail system. If you look at the source of a bounced email in your inbox, you'll see what it looks like. The syntax of an RFC 1892–compliant message is exactly like the more

---

[35]http://www.ietf.org/rfc/rfc1891.txt?number=1891: SMTP Service Extension for Delivery Status Notifications

[36]http://www.ietf.org/rfc/rfc1892.txt?number=1892: The Multipart/Report Content Type for the Reporting of Mail System Administrative Messages

familiar multipart/mixed that you use when you send mail attachments. This means that a multipart/report-encoded message is a *container* for other submessages that would have their own MIME types.

That's where RFC 1891 comes in. It defines a format for messages describing the delivery status of messages. Failure, for example, is a delivery status that can be reported by a RFC 1891–encoded message.

Let's look at the source of an actual bounced message. I sent a message to an email address that I knew didn't exist, and when I received the bounce notification, I viewed the message's source in my mail client. Here it is in pieces, starting with the headers:

HandlingBouncedMail/bounce_example.txt

```
Return-Path: <MAILER-DAEMON@ns1.chadfowler.com>
Received: from localhost (localhost)
        by ns1.chadfowler.com (8.12.10/8.12.10) id k25GHX28007404;
        Sun, 5 Mar 2006 11:17:33 -0500
Date: Sun, 5 Mar 2006 11:17:33 -0500
From: Mail Delivery Subsystem <MAILER-DAEMON@ns1.chadfowler.com>
Message-Id: <200603051617.k25GHX28007404@ns1.chadfowler.com>
To: <Chad@chadfowler.com>
MIME-Version: 1.0
Content-Type: multipart/report; report-type=delivery-status;
        boundary="k25GHX28007404.1141575453/ns1.chadfowler.com"
Subject: Returned mail: see transcript for details
Auto-Submitted: auto-generated (failure)
```

Notice the line that sets the Content-Type of the message. If you've dealt with multipart/mixed messages in the past, you'll recognize the pattern here. The Content-Type is set, the type of report is specified, and the boundary is declared. This boundary will be used by the receiver of the mail as the delimiter for breaking the message into its parts.

Next is a human-readable text message. This is the part you usually see in your mail client when you receive a bounced email:

HandlingBouncedMail/bounce_example.txt

```
-k25GHX28007404.1141575453/ns1.chadfowler.com

The original message was received at Sun, 5 Mar 2006 11:17:22 -0500
from c-67-190-70-79.hsd1.co.comcast.net [67.190.70.79]

    --- The following addresses had permanent fatal errors ---
<randomaddress@pragprog.com>
    (reason: 550 <randomaddress@pragprog.com>: Recipient address rejected:
        User unknown in local recipient table)
```

```
    --- Transcript of session follows ---
... while talking to mail.pragprog.com.:
>>> DATA
<<< 550 <randomaddress@pragprog.com>: Recipient address rejected:
        User unknown in local recipient table
550 5.1.1 <randomaddress@pragprog.com>... User unknown
<<< 554 Error: no valid recipients
```

You've seen that one before, and we're not going to have to do anything with it. The part we're most interested in is the following:

`HandlingBouncedMail/bounce_example.txt`

```
-k25GHX28007404.1141575453/ns1.chadfowler.com
Content-Type: message/delivery-status

Reporting-MTA: dns; ns1.chadfowler.com
Received-From-MTA: DNS; c-67-190-70-79.hsd1.co.comcast.net
Arrival-Date: Sun, 5 Mar 2006 11:17:22 -0500

Final-Recipient: RFC822; randomaddress@pragprog.com
Action: failed
Status: 5.1.1
Remote-MTA: DNS; mail.pragprog.com
Diagnostic-Code: SMTP; 550 <randomaddress@pragprog.com>:
    Recipient address rejected: User unknown in local recipient table
Last-Attempt-Date: Sun, 5 Mar 2006 11:17:33 -0500
```

This section is a computer-readable explanation of the status of a specific delivery attempt. All the fields here may be useful at some point, but the really important ones to us right now are the Final-Recipient and Status fields. Final-Recipient is, of course, the ultimate destination address that the message was to be delivered to, and Status is a special code (defined in RFC 1893)[37] that represents the delivery status.

We won't go into detail on the specific meanings of the codes here, but what you're going to want to know is that the first segment of the dot-separated code indicates the *class* of delivery status. Namely:

- 2.X.X means the message was successfully delivered.

- 4.X.X indicates a temporary failure to deliver the message. Later retries may still succeed. This might happen if the recipient's email server was temporarily unavailable.

- 5.X.X means that there was a delivery failure, and there will be no more attempts. That's what you get, to use our current example,

---

[37]http://www.ietf.org/rfc/rfc1893.txt?number=1893

when you attempt to send a message to a bogus email account. The receiving server definitely says, "Wrong number. Buzz off."

Finally, a multipart/report-encoded message contains the original message, including the headers that were sent with the original message. This is useful when you get a bounce message in case you can't remember what you originally sent. It's also important when programmatically processing bounced mail, because we have access to the message ID of the original mail. This is important and will be what we use to match failed deliveries with the messages we were attempting to send.

HandlingBouncedMail/bounce_example.txt

```
-k25GHX28007404.1141575453/ns1.chadfowler.com
Content-Type: message/rfc822

Return-Path: <Chad@chadfowler.com>
Received: from [192.168.0.107] (xyz.comcast.net [67.190.70.79])
        by ns1.chadfowler.com (8.12.10/8.12.10) with ESMTP id k25GH628007376
        for <randomaddress@pragprog.com>; Sun, 5 Mar 2006 11:17:22 -0500
Content-Transfer-Encoding: 7bit
Message-Id: <6624C411-80B4-40AD-AF6D-DFA5878A1A3C@chadfowler.com>
Content-Type: text/plain; charset=US-ASCII; format=flowed
To: randomaddress@pragprog.com
From: Chad Fowler <Chad@chadfowler.com>
Subject: You will never get this...
Date: Sun, 5 Mar 2006 09:16:52 -0700
X-Mailer: Apple Mail (2.746.2)

...because you don't exist.

-k25GHX28007404.1141575453/ns1.chadfowler.com-
```

OK. Now we know how bounced messages are reported, and we know what the report format looks like. We're ready to write some code. We'll start with a quick mailer, which will send out fictitious meeting reminders and will store the *fact* that the reminders were sent. Here's the mailer code:

HandlingBouncedMail/app/models/reminder.rb

```ruby
class Reminder < ActionMailer::Base
  def reminder(recipient, text)
    @subject    = 'Automated Reminder!'
    @body       = {:text => text}
    @recipients = recipient
    @from       = 'chad@chadfowler.com'
    @sent_on    = Time.now
    @headers    = {}
  end
end
```

Nothing too special. It just takes a recipient's email address and some text to send and does the needful. We invoke this mailer with the following super-simple controller code:

`HandlingBouncedMail/app/controllers/reminder_controller.rb`

```ruby
class ReminderController < ApplicationController
  def deliver
    mail = Reminder.deliver_reminder(params[:recipient], params[:text])
    Delivery.create(:message_id => mail.message_id, :recipient => params[:recipient],
                    :content => params[:text],        :status => 'Sent')
    render :text => "Message id #{mail.message_id} sent."
  end
end
```

The controller accepts the same parameters that the mailer accepts and invokes the mailer. What's notable is that it then takes the message ID from the delivered mail object and stores it in the deliveries table in our local database. This is the table we will use to keep track of all the reminder notifications we've sent and their delivery statuses. Here's the migration that defines that table:

`HandlingBouncedMail/db/migrate/001_add_deliveries_table.rb`

```ruby
class AddDeliveriesTable < ActiveRecord::Migration
  def self.up
    create_table :deliveries do |t|
      t.column :message_id, :string
      t.column :recipient, :string
      t.column :content, :text
      t.column :status, :string
    end
  end

  def self.down
    drop_table :deliveries
  end
end
```

The default generated model, Delivery, is sufficient for our needs on the Ruby side of the house.

So now we're delivering messages (or attempting to, at least) and storing enough information that if a message were to bounce back to us, we could update the status of the delivery in our local database for display to our users. Let's do that.

First we'll make a new mailer whose exclusive job it is to receive bounce messages. We'll call it BounceReceiver. Here's what our receive() method looks like:

HandlingBouncedMail/app/models/bounce_receiver.rb

```ruby
def receive(email)
  return unless email.content_type == "multipart/report"
  bounce = BouncedDelivery.from_email(email)
  msg    = Delivery.find_by_message_id(bounce.original_message_id)
  msg.update_attribute(:status, bounce.status)
end
```

Our receiver is simple. If a message is not a multipart/report, the receiver
ignores it. Otherwise, it parses the bounce notification (more on that in
a minute) and updates the delivery record with its status.

The receiver method was simple, because we hid the hard stuff away in
the BouncedDelivery class. We defined that class right in the same file
as our BounceReceiver. Here's what it looks like:

HandlingBouncedMail/app/models/bounce_receiver.rb

```ruby
Line 1  class BouncedDelivery
   -      attr_accessor :status_info, :original_message_id
   -      def self.from_email(email)
   -        returning(bounce = self.new) do
   5          status_part = email.parts.detect do |part|
   -            part.content_type == "message/delivery-status"
   -          end
   -          statuses = status_part.body.split(/\n/)
   -          bounce.status_info =  statuses.inject({}) do |hash, line|
  10            key, value = line.split(/:/)
   -            hash[key] = value.strip rescue nil
   -            hash
   -          end
   -          original_message_part = email.parts.detect do |part|
  15            part.content_type == "message/rfc822"
   -          end
   -          parsed_msg = TMail::Mail.parse(original_message_part.body)
   -          bounce.original_message_id = parsed_msg.message_id
   -        end
  20      end
   -      def status
   -        case status_info['Status']
   -        when /^5/
   -          'Failure'
  25        when /^4/
   -          'Temporary Failure'
   -        when /^2/
   -          'Success'
   -        end
  30      end
   -    end
```

The job of the BouncedDelivery class is to parse a multipart/report-encoded message into its relevant parts. That job is made substantially easier by the fact that Rails (via the bundled TMail library) does the basic parsing for us automatically.

Let's not get bogged down in the details of BouncedDelivery's implementation. We'll just walk through the major points that are essential for understanding what's happening. First, from the multiple parts of the incoming email, on line 5 we locate the part that contains the computer-readable status information. We then convert the text of the status information to a nice, convenient Hash with the block starting on line 9. Next we locate the message part that contains the original message text, and on line 17, we use TMail to parse it into an object from which we can easily grab the original message ID.

The final interesting part of the implementation is on line 21, where our status method returns a friendly status code that we'll use to update the status field of our deliveries table.

With this code deployed and configured to receive incoming mail for the account to which the bounce messages will be delivered (the account the outgoing message was *from*),[38] our receiver will update the deliveries table, so our users can easily see which messages have had delivery failures.

Though it's impossible to accurately measure which messages get *delivered* (unless, of course, you want to call all intended recipients on the phone and ask them whether they received the email), we're now at least one step closer to a feeling of confidence that when we send a message, it's not being sent to a bogus email address.

---

[38]For detailed information about setting up your system to process mail with Rails, see Chapter 19 of *Agile Web Development with Rails* [TH05].

Part VII

Appendix

Appendix A

Resources

A.1 Bibliography

[HT00]   Andrew Hunt and David Thomas. *The Pragmatic Program-
          mer: From Journeyman to Master.* Addison-Wesley, Reading,
          MA, 2000.

[TH05]   David Thomas and David Heinemeier Hansson. *Agile Web
          Development With Rails.* The Pragmatic Programmers, LLC,
          Raleigh, NC, and Dallas, TX, 2005.

A.2 Source Code

The source code in tis book is available for download from our website:

- http://pragmaticprogrammer.com/titles/fr_rr/code.html

If you are reading a PDF version of the book, you can click on the gray
lozenge above a listing to link directly to the code in that listing.

Index

Symbols

A

B

R

Facets of Ruby Series

Now that you're a Ruby programmer, you'll want the definitive book on the Ruby language. Learn how to use Ruby to write exciting new applications. And if you're thinking of using Ruby to create web applications, you really need to look at Ruby on Rails.

Programming Ruby (The PickAxe)

• The definitive guide for Ruby programmers.
• Up-to-date and expanded for Ruby version 1.8.
• Complete documentation of all the built-in classes, modules, and methods. • Complete descriptions of all 98 standard libraries. • 200+ pages of new content in this edition. • Learn more about Ruby's web tools, unit testing, and programming philosophy.

(864 pages) ISBN: 0-9745140-5-5.
http://pragmaticprogrammer.com/titles/ruby

Agile Web Development with Rails, Second Edition

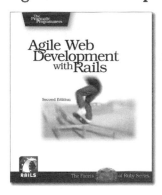

• The definitive guide for Rails developers. • Tutorial introduction, and in-depth reference. • All the scoop on Active Record, Action Pack, and Action View. • Special *David Says...* content by the inventor of Rails. • Chapters on testing, web services, Ajax, security, e-mail, deployment, and more.

(600 pages) ISBN: 0-9776166-3-0.
Beta-book available from our website May 1, 2006.
Final book available in the Fall, 2006.
http://pragmaticprogrammer.com/titles/rails2

The Pragmatic Bookshelf

The Pragmatic Bookshelf features books written by developers for developers. The titles continue the well-known Pragmatic Programmer style and continue to garner awards and rave reviews. As development gets more and more difficult, the Pragmatic Programmers will be there with more titles and products to help programmers stay on top of their game.

Visit Us Online

Rails Recipes Home Page
pragmaticprogrammer.com/titles/fr_rr
Source code from this book, errata, and other resources. Come give us feedback, too!

Register for Updates
pragmaticprogrammer.com/updates
Be notified when updates and new books become available.

Join the Community
pragmaticprogrammer.com/community
Read our weblogs, join our online discussions, participate in our mailing list, interact with our wiki, and benefit from the experience of other Pragmatic Programmers.

New and Noteworthy
pragmaticprogrammer.com/news
Check out the latest pragmatic developments in the news.

Save on the PDF

Save more than 60% on the PDF version of this book. Owning the paper version of this book entitles you to purchase the PDF version for only $5.00 (regularly $13.00). That's a saving of more than 60%. The PDF is great for carrying around on your laptop. It's hyperlinked, has color, and is fully searchable. Buy it now at pragmaticprogrammer.com/coupon

Contact Us

Phone Orders:	1-800-699-PROG (+1 919 847 3884)
Online Orders:	www.pragmaticprogrammer.com/catalog
Customer Service:	orders@pragmaticprogrammer.com
Non-English Versions:	translations@pragmaticprogrammer.com
Pragmatic Teaching:	academic@pragmaticprogrammer.com
Author Proposals:	proposals@pragmaticprogrammer.com